What People Are Saying About Steve D. Bullock

"Steve is the peacemaker. The country was undergoing changes that coincided with a lot of civil rights activity. In his own way, Steve began to open the Red Cross to the possibility of people of color being engaged at higher and higher levels. He did that without challenging or confronting people, but instead made change through excellent work, careful coaching, and living with situations that people learned to respect. Thanks to his personal style, he made an extraordinarily big difference in terms of how quickly he brought change to the organization. Steve's ascent into leadership roles enabled him to apply a non-work agenda about acceptance and as such was a leader for minorities. He did it in a thoughtful, quiet way that was extraordinarily impressive. All the people who worked for him either liked him or loved him."

~ Robert Bender
Former CEO, American Red Cross in Greater New York

"I have to salute a person like Steve Bullock. He is part of that tradition that created a Dr. Martin Luther King Jr., a Muhammad Ali, a Mary McCloud Bethune, a Dorothy Height, and a Barack Obama. Steve is an individual of great integrity, great commitment, and esteem. I cannot think of anyone over my six decades of public service for whom I have greater respect and admiration than Steve Bullock. We should study his story, and learn and teach from his narrative."

~ Reverend Dr. Otis Moss Jr.
Pastor Emeritus, Olivet Institutional Baptist Church, Cleveland, Ohio

"Steve always encouraged me to be myself and to feel that I deserved to take a seat at the all-male leadership table. He was sensitive to my feelings… very thoughtful in helping me feel included and respected. He encouraged me to speak up and add my perspective. He took the time to listen. It sounds so simple, but it was very significant. Some people had confrontational communication styles. But Steve was very principled and thoughtful about different perspectives on the local and national levels. He always said his mother told him to 'make some dust' by making a difference, and Steve was definitely trying to kick up some dust. He was always listening for a way to make things better. We had many difficult days dealing with controversial issues. But Steve had a way of dealing with them in a way that maintained everyone's dignity and integrity."

~ Linda Mathes
CEO, American Red Cross in the National Capital Region

"Steve led a rebirth of the Red Cross that was extraordinary. Steve was a wonderful, wonderful leader. He provided excellent inspiration and mentoring to many of us. He'll always have a place in the heart of the Red Cross because the organization is only great because of great people, and Steve was definitely one of the greater ones to come and share his talents with the organization."

~ Harold Brooks
Former Senior Vice president of International Operations and
Former CEO of the American Red Cross San Francisco Chapter

"My dad is my hero. It brings tears to my eyes. It took me a long time to figure it out. Now I respect everything he ever said, because I wouldn't be who I am and where I am, had I not grown to understand everything that he's done. When I started my undergraduate degree, I never would have believed that I would have a doctorate in education. My daughter was four-months old when I began taking classes from Walden University online. It took six years, three face-to-face visits with professors, and an intense thesis defense via

Skype. My dad taught me the power of hard work and perseverance. I used to think he was mean, but he had values that he stood by them. He taught us that everything is earned. He earned his; I'm going to earn mine."

~ Kelly A. Bullock Daugherty, EdD

Daughter & Educator

"When I saw pictures of Steve in Honduras carrying sacks of food on his shoulder, I was amazed that he was doing that during the time of his first 100 days of goals. I thought, 'Oh my gosh, he's acting president and doing all these things, and these photos exemplify his work great work ethic. Steve was hands-on and showed that no job is too small, no matter what your level is in the organization."

~ James Krueger

Former Senior Vice President, American Red Cross

"Here's a guy who can afford to wear a custom-made suit with his name stitched on the inside, and he's taking it off to go sing to prisoners and inmates in a state prison. It speaks to his capacity as a person and his humility to go participate with his church in a worship service behind bars. Not all deacons would take that trip to a prison. He had a very deep commitment not just to going to church, but doing the work of the church, even if it meant going to the prison."

~ Reverend Dr. Marvin A. McMickle

Former pastor, Antioch Baptist Church, Cleveland, Ohio

President of Colgate Rochester Divinity School, Rochester, New York

"We really have lived a charmed life. We rose from a rural lifestyle in Virginia to traveling the world. Our story is proof that with education, hard work, devotion to your religion, and a strong family, anything is possible."

~ Doris Bullock

Wife of 56 Years, Retired Teacher

"We were farmers. We lived back in the woods. We didn't see people who were educated. Steve was a distinguished man and we needed someone else to emulate. The way he carried himself with dignity, grace and purpose was impressive and made us want to be a part of what… made him an exceptional man. He began a tradition in our family that wherever possible, the Kelly men following after him would be proud Alpha Phi Alpha fraternity men also. I and my two brothers ultimately became Alphas because of Steve Bullock. We discovered that the same quiet determination displayed by our brother Steve could be ours also, if we just tried to follow in his huge footsteps. We worked to be like him. We strived for excellence in the way we lived our lives."

~ Charles Kelly
Brother-in-Law, Pastor, Chesapeake, Virginia

"I went to college because of Steve Bullock. He showed us that you can have a greater life than the one you're leading."

~ Mark Kelly
Brother-in-Law
U.S. Army Colonel and Real Estate Broker, Clarksville, Tennessee

"I grew up in a rough section of Cleveland… and wanted to make a difference. But none of the black business leaders would meet with me… When I met Steve, he affirmed that self-worth in me… He embodied this wisdom with the way he spoke and how he allowed me to sit there and talk to him about my life and my future. I said, "Here's my dream," and he… was encouraging and made me feel like I could do it. I said, "I will never ever treat nobody like these other people treated me; instead, I will always treat people the way Steve treated me." Now, at 51, I always take the time to talk with young men and young ladies just to hear them. Now I have two schools modeled after HBCUs, with 300 students, and have since earned my PhD from Case Western Reserve University."

~ Timothy D. Goler, PhD
Founder and CEO of HBCU Preparatory Schools Network, Cleveland, Ohio

"My dad sets the bar on how to be a good citizen. He's a good man. And that's what he's trying to teach us; to be good men and women. My mom has done the same thing. As leader of the Red Cross, as a city councilman, and as school board president, he set the example that you help your neighbors and your friends.

It wasn't until we got to Cleveland that I understood how important my dad was, as the first African American leader of a Red Cross chapter. The phone rang… a woman with a southern accent was on the line and said: 'This is Elizabeth Dole.' I knew she was the President of the American Red Cross, and it was really impressive that she was calling for my father. I took a message… called my dad and said, 'Elizabeth Dole just called.' I was awestruck!"

~ Eric Bullock
Son and School District Security Officer

"Dad set extremely high standards for himself and for us. He would always stress working hard, and he would show us. I used to love going to work with my dad. We would walk in and it was so cool that my dad was the boss and was so well-respected. He was in a suit and I was there with him all day. We sat in his office while he held meetings. He had a cool office with people coming in and out, asking him questions. You could tell he was important, the leader, but he was not pretentious. He had the same humility about him that he has today. I wish he had beat his chest a little more and said, 'Hey, look I'm the man!'"

~ Brian Bullock
Son and Filmmaker

"When the Cleveland chapter hosted The Boulé's national conference, Steve was tremendous in getting organizations to join, securing venues, and setting up programs, particularly with respect to young people. He was critically involved in trying to realize what we need to do to help these young African American boys and girls become better citizens. Steve spearheaded that effort. It was an extremely successful gathering of 1,300 men committed to leadership and service."

~ Robert P. Madison
Retired Architect and Longtime Friend

MY NAME IS STEVE DELANO BULLOCK

How I Changed My World and The World Around Me Through Leadership, Caring, and Perseverance

Steve D. Bullock

Copyrighted Material

My Name is Steve Delano Bullock: How I Changed My World and
The World Around Me Through Leadership, Caring, and Perseverance

Copyright © 2018 Steve D. Bullock.

All Rights Reserved.

No part of this publication may be reproduced, stored in a retrieval system
or transmitted, in any form or by any means – electronic, mechanical,
photocopying, recording, or otherwise – without prior written permission
from the publisher, except for the inclusion of brief quotations in a review.

For information about this title or to order other books
and/or electronic media, contact the publisher:

Published by Atkins & Greenspan Writing
18530 Mack Avenue, Suite 166
Grosse Pointe Farms, MI 48236
www.atkinsgreenspan.com

ISBN 978-1-945875-26-7 (Hardcover)
ISBN 978-1-945875-25-0 (Paperback)
ISBN 978-1-945875-27-4 (eBook)

Printed in the United States of America

Cover and Interior design: Van-garde Imagery, Inc.

All photographs used with permission. All uncredited
photographs courtesy of the Bullock Family Collection.

Cover Photo: Brian Bullock

"What lies behind us and what lies before us are small matters compared to what lies within us. And when we bring what is within us out into the world, miracles happen."

Ralph Waldo Emerson
American Essayist & Poet

Contents

Dedication xiii

Acknowledgements xv

Foreword by Dr. Otis Moss xvii

Introduction xxi

Chapter 1 – Beating the Odds 1

Chapter 2 – The First in my Family to Attend College 39

Chapter 3 – Joining the Army & Getting Married 69

Chapter 4 – The American Red Cross 81

Chapter 5 – CEO of the St. Paul Chapter 131

Chapter 6 – CEO of the Greater Cleveland Chapter 161

Chapter 7 – Interim President of the American Red Cross 207

Chapter 8 – Making Change with the Bullock Group 243

Chapter 9 – Bullock Family Legacy 255

Epilogue 261

Appendix 265

Index 269

Dedication

This book is dedicated to:

My mother and father

Ida Mayo Bullock and William Henry Bullock

My 21 brothers and sisters

My two siblings who played a parental role:

William Harvey Bullock and Selma Doris Bullock Harvey

My wife, Doris

Our three children:

Eric Delano Bullock

Brian Dennis Bullock

Kelly A. Bullock Daugherty

Our Six Grandchildren:

Marcus Delano Bullock

Elizabeth Lynn Bullock

Brianna Clyde Bullock

Blair Ali Daugherty

Steven Kyle Daugherty

Kylee Alicia Daugherty

Acknowledgements

IT IS WITH IMMENSE gratitude that I acknowledge the men and women whose influence has motivated me to excel and achieve far beyond my circumstances of every phase of my life. They are:

Ms. Watson, principal of my elementary school.

Ms. Willa Cofield Johnson, my senior high school advisor who helped me apply for college.

The top two leaders at Virginia Union University – Dr. Thomas Howard Henderson, the dean and academic advisor, and Dr. Samuel DeWitt Proctor, the President – who enabled me to stay in college.

William "Mike" Miracle, an American Red Cross (ARC) field chapter director who called on me to manage the ARC Community Service Center in the black and Latino population in Washington, D.C.

Paul M. Moore, my boss at the American Red Cross Southeast Area Office, whose protective guidance enabled me to help the organization better serve the black and Latino communities.

Isaac McKee, an assistant director for services at military installations for the Red Cross, who encouraged me to persevere until better opportunities opened up for African Americans in the organization.

Spiritual leaders: Reverend K.P. Battle, my first pastor who baptized me; Reverend Earl F. Miller, my pastor in St. Paul, Minnesota where I first became a church leader as a trustee at Pilgrim Baptist Church; Reverend Dr. Marvin A. McMickle of Antioch Baptist Church in Cleveland, Ohio where I became a deacon; Reverend Dr. Otis Moss Jr., pastor emeritus of Olivet Institutional

Baptist Church in Cleveland, Ohio, and his wife, Edwina Moss, who are true friends and trusted counselors; and my current pastor, Reverend Dr. Todd C. Davidson, Senior Pastor at Antioch Baptist Church.

Lastly, I would like to thank Elizabeth Ann Atkins and Catherine M. Greenspan for assisting me in the composition and publication of this book. They skillfully wove my life story with the major themes that have driven my personal and professional life, enabling me to excel far beyond the harsh realities of the world into which I was born. Their assistance enabled me to bring this longtime dream of writing to fruition, so that I may share my story and success principles with you.

Foreword

I WANT TO COMMEND Mr. Steve Delano Bullock for setting an extraordinary standard, both personally and professionally, that few can surpass, and that all of us should emulate.

As such, I deeply admire and respect my friend who has demonstrated an indefatigable commitment as a leader in our local, national, and global community through his work with the American Red Cross.

Steve Bullock's narrative records how he demonstrated excellence on a daily basis as a leader and administrator of the Red Cross, an organization with local, state, regional, national, and international units of service.

He faced tremendous challenges at every level and had to be prepared seven days a week, to exercise the wisdom and love of a Martin Luther King Jr., the courage of a Rosa Parks, the leadership skills of a Samuel DeWitt Proctor, the fighting spirit of a Muhammad Ali, and the teaching genius of a Mary McCloud Bethune and a Dorothy Height.

However, the above individuals fought most of their battles in the public arena.

Steve Bullock was fighting the same battles behind closed doors "through many dangers, toils, and snares," to quote the hymn *Amazing Grace* by John Newton. These dangers, toils, and snares included a Mississippi hotel in KKK territory, to the battlegrounds (literally) of Vietnam with Viet Cong often in the same space. The Viet Cong were working beside Steve in the daytime and practicing sabotage at night. His story is necessary and compelling.

The Steve Bullock narrative is a lesson in family commitment, education for liberation, and excellence as a lifelong commitment.

This is a message to everyone concerning the necessity of a profound faith, devotion to family, service, and an anchoring in church from childhood through the high-achieving years of his adulthood. He has been sustained by deep faith that equipped him for storms, hurricanes, and floods, both literally and experientially.

This book, the Steve Bullock narrative, is a study in leadership, family, faith, struggle, and achievement. I maintain that the greatest mistake made in the history of the National Red Cross, was the missed opportunity to appoint Steve Bullock as its national president. Steve Bullock's life story is a teachable history in institutional blunders when great leadership is available and boards of directors are not wise enough to embrace it. This is self-imposed organizational robbery.

Steve Bullock is a great leader and remarkable human being by the highest standards of excellence. We should study his story, learn, and teach from his narrative.

Mr. Bullock's exemplary integrity and commitment to helping others are rooted in his strong family values, his deep Christian faith, his education, and his meager beginnings. Growing up as a sharecropper's son in the segregated South instilled in him a profound empathy that inspired his life's work. It also sparked a fierce ambition to not only overcome the oppression of poverty and racism, but to lead others onward and upward. He continues to do this in his family, in his church, in his consulting business, at his alma mater, Virginia Union University, and in the community at large.

Steve's steady and strategic approach to breaking down barriers within organizations and the people they serve has been his hallmark. His quiet yet unwavering commitment to cultivating diversity and inclusion – decades before it was widely accepted or vogue – has enabled him to make institutional change that may have seemed impossible or at least unlikely at the onset.

Allow me to also illuminate the fact that his narrative mirrors my own journey of growing up in the rural south facing racism, segregation, and the debilitating circumstances triggered by these injustices. Like Mr. Bullock, I attended dilapidated schools, but learned from excellent teachers. I was also blessed by the powerful presence of the African American church and community.

At the age of 12, I experienced the lynching of a cousin in our community where the KKK was a living presence. However, thanks to loving and encouraging parents, neighbors, church leaders, and teachers, I always felt and saw something better, something greater, and something more than what we experienced on a daily basis in the wider, white racist community.

Also, similar to Mr. Bullock, my college experience was one of the most liberating in my life. My participation in the student sit-in movement in Atlanta was experienced as a calling, a moral necessity. Going to jail in that experience was a small sacrifice compared to the history of slavery, lynching, Jim Crow, injustice, and discrimination.

As I view Mr. Bullock's life through my personal lens of experience, it is clear that he has given to us a narrative that lives out the lyrics of *We Shall Overcome*. We cannot say that we have overcome, but we do say that we will never give up, and we will never accept injustice as the final word in our existence.

Mr. Bullock speaks to present and future generations by giving to us his narrative, his response to tragic, debilitating injustice and challenges that destroyed so many and deferred so many dreams. But his life speaks as a clear trumpet sound saying that a life of fulfillment can be achieved with preparation, liberation, sometimes suffering, sometimes sacrificing, but all geared toward service.

It is my prayer that Mr. Steve Delano Bullock's autobiography will be read by many for generations and years far beyond his time and place. I predict that all readers will find a lesson of hope, a lesson of faith, and a lesson of triumphant love. And with these, a lesson in liberation.

Thank you, Steve Bullock, for sharing your story and enriching our lives.

~ Reverend Dr. Otis Moss Jr.

Pastor Emeritus, Olivet Institutional Baptist Church

Cleveland, Ohio

Introduction

"Hey, bellhop!"

That's what guests and staff alike called to get my attention in the lobby of the Jefferson Hotel in Virginia Beach, Virginia, during the summer of 1955. I had just graduated from high school, and took the job to save money before attending Virginia Union University in the fall.

Neither my employer nor the hotel patrons ever called me Steve. To them, I was simply called by my job description. In the evening, I left the hotel for my second job at a bowling alley.

"Your name is John Two," the manager declared.

"My name is Steve," I corrected.

"Your name is John Two," he repeated, this time writing it on the brown envelope that contained my pay. "John One" was my friend and classmate, Curtis Wright, who towered four inches over my height of 5'11".

What did I do in response to being misnamed? Nothing.

This was a dangerous time for black men. We were acutely aware that we could be beaten or killed at any time, in any place, for no reason at all. Never had the world received a more brutal reminder of this horrific truth about the American South than that same summer when two white men in Money, Mississippi, slaughtered 14-year-old Emmett Till, after he had allegedly flirted with one of the men's wives.

We understood that we had to choose our battles. And battling over my name was not worth the risk of losing my life or my jobs. I needed to work at that hotel and at the bowling alley. I needed to earn the money in the brown envelope for "John 2."

Going along with this did not mean that I liked it. I was profoundly troubled by the fact that nobody respected me enough to look me in the face and call me Steve.

At the time, I was mature enough to understand that it was nothing personal; by focusing my mind's eye on the big picture – that I was on my way to college and a career that would create a better life than I'd had growing up in the rural, segregated South – I could endure this societal practice of attempting to diminish my humanity and value.

Though I was being psychologically victimized, I decided that I would never be a victim. Therefore, no matter what the world called me, I quietly cultivated pride and confidence that my name is Steve Delano Bullock, a person of power and value who would one day do great things.

My name is very important because it helps me understand who I am and from where I've come. My name speaks to my history, my present, and my future. The name Steve derives from the Greek name Stéfanos, which has origins in the words: wreath, crown, honor, and reward.

This knowledge serves as a motivating reminder that being a leader is essential to my life's journey. This phenomenon has the same impact on my grandson, Steven, who looked up the definition of his name and walks proudly as a result.

"What's in a name?" Shakespeare wrote in *Romeo and Juliet*. "That which we call a rose / By any other name would smell as sweet."

I disagree. If you were to ask, "What's in a name?" I would respond that a name contains a fundamental understanding of oneself and serves as a label and a blueprint that can inspire positive thoughts and behavior within oneself, and elicit the same from other people. Say "lion" and you may think "powerful" and "majestic." Say "rat," however, and it probably evokes images of garbage and filth.

Our names have the same power to conjure up good or bad feelings or ideas, and therefore should be embraced and celebrated accordingly. Great thinkers such as Albert Einstein and Nostradamus understood this. In fact, they're believed to have said that the name Steve should be retired from further use because it imposes a heavy burden on its bearer. I would argue the contrary: that the name motivates greatness. That is what my parents had in mind when they selected my middle name: Delano.

They were inspired by President Franklin Delano Roosevelt, who was in office when I was born and whom my parents, especially my mother, truly admired. In fact, my father's normally somber personality became more pleasant when he spoke of FDR and his New Deal Work Projects Administration. My father had worked for the WPA, which provided nearly eight million jobs constructing public buildings and roads during the Great Depression. By naming me after the president, my parents were essentially instilling in me the potential for greatness and leadership.

Finally, my last name is Bullock. Some argue that it was Bulluck; both are synonymous with power and strength. The dictionary defines it as "a young bull."

To underscore my point that the world responds to one's name, my children's athletic prowess inspired friends, family, and spectators alike to affectionately call them "Bull" in high school.

"Good job, Bull!" fans shouted for Kelly as she dominated the volleyball court and the track, earning all-conference and statewide honors.

"Get 'em, Bull!" people yelled as Brian and Eric played football and other sports.

As for the origin of Bullock, I don't know the names of my ancestors who were captured in Africa and brought to the United States. However, I do know that when slavery was abolished, they chose to take our family name from the former plantation owner and slave owner named Bullock.

As an African American male who grew up in the Jim Crow South, I learned that the bigoted oppression of that era attempted to diminish the humanity of people like myself by refusing to acknowledge that we even had names of our own. Given this personal history, I insist to this day that people call me by my proper name.

"Your name is Bull-LUCK," said the wife of a former governor who is a good friend.

"No, my name is Steve D. Bullock," I told her, pronouncing my name with emphasis on "LOCK." I then said, "If you speak to me and don't say the D, then it's not me."

"I appreciate that," she said. "From now on, when I say your name, you will be Steve D. Bullock."

For a period during college, I altered my name for political impact as an expression of intense rage over injustices toward black people. Had we met on the Virginia Union University campus back then, I would have introduced myself this way:

"My name is Delano Korsakov, and I'm from Money, Mississippi."

I had chosen the name of the Russian musician, Nikolai Rimsky-Korsakov, whom I admired at the time, because I wanted to declare myself as a foreigner. I also wanted to disassociate from a country that perpetrated inequality and injustice toward black men. That's why I claimed that I was from the town where Emmett Till was killed.

I ultimately resumed the use of my birth name and found a more productive way to channel my energy to make a positive impact on America and the world. Our name represents our family brand. We have a responsibility to respect and protect it. We owe this to our parents, grandparents, and others who carried the name before us. Your name should represent who you are.

While this book is not about names, my message is that names are important, but what's within you matters most. The American Essayist and Poet Ralph Waldo Emerson wrote it best: "What lies behind us and what lies before us are small matters compared to what lies within us. And when we bring what is within us out into the world, miracles happen."

That has been the driving tenet of my life. Finding the courage to discover what was within me, and bringing it out to influence the world, has not made me perfect, but it's made me better.

While it was my responsibility to cultivate myself from the inside out, I credit four institutions for nurturing and supporting me – from the outside in – throughout my life. I call these "The Four Pillars," and they are, first, the Christian Church, or more specifically, the Missionary Baptist Church, in which I grew up and am still active today. The second pillar is Family, which after God is first and foremost in all of my world. Third is Virginia Union University, which found me and covered me from the cruelties of the world, then helped to transform my life. The final pillar is the American Red Cross, where I spent almost 40 years of my life working to improve the human condition for myself, my family, and all others within my reach, which ultimately extended around the world. These four institutions have had a profound impact on my life and I have worked hard to return the favor.

I hope that you can glean guidance from my life story and my philosophies and use it to maximize your potential.

Furthermore, please pay special attention to one key strategy that I learned in college. It has enabled me to excel in every endeavor, and it involves Purpose, Preparation, Performance, and Results. These four principles of achievement constitute the foundation of my personal success formula. It begins with purpose. Very early in life, I established my Purpose: to improve the human condition. That core motivation has propelled every step of my personal and professional life.

As you determine your own Purpose, it's imperative that you define what success looks like for you. It's not simply to live in a beautiful home, take wonderful trips, and drive a luxury car. You need to create your own definition of success for every level of your life, including: your health; your emotional state and personal well-being; your relationship with your spouse, your family, your spiritual and religious life; your financial status; your friendships; your professional relationships; your philanthropy; your contributions to your community and the world; et cetera.

It's also important to define your personal brand of success, so that when you achieve it, you will recognize it. So, what does success look like to you? What does achieving excellence look like to you? For me, success is defined by reaching the point where I and my family can live comfortably as I simultaneously make a positive contribution to improving the human condition to help others live a better life. I want to leave some footprints in the sand that say I came through that area and I made a difference. That's what satisfies me and gives me a sense of fulfillment. Take some time to determine what satisfies and fulfills you. These points have enabled me to set goals, realize them, and evaluate how I can do better next time.

In addition, I intend to add value to your life by presenting strategies for managing and overcoming the challenges and barriers that all of us encounter in the pursuit of our life's goals, including those involving gender bias, poverty, education, racism, youth, and aging.

Throughout my career, I have worked with people from all walks of life, and this book is written for everyone. That's why, rather than playing "the race card" or "the gender card," I am playing "the reality card."

In doing so, I pray that the stories, lessons, and life achievement strategies on the following pages will help you discover your potential and power within, so you can, as Emerson so eloquently said, make miracles happen for yourself and the world.

Sincerely,
Steve D. Bullock
Former Interim President of
The American Red Cross
CEO, The Bullock Group

Chapter 1

Beating the Odds

My father, William Henry Bullock, was one of seven children born to a freed slave and his wife in Enfield, North Carolina. Pa came into the world circa 1865, based on a family oral history, just five years after President Abraham Lincoln issued the Emancipation Proclamation declaring that all people who were enslaved "are, and henceforward shall be free."

But the Bullocks, like many of America's four million newly freed blacks, were relegated to a new form of economic slavery called sharecropping. Plantations were divided into plots of land, and blacks lived on them to plant, cultivate, harvest and sell the cotton, tobacco, peanuts, and other crops that they produced.

These black tenant farmers were supposed to receive a 50-percent share of the profits when the bountiful crops sold at the market in Enfield, which was booming as the world's largest raw peanut market. But white farmers used deceptive tactics to prevent blacks from receiving their fair share, keeping them indebted in a vicious, endless cycle of servitude.

Protesting or reporting the unfairness to authorities was not an option; the landowners were the authorities – and they were the faces behind the white hoods of the Ku Klux Klan who beat and killed black men for being "uppity."

This was the reality for my grandparents when they lived on the farm of "Foot" Bullock, a white man who shared their name because his family had recently "owned" my relatives. They were freed and promised land; this promise was upheld when my grandfather received land, then helped his children become landowners. They chose to keep the name.

Having survived slavery and now hoping for a better life for their family, my grandparents encouraged their children to strive above and beyond their oppressive circumstances.

"Someday you'll go to school and make something good of yourselves," my grandfather told Pa and his siblings. "You will own land. And you'll marry light-skinned spouses. That will give you and your children more privileges that darker-skinned folks don't get."

My grandfather meant well. Having fair skin like my grandmother, he was espousing the conventional wisdom of the day that lighter-skinned blacks enjoyed better treatment than blacks with darker complexions.

Those were my grandfather's rules, and Pa was determined to follow them as best he could in Enfield, the oldest town in Halifax County, located 100 miles west of the Atlantic Ocean and a short distance south of the Virginia border. The town had about 700 residents when my father was born; the booming peanut industry helped spike its population to nearly 4,000 during his lifetime.

All the while, Pa regarded becoming a landowner as the pinnacle of success, and he was determined to achieve that goal. So, he set out to purchase the farm where he was raising children with his light-skinned wife.

But as was the case for most black sharecroppers around the turn of the century, white farmers' deceptive tactics forced him to borrow money to support the farm throughout the year. When it came time to sell the crops at the market, the transaction with the farm owner usually sounded something like this:

"Here are your profits, William Henry, and when I subtract what you owe me, you get this."

Too many times, "this" was little or nothing, forcing my father further into debt by borrowing more to survive another winter, before embarking on yet another profitless cycle of planting, cultivating, harvesting, and selling.

"Someday I will buy the farm," Pa declared over and again. Even when he thought he had saved enough to purchase the property, landowners were notorious for changing the sale prices and terms, making it impossible for my father to achieve his greatest goal.

Hardship haunted my father in other ways as well. His first wife died. His second wife was sent to a sanatorium with tuberculosis. This left him alone with many small children.

Then a foster parent placed a 13-year-old girl with him; she became his unpaid nanny, cook, and housekeeper. Her name was Ida Mayo, and she was a dark-skinned orphan. She and her sister Annie had been placed with one family, while their two sisters went to another home. Despite their 34-year age difference, Ida Mayo ultimately became my father's third wife.

Together my parents had 14 children, 10 of whom survived infancy. My father's children from prior marriages brought the total to 22 sons and daughters. I was born at home with the help of a midwife on July 20, 1936. Pa was 72 years old; Mom was 38.

Sometime either before my birth or before I can remember, the farm owner had told my father to tame two mules that the farmer had just purchased.

"You better not let anything happen to those mules," the farmer warned. My father – who was 5'11" with a regular build like myself – was on a wagon, attempting to steer the mules. They ran wild. The wagon broke up, dragging my father and crushing his bones. Back then, poor blacks had no access to a hospital, insurance, or money to pay a doctor. He was treated at home. As a result, he could not walk well, sometimes using two canes to maneuver.

He interpreted the accident and its disastrous aftermath as evidence that he was indeed doomed to a life of suffering for breaking his father's rule by marrying a woman with dark skin. That belief was reinforced as my father witnessed his six siblings earning educations, becoming professionals, purchasing land, and sending their children to school to become high-level professionals.

This is the only photo that I have of my father, and it reflects exactly how I remember his demeanor and appearance.

All the while, Pa was confined to the pitiful existence that became my first memory of him: sitting in a chair, holding a cane, embittered that a farming accident had broken his body, and that his subsequent inability to support our family or become a landowner had crushed his spirit.

Struggling Through the Great Depression

Before I was born, and farming work was failing to provide enough money, my father worked on road construction for President Franklin Delano Roosevelt's Public Works Administration. Known as the PWA, it provided more than eight million jobs for men and women as the nation recovered from the Great Depression.

"We got paid for standing by the side of the road, not doing anything," he would later tell me, describing how he had "worked" on building roads during the Depression.

Throughout my childhood, we lived in a series of small, one-story farmhouses throughout Enfield and, for three years, in South Carolina. Each home typically had four bedrooms inside an unpainted, wooden exterior that had faded to a weather-beaten gray. A one-step stoop led to the front door, which opened to a wall covering the chimney. To the left was a living room, cramped with a wood-burning heater, an upright piano, a bed, a dresser, chairs, and clothes – all surrounded by colored wall paper, secured with homemade paste.

To the right of the front door was our parents' bedroom, which contained a bed, a dresser, another wood-burning heater, and spaces for clothes. Walking through my parents' room led to a step down into the kitchen, which had a stove, a table, cabinets containing pots and pans, and chairs. The kitchen's two doors led outside and to the bedroom where Morris and I shared a bed, and Floyd slept in another bed. It had a window and a table that held a kerosene lamp.

The circumstances were always the same: we had no running water and no electricity – but a lot of farm work to do. This work fell upon my parents, my youngest sister Esther, myself, and my three brothers: Paul, Floyd, and Morris.

As the youngest child, I grew up with nieces and nephews who seemed more like brothers and sisters. Some of my father's children by his first wives were older than my mother, and some of my grown siblings and their children lived in sharecroppers' homes near us. Several of my siblings had moved away, and I did not know them. The brothers and sisters whom I did know, from oldest to youngest, were:

- Percy Sherrod Bullock
- Estee Bullock
- William Harvey Bullock
- Lillie Bullock DeCosta
- Margaret Bullock Vaughan
- Selma Doris Bullock Harvey
- Esther Bullock Muldrow
- Paul Roman Bullock
- Floyd Douglas Bullock
- Morris Vernon Bullock

My father had several other children with his first two wives. I knew three of them: Savannah Alfonso Bullock (Van); Leslie Bullock; and Raymond L. Bullock.

Back then, white farm owners viewed the children of large black families as a free labor force. This resulted in a lot of black children being forced to quit school around the age of 12 to spend the rest of their lives working on someone else's farm.

"You have to go to college, Stevie," my older brother, William Harvey, told me every day like a mantra. I had no idea what college was, but I respected and trusted him, so I believed him. Harvey had moved to New York for a time, but returned to Enfield to raise his family on a farm adjacent to ours. He became a father figure to me, and because his son James was close in age, he was more like my brother than my nephew.

"Get as much education as you can and be whatever you want to be," Harvey drilled into me. "You CAN DO IT." He spoke this over me nearly every day, echoing my parents' emphasis on education as the ticket to escaping the harsh circumstances of their lives.

"You are very smart," Harvey would tell me, "and the world has more to offer you than anything that life here on the farm can give you."

Like him, many of my older siblings had moved to New York City – where my mother's sisters and some of my father's older children lived – to pursue better lives. Our parents wanted the same for us. We occasionally saw my older brother, Savannah, whom we called "Van," who lived in Philadelphia. For a time, he stayed in Tolka, North Carolina, then moved back to Enfield and lived with Harvey. Leslie, whom we nicknamed "Little Bud," resided in Enfield, where he enjoyed a close, supportive relationship with our family. Morris and I lived with Leslie, his wife, and their children during our senior year of high school.

Raymond Bullock lived in Emporia, Virginia through my high school years and visited us often. After he moved to New York City, I did not see him for many years. However, he always stayed in contact with Mom, Dad, and William Harvey, who became and remained the cornerstone of our family.

As I grew up in Enfield, our parents needed me and my siblings to work the farm because Pa was too disabled and sick to do so.

Fighting White Farmers to Stay In School
The white farmers who owned the land where we lived and worked routinely tried to intimidate my mother into making us quit school and work full time: planting, cultivating, harvesting, and selling crops. The farmer spoke in an intimidating tone toward my mother when he said:

"Keep these kids here working until we get this work done!"

"No, my children are going to go to school," she retorted, time and again. She exhibited great courage as a poor black woman standing up to a white male farmer. It was a fight all the way, but my mother never gave in, so we remained in school.

However, in March, April, and May, we did miss some class time because we had to plow the land in preparation for planting seeds. Work continued when the academic school year ended in the spring, until we returned to classes in the fall. September and October were cotton picking season, so we missed some school then as well.

"I want you to work," my mother told us, "but I want you to go to school. You're going to go to school, even if we have to move after this year."

While I have no photos of my mother during my childhood, this portrait was taken during her later years by Olan Mills.

Her defiance to keep us in the classroom caused friction with the farmers. As a result, we moved often. And at times, our family endured such extreme hardship that I was not eating well. These difficult times made my mother even more determined to keep us in school. No matter how much pressure she felt from the farmers, my mother always told us, "You have to stay in school and get a good education."

When not farming, she worked every day for white families as a housekeeper, cook, and nurse, and wanted us to achieve more.

"You are something," she reminded us. "You can do important things in the world."

Pa would add, "And don't let anybody tell you anything different."

With that in mind, I relished the opportunity to attend elementary school with my two brothers and my nephew, James. He recalls how his father dealt with the farmers' edict that his nine children work the fields.

"My daddy would send us to school on Monday in the morning and he'd pick us up at noon and we'd go home and work," recalls James, 78, a retired educator and business owner who is a pastor at Union Missionary Baptist Church in Newburn, North Carolina. "The next day we'd work in the morning and go to school at noon."

During the spring and summer, my siblings and I were accustomed to starting our days with two hours of farm work. Our father was too disabled and sick to do much beyond toss corn to feed the chickens and pigs. So, he relied on us to do the planting, cultivating, and harvesting of peanuts, tobacco, cotton, and corn – all by hand.

"Here's how you do it," Harvey said, demonstrating how to "chop" the fields, which meant using crude plows pulled by mules to till the soil to prepare it for planting peanuts and cotton.

"Do it right," he said, showing me how to keep the weeds away from the plants so they got maximum exposure to the fertilizer that we gave them. "You have to get the little tiny weeds, all of them, and make the ground around the plants fresh and clean. Make sure no growth is left behind that will grow and steal what you put in the fertilizer to grow the cotton, peanuts, and tobacco."

My dad sat and watched and judged, but did not help.

Picking cotton was brutal, because pulling it from inside the hard, sharp boll poked and sliced the fingertips.

As for "priming" tobacco, the 25 leaves on the big stalks ripened from the bottom, usually four at a time. They would turn yellow, and we would bend down to break them off, working higher and higher up the stalk for about five weeks during harvest time. Then we had to put them on a stick in a barn and heat the tobacco until it cured, turning brown and becoming ready to be smoked. That's when we took it to the market.

We also planted peanuts in the spring. In the fall, the 18-inch bushes turned yellow, signaling harvest time. The peanuts grew in pods, or shells, which sprouted from the plants sprouting from the roots. We harvested them by using a mule pulling a plow whose blade cut the peanut plant roots. Later, we used tractors to plow up the plants. The next step was to use our hands to pick up the plants and put them on a stack pole. Coming from the ground, the still-green peanut pods were very moist, so we stacked them in the field on a "stack pole," which enabled the sun and the wind to dry the moisture from the peanut plants and pods. If you drove past a peanut farm, you'd see rows of stacks sometimes a quarter-mile long. After that, we took them to the market.

Harvesting corn was as simple as pulling the ears off the stalks, then storing them in the barn as feed for pigs, horses, and mules. We also sold corn at the market.

When we weren't planting and tending to the crops, we were taking care of the chicken house or feeding the pigs. We also helped in the pork house where pigs were slaughtered, drained of blood, salted, and put in the smokehouse to make bacon, pork chops, and other meat.

We grew most of the food that we ate: potatoes, collard greens, beans, lima beans, green beans, tomatoes, apples, and pears. My mother would can and pickle foods for the winter, and we always had a few animals, mostly pigs and chickens, for meat and eggs. Sometimes we had beef. Pa purchased barrels of herring that we ate for breakfast and supper. We also ate fish if we went fishing or bought from "the fish man." He and "the ice man" came around once a week to put a block of ice in our icebox, where it lasted a few days. Having no electricity, we had no refrigerator. We also made sausage that we enjoyed for breakfast with rice or grits.

I Loved Going to School

When school resumed in the fall, I could hardly eat breakfast quickly enough, because I wanted to get out the door, walk with my siblings through the woods and over a bridge above a swampy stream, and spend the day in our public school house.

I did not attend kindergarten, because it was not offered at the one-room, all-black Hardee Elementary School, located in the country near Enfield. Instead, I started school in first grade and attended Hardee for one year before we moved to South Carolina (I'll explain in a later passage) where my brother Morris and I were in the same class for second and third grade.

I loved school, especially geography and history. Through books and lessons, I explored the world. And because World War II was raging, our teacher often spoke of news about President Franklin Delano Roosevelt. Sharing his middle name, and knowing that my parents respected him, piqued my interest to learn more about politics and how the United States functioned at home and abroad. Learning about President Roosevelt also intrigued my young mind about the concept of leadership. I was fascinated that one individual with courage, vision, and determination could make decisions and take action in ways that impacted millions of people around the world.

My desire to become a leader was also honed by observing my peers. I was beginning to notice that some of my classmates were followers, while some of us were natural leaders. For me, this was manifest as an innate need to help people, after quickly conceiving strategies to guide others along the best route for achieving a goal. I believe this quality was honed by my parents and teachers when they encouraged me to be my best. I'm thankful for their guidance that encouraged my intense yearning to be in charge.

My siblings and I attended the four-room Eden Rosenwald School in Enfield after returning from South Carolina when I was in fourth grade. Jewish philanthropist Julius Rosenwald (whose family helped construct Chicago's Sears Tower) built schools for black students and homes for black teachers throughout the South. This dramatically improved the quality of our education because segregation resulted in terribly underfunded black schools.

This observation occurred as early as fourth grade, when we attended the four-room Eden Rosenwald School in Enfield after returning from South Carolina. Back then, schools were legally segregated, and black schools were miserably underfunded. To improve our conditions, Jewish philanthropist Julius Rosenwald (whose family helped build the Sears Tower in Chicago) established The Rosenwald Fund and built schools throughout the South for black students, as well as homes for black teachers. Many of these buildings still exist.

I adored the principal, Miss Watson. She tasked me with the responsibility of firing up the coal stove every morning to warm the school. Coal and wood were delivered outside, and my job was to retrieve it with a bucket-like scuttle, carry it indoors, start the fire, and keep it stoked throughout the day. I was so proud to have that responsibility! I always took care to do it right, learning to apply the same effort to my class work. This established a major message that I would, later in life, espouse to my staff, our children, my trainees, and my clients: "Take pride in your work!"

Miss Watson reinforced this when I struggled with a math problem or reading assignment. "Try, try again," she said. "Never quit when you fail. Keep trying."

With two grades in each classroom, Miss Watson also taught us life skills.

"This is how you wash your face," she demonstrated. "Stroke your fingers in circles, moving up your face from your jaw. Don't pull your cheeks down. Use upward motions. This helps your face to stay in place."

And while my mother was also teaching us hygiene at home, Miss Watson explained that should we ever find ourselves without a toothbrush, we could use a small branch of a sweetgum tree to brush our teeth. She told us where to look for it and demonstrated how its wood splintered into fine bristles like a toothbrush. She also said baking soda was a good alternative if we lacked toothpaste.

All the while, Miss Watson echoed my mother's edict to always obey the rules. One day in fifth or sixth grade, a girl whom I liked very much wanted me to kiss her as we walked home from school. I obliged, in front of our classmates. Embarrassed, she ran home and told her mother. The next day, the girl brought a note to the teacher.

"Stand in front of the class!" Miss Watson ordered. She held the tips of my fingers, bending them back to expose my flat palm. Then she spanked my hand until she got tired.

"I promise I'll never do it again," I cried.

At home, my mother was a strict disciplinarian who expected the best behavior from me, my siblings, and the children of our extended family who lived nearby.

"Grandma Ida was the pusher," recalls James, 78, a retired educator, a pastor, and business owner in Pollocksville, North Carolina. "She would say, 'You go to school, your clothes will be clean, your hair will be combed, and you're going to listen. It is not a place to act foolish. You are there for a reason, to learn.' If you were disobedient, she could pull an ear until it felt like your ear would fall off your head, so you would dance to her tune or suffer the consequences."

The Parable of the Talents

Our family held Bible study and prayer at home on Sunday mornings when we did not attend church. We sat around the kitchen table, facing my mother, who laid before us her most cherished possession: the Holy Bible.

"Today we're studying Corinthians Chapter 13," she said, looking at me, my siblings, and our father.

Mom pressed her finger to the page and read, starting with Verse 1: "If I speak in the tongues of men or of angels, but do not have love, I am only a resounding gong or a clanging cymbal. If I have the gift of prophecy and can fathom all mysteries and all knowledge, and if I have a faith that can move mountains, but do not have love, I am nothing. If I give all I possess to the poor and give over my body to hardship that I may boast, but do not have love, I gain nothing."

Then my mother read what became one of my favorite Scriptures: 1 Corinthians, Chapter 13, Verses 4 through 7. It says, "Love is patient, love is kind. It does not envy, it does not boast, it is not proud. It does not dishonor others, it is not self-seeking, it is not easily angered, it keeps no record of wrongs. Love does not delight in evil but rejoices with the truth. It always protects, always trusts, always hopes, always perseveres." (Please see appendix for the entire Corinthians chapter).

Those words delighted my spirit. I held tight to them, even though the world seemed to contradict love as black people were hated, tricked, beaten, and killed for no reason at all. Why didn't these beautiful words that my mother was reading apply to people who were not showing love to everyone? What could happen to make them do so? These questions deeply puzzled and troubled me.

As much as I loved our family Bible study, I was eager to conclude it and enjoy homemade sausage and grits.

"I'm hungry," Morris announced.

"Hush," Mom said. "We'll eat as soon as we give the Lord our attention, and after your Pa does the prayers."

Then she read Verse 13: "And now these three remain: faith, hope and love. But the greatest of these is love."

She gazed at each of us, punctuating the importance of that message. Then she turned to our father and said, "Mr. Bullock, it's time for the prayers."

He bowed his head, and we did the same, as he said, "Psalm 23 says 'The LORD is my shepherd; I shall not want.' So, we pray to you today, Lord, to be our strength so that only good can come to this house and this family. We humbly ask you to let me own this farm where we live, and that these children can go to school and be something in life. We pray to you, Lord, that you let the harvest be a good one so we have plenty of money and food to take us through the winter, and that no harm comes to us or anyone we know."

As my father prayed, a deep sense of peace filled me. At times I wondered, since everyone had the ability to pray and ask God for help, why did bad things still happen to people, especially black people?

Almost all of the white land owners that we worked for were evil and dishonest, and they operated within a system that was firmly rigged against us. However, I drew hope that all white people were not the same way, because we knew some individual whites who were kind. While they were not leading the way for equality, they were also not standing in your way. Many of these individuals were my mother's employers. They helped her in ways that included giving her books and magazines to bring home for her kids. They also gave us a lot of used clothes.

At the same time, the merchants in town demonstrated both fair and unfair treatment toward my mother. White merchants allowed blacks to buy food and other items on credit, which resulted in "carrying charges," the modern equivalent of interest charges. For example, for a five-pound bag of sugar, a mean-spirited merchant might impose carrying charges of $1.25, while a decent merchant might charge only 50 cents by saying, "You owe me 50 cents now and 50 cents next month."

The ways of the world always inspired me to reflect during our family prayer services, as I was growing to understand love and hate, fairness and unfairness, kindness and cruelty, in the context of Biblical principles.

"God is always watching and listening," my mother said often.

"Lord," my father would say during our prayers, "we thank you for the bounty we are about to receive in the meal prepared by Miss Ida for this family. And we thank you for blessing us with the words of the Bible that keep us living right in a world that doesn't always treat us right. You teach us right from wrong, so we know how to live in a way that honors you, and we keep the faith that we'll be rewarded for that someday. In Jesus' name, Amen."

"Amen," I said in unison with my family. Psalm 23 touched me so profoundly that after our family Bible study, I studied it on my own; its words became a guiding force in my life. Here is the King James Version of Psalm 23:

> The LORD is my shepherd; I shall not want.
>
> [2] He maketh me to lie down in green pastures: he leadeth me beside the still waters.
>
> [3] He restoreth my soul: he leadeth me in the paths of righteousness for his name's sake.
>
> [4] Yea, though I walk through the valley of the shadow of death, I will fear no evil: for thou art with me; thy rod and thy staff they comfort me.
>
> [5] Thou preparest a table before me in the presence of mine enemies: thou anointest my head with oil; my cup runneth over.
>
> [6] Surely goodness and mercy shall follow me all the days of my life: and I will dwell in the house of the LORD for ever.

Hearing this scripture in church always delighted me. Back then in the rural South, churches held services only once or twice per month. On the first Sunday, we attended First Baptist Church, where we were members. That's where Reverend K.P. Battle baptized me in a nearby river, whose water was red due to the soil composition. On the second Sunday of the month, we attended Pleasant Hill Baptist Church, where my brother William Harvey and his family were members. On the third Sunday, we visited Daniel's Chapel out in the country north of Enfield. On the fourth Sunday, we often went to St. Paul's Baptist Church, where the pastor was my cousin, Reverend Frank Leon Bullock. One of his sermons in particular would become a major tenet of my life's philosophy.

"Today I'm going to share with you The Parable of the Talents," Reverend Bullock said, staring out at the congregation. "It tells us how, when God blesses you with something, you have to use it for good, or it will be taken away."

He told everyone to open their Bibles to Matthew Chapter 25, Verses 14 through 30. Then he read the entire passage, including: "For it will be like a man going on a journey, who called his servants and entrusted to them his property. To one he gave five talents, to another two, to another one, to each according to his ability. Then he went away.'"

My cousin continued reading: "He who had received the five talents went at once and traded with them, and he made five talents more. So also he who had the two talents made two talents more. But he who had received the one talent went and dug in the ground and hid his master's money."

Then he described how the master returned and rewarded the servant who had doubled his five talents by saying, "Well done, good and faithful servant. You have been faithful over a little; I will set you over much. Enter into the joy of your master."

First Baptist Church, Enfield, North Carolina.

The master, my cousin said, also rewarded the servant who had doubled his two talents.

"Here's what happened to the servant who received one talent but was afraid and hid it in the ground," Reverend Bullock said, his voice crescendoing in the traditional style of southern black preachers. "The master became enraged and said, 'You wicked and slothful servant!' and he took the one talent away and gave it to the servant with ten talents."

I listened in awe, trying to figure out how this applied to my life.

"For to everyone who has will more be given, and he will have an abundance," Reverend Bullock read from the Bible. "But from the one who has not, even what he has will be taken away. And cast the worthless servant into the outer darkness. In that place there will be weeping and gnashing of teeth."

That sounded horrible. I certainly wanted to honor God's Word to avoid a punishment like that.

"I'm here to tell you," Reverend Bullock bellowed, "when God blesses you with a talent, an idea, a skill to give to the world, you must use it for the greater good of all! And if you don't, you will be punished. God will see you as ungrateful for ignoring the help that he tried to give you. It is your holy duty to take that talent and multiply it! And how do you multiply it? By using it to help others and by giving it away! Only then will you and everyone you help be abundantly rewarded!"

Those words penetrated my very soul. As we walked home from church, I asked my mother about it.

"It means that God wants us to help people," she said, "especially people who are disadvantaged because they're sick or have no food or are the victims of something bad happening to them. It's up to us folks with the talents to help them."

Don't Park on Somebody Else's Nickel

My cousin, the Reverend Bullock, also imparted some of the best wisdom I've ever heard. It happened during my graduation ceremony after sixth grade.

"Boys and girls," he said, looking out at our impressionable, 11-year-old faces before launching into a spirited, 20-minute speech that boiled down to this:

"I don't want you to do what I'm about to describe to you. When you go into Enfield, you'll find that parking meters cost a nickel for an hour. When

I'm in town, I see people driving around the block, circling and circling, just waiting for someone to move their car. Why? So, they can park their car on someone else's nickel!"

His message was about personal responsibility, and doing as much as you can for yourself. He was telling us not to waste time driving around the block or waiting for somebody else to do something that we can take advantage of. Instead, we must all take responsibility for ourselves and use our time and effort creatively.

Reverend Bullock explained the importance of working hard to earn one's own money.

"Nothing is free," he said. "Parking on someone else's nickel means they already used up some of the time. And by driving around the block, desperately seeking a freebie, you're only cheating yourself out of time and energy for something that you might not even find."

The message became a powerful lesson on personal responsibility. I decided right then that I would never go through life "parking on somebody else's nickel." Instead I vowed to achieve my goals and pay my own way with education, hard work, and leadership to serve as an example of this important lesson.

Education Outside the Classroom

Terror jolted through me as I stood watching a caravan of Ku Klux Klansmen drive past in pickup trucks. Wearing white hoods and robes, they were heading to a rally. Though I was eight years old, I didn't know their names, but I knew they were "that old Klan," as my parents called the white men who killed "uppity" blacks.

They were the domestic terrorists of my day, because they used violence and fear to control, torment, and kill people. Their goal was to force blacks to conform to the racist power structure back then. One wrong move – or simply being in the wrong place at the wrong time – could mean death.

"Stay away from Mr. So-and-So and those old Bellamy boys," Mom warned, referring to members of the wealthy, prominent family that owned Bellamy's Mill. "They're always causing problems."

One afternoon, my mother burst into the house, visibly upset.

"I was walking on the road," she said, as she tried to clean dirt off the sack of items she'd been carrying. "A truck full of teenagers tried to hit me!"

My mother was shaking. "They came close," she said. "Knocked the bag out from under my arm!"

I hugged my mother, hating that anyone would treat her that way.

"Why did they do that?" I asked. "What is wrong with them?"

"They don't have any respect for you," she said. "They don't consider you to be human. But you're not going to let them make you believe that. Just leave them alone. Stay out of their way."

After that, if I were walking alone on a country road, and I heard a car coming, I would hide in the woods until it passed. It was a well-known fact of life that it was not safe to walk at night on the road. Somebody was always missing, and people got killed intentionally. At church and around the farm, everybody knew what happened, but arrests almost never happened.

In fact, people in our community believed that Elmo Spade, a good friend of our family, was beaten to death by state troopers, but no arrest was ever made.

"You'll Never Own this Farm"

My father dreamed of purchasing a farm and becoming a landowner. He was motivated by the financial stability that land ownership could bring, as well as by the desire to prove that he could be just as successful as his landowning siblings. However, being a black sharecropper in the bigoted South during the 1940s was like running on a treadmill, exerting tremendous effort but literally getting nowhere.

Sharecroppers typically borrowed money to live on during the year. When crops were sold, the tenant was supposed to receive a 50-percent split of the profits. However, white landowners used trickery and deceit to block blacks from ever having enough money to purchase the land.

An old country western song about owing one's soul to the company store summarized this dilemma for black sharecroppers, because they could never pay off the debt incurred throughout the year; the landowners ensured this by paying the farmers too little to cover the purchase price of the farm.

Every time my father thought he was ready to make a payment to buy the farm, the landowner told him he came up short.

"I added everything up," the farmer would say, "and you don't get anything."

Adding insult to injury, the white farmers had impolite behavior that conveyed extreme disrespect as they talked to blacks. One farmer who would arrive at our farm in a pickup truck would run a finger under his nose, then rub his hands over his hair, and down his side. Then he would scratch his behind. All while looking my father in the eye and telling him once again that he did not have enough money to buy the farm. This happened time and again.

When I was eight years old, in 1944, the farmer who owned the land where we lived and worked told my father:

"As long as you work for me, nigger, you'll never own the farm."

Moving to South Carolina

"I'm going to kill that man," my father announced.

"We've got to get him out of here," my older brother Estee said.

"Or they'll kill him," my mother added in a conversation that I would learn about many years later.

At the time, I was told that Estee – who owned a cesspool cleaning company in Port Chester, New York – had decided that it was time for our parents to own a farm. So, he purchased land on a tax sale and gave it to them. The catch was that the land was 375 miles away in South Carolina. So, Estee brought his quarter-ton truck to Enfield to move us.

My brother, Reverend Floyd Bullock, vividly recalls how Estee had built a rack over the cab of his truck so he could almost double the cargo space of the truck bed. We loaded everything we owned – including furniture, chickens, and a cow – into the back of the truck for the long drive.

"Estee, are you sure your truck can handle this load?" my mother asked with a skeptical tone, as she stood by the truck, eyeing its worn tires under the weight of our huge load.

"Sure, it can," Estee assured her.

"How old are these tires?" she asked over clucking chickens, a mooing cow, and rattling furniture.

"Ma, you know with the rations, nobody can get rubber tires," Estee said, referring to rules during World War II when rubber tires were allocated for combat vehicles.

Unconvinced, my mother climbed into the cab with my father and Estee, who would drive us to our new home in a town called Lugoff, just south of Camden, South Carolina. Meanwhile, I was crammed in the back with my brothers, Paul and Morris, and my sister, Esther.

As we drove toward our new home, the tires gave out, just as my mother had feared.

"We had more blowouts than I've had in a lifetime," recalls Floyd, 85, who would go on to pastor churches for more than 50 years in Los Angeles and Riverside, California. "We kept patching the tires, but after a while, we couldn't go any further."

That's when Estee set off by foot to get help in the nearest town: Blaney, South Carolina. Meanwhile, my mother knocked on the door of a small house where a woman answered.

"Can we come in to wash up and fix food?" my mother asked. Her kind personality endeared her to others very quickly.

"Yes," said the woman, who allowed us to eat in her family's home. However, we had to sleep outdoors, around the truck. It took Estee several days to reach Blaney and return with help to repair the truck. The entire ordeal lasted at least a week.

We finally made it to South Carolina. While living there, my brother Morris and I had to walk about a mile to our one-room school, which was far less enjoyable than my educational experience in Enfield. Meanwhile, our father would hitch a slide to a mule and go into town to hang out with men he knew, eating baloney sandwiches and talking all day before returning to our house at night.

Unfortunately, we soon learned that the reason our new farm had been available for such a cheap price was that the land was not fertile. It was not producing enough peanuts, corn, tobacco or cotton to feed our family.

"Stevie, I have to go work in Connecticut," my mother announced one day. "I'm going to be working for a family there, and I'll send money home to take care of you, Pa, and Morris."

My mother's departure, and my elderly father's inability to support us, prompted me to wonder, "What is in this world for me and my brother and my dad who can't do much for himself?"

After my mother left, our family's harsh circumstances were literally making me ill. I was not eating well, even though our school provided lunch. One day, I was watching a teacher stir a large jar of peanut butter to mix in the oil that pooled on top. It looked so unappealing, and I was feeling so bad from my family's difficult situation, that I fainted. The teacher poured water on me and gave me a peanut butter sandwich. After I ate, I felt better.

After three years, the failure of the farm in South Carolina prompted my brother to decide that we needed to return to North Carolina. It was 1947, and South Carolina represented yet another failure for my father. As a result, my mother quit her job in Connecticut, came to South Carolina, and helped us return to Enfield. Estee and Harvey brought a truck to move us and everything we owned – minus a cow this time – into another typical sharecropper's house behind the home where my brother William Harvey lived with his family.

At left is a close-up of the house where my brother William Harvey lived. I lived with Morris and my parents in a small, two-room house directly behind this house, which has since been torn down. This house has been restored and painted (it was not painted when we were there). At right, Neville's was a general merchandise store near where we lived, where we would purchase snack items such as bologna, cheese, and Coca Cola.

Our circumstances did not improve after my mother, father, Floyd, Morris, and I moved into a second house of our own about 3.5 miles from where my brother William Harvey lived. In our attempt to farm, we bought a mule. The man who sold it to us left the mule at the end of our dirt path that led from the house to the main road. Then he just stood there like he was waiting for something to happen. The mule died that night. It was old and sick. That year we used Harvey's mules and equipment after traveling three miles to get it.

These experiences, and my observations, provided powerful lessons that no classroom could provide. Already familiar with the economic oppression that my family endured, I was poignantly fascinated by the way my father responded to the cruel blows that life had dealt him. I came to understand that my father was a defeated man. He was both physically and financially crippled by the severe conditions in which he lived. His spirit was crushed; I don't remember him smiling or telling jokes. I say this not with judgment or pity, but with the objective observation that enabled me to conclude as a boy that although I might be victimized, I would never allow myself to be a victim.

Bad things may happen, I declared to myself, *but I'm not going to give in. I will not be defeated. I will never be anybody's victim.*

From this I also cultivated a deep desire to make my own way and provide for myself and my family, should I be blessed in the future to have a wife and children of my own. Again, I say this not with negativity toward my father, but instead with the ability to filter the world through his experience and determine how I might proceed more effectively.

This feeling was only bolstered by watching my mother shoulder the burden of supporting us. At times, it seemed she had 16 jobs, working as a housekeeper, a cook, and a nurse for white families. On top of that, she was studying diligently and taking tests to become a Licensed Practical Nurse by earning a degree through a mail-in study program; it required her to take a licensing examination to earn her diploma.

God in the Garden

My mother's seemingly miraculous ability to make something out of nothing was manifest in one of my most cherished memories. It happened in 1948, a year that was a complete farming failure for us. That year, I was 12 years old, and I was happy that we had food and clothes for school as I looked forward to graduating from the sixth grade and going on to middle school.

When the Christmas season began, we cut down a tree and decorated it with paper. I approached the holiday knowing that we had nothing; I expected no gifts and knew that food would be sparse. I woke up Christmas morning to see a light snow on the ground – not more than an inch. It was absolutely beautiful, like a perfectly clean, white carpet. It was untouched except for footprints made by a few small birds looking for food. I enjoyed that time alone with what I called "nature" as a child.

I went inside and woke up my brothers, Floyd and Morris. We entered our parents' room where the Christmas tree was located. There we found three small brown paper bags, one for each of us. Each bag contained one apple, one orange, one tangerine, some walnuts, and peppermint candy. Underneath each bag was a pair of gloves. My gloves were brown.

I stared at them in awe! My mother had performed another miracle! I would later learn that somehow my mother had purchased the gloves on credit.

As I matured and reflected on that beautiful day, I realized that her faith and God had worked together to create the happy surprise for me and my brothers. Likewise, years later, I learned the hymn entitled "In the Garden," whose lyrics effectively described my experience:

I come to the garden alone, while the dew is still on the roses;
And the voice I hear, falling on my ear, The Son of God discloses.

This has since become one of my favorite hymns. Even much later in my life, I realized that I did come to the garden alone, early Christmas morning in 1948. What I called nature was God's creation, and He had brought me to that special moment to witness and appreciate it.

It was His lesson for me that, despite our family's material lack, we were rich with God's presence. Little did I know how luxuriously God would later bless my family to celebrate elaborate Christmas days with our children and grandchildren, as well as our wedding anniversary on a Greek Island, and so much more. But nothing compares to my childhood memory of that early morning alone with nature, the one-inch carpet of snow, and the unexpected gifts from God through my mother.

Reading Opens the World of Possibilities

After my mother finally earned her LPN certificate, she put her skills to use by doing domestic work for white families in Enfield. From their homes, she often brought home a lot of books, magazines, and newspapers for us to read. One day, she handed me a copy of *Life* magazine.

"Here, Stevie, read it. Read it."

"Thank you, Mom," I said, eagerly devouring the publication by the light of a kerosene lamp. I became enthralled by an article about the Vanderbilts, one of the richest families in the world, thanks to their shipping and railroad empire. Beautiful photographs showed Biltmore Estate in Asheville, North Carolina. Though only 318 miles from Enfield, its 250 rooms and gilded opulence were worlds away from my family's reality.

How is this possible, I wondered, *that people can live like that, when I've got two pairs of shoes – my old shoes, and my good shoes. No running water. No electricity. One day,* I promised myself, *God must have something planned for me that's somewhere between where I am and where those people are. It's going to be up to me to figure out where that is, with His help.* I often discussed this with my brother Morris.

"I'm going to the Army," he said confidently. "That's my ticket to a better life. When you're in the Army, you can travel the world and have everything paid for."

With my mind opening to the vast possibilities that life seemed to offer white people – as I did not see any photos or articles of blacks living like the Vanderbilts, or even excelling as professionals, for that matter – I decided that I would strive for a comfortable, and maybe even luxurious, lifestyle. The way to do that, I concluded, was to learn about opportunities that the world offered. I did that by studying hard at school and by reading as much as possible.

"Steve's oldest brother would bring books to read to us," James recalls. "I remember my uncle sitting in the corner of the one heated room, and us kids would all sit around him as he read to us. My daddy would read comic books to us and detective stories for himself. He wanted to be a lawyer, but school only went to the eleventh grade."

My learning quest taught me that most Southern blacks never exercised their Constitutional right to vote. Those who did risked being beaten or killed. Others were threatened or forced to take a literacy test or pay a poll tax that they could not afford. The more I learned about the world, the more I wanted to change it.

In junior high school, my homeroom teacher was also my cousin, Mrs. Bertha Bullock, who encouraged me to learn and accomplish important goals in life. Every day I was eager to attend her class, after my brothers Floyd, Morris, and I walked a quarter-mile through our farmland to the road. There we boarded a yellow bus that took us seven miles to school.

At home, my mother was always building my character with words and actions. She fueled my spirit with words of motivation, most notably: "Stevie, keep trying until you succeed, and celebrate success." She also told me that after I earned my education, I should head out into the world and "make some dust." She was using a common occurrence on the farm as a metaphor.

On the farm, when you're working hard and moving quickly, which I did a lot with two mules pulling a plow or some other instrument like a cultivator or rake, the work stirred up a cloud of dust around me, the mules, and the equipment. Making a lot of dust resulted in success. So, when I was working on the farm, I was expected to go out and make some dust.

"Stevie," my mother said, "when you leave this farm, I want you to go make some dust." I interpreted that to mean that I should work hard, do things well, and try to make a difference with all my endeavors. It reinforced her message to, "Leave everything you touch better than when you found it."

My mother's guidance planted seeds deep within me that would, indeed, inspire me to find the courage to disrupt the proverbial dirt in the world to draw attention to something that needed changing, even if people didn't like it. Kicking up the dust was necessary to make better things happen.

My brother Floyd took our mother's encouragement to make some dust in the world by becoming a boxer. Inspired by Sugar Ray Robinson, he convinced our mother to let him drop out of school, go to Brooklyn, New York, and become a member of the Golden Gloves. He was pretty good for a while, until a defeat by an Italian boxer inspired him to leave boxing and volunteer for the U.S. Air Force.

My mother's strong faith permeated her guidance.

"Always make the most out of what God has already given you before," she told me. "As you ask for more, be sure to make the most of yourself and what you own." My mother demonstrated this quality every day of her life or until she was no longer physically or mentally able to do so. When we had no meat, she used the gravy to make more gravy in an effort to make the rice or potatoes more flavorful. She also made underwear, shirts, and other items – such as sheets and bedding items – from cloth bags which had contained flour or other food products that she bought.

Learning about Leadership and Character
Throughout my childhood, as I watched my mother struggle to provide for us, and as I labored in the fields where many others were destined to spend their entire lives repeating the back-breaking oppression that their share-cropper parents had suffered, I was constantly contemplating how education could serve as the life raft that would rescue me from such a miserable future.

I desperately wanted to figure out a plan for my life to help myself, while elevating my family, community, and all people of color, thus simultaneously enhancing society at large. My mother's oft-spoken words reverberated through my thoughts. "Get an education," she said. "Add value, and leave things better than you found them."

These concepts were drilled into me during participation in 4-H and the Boy Scouts of America. Starting in elementary school, the agriculture-based 4-H youth development program engaged me and Morris in activities based on its motto of "head, heart, hands, and health." As junior high school students, we camped in the woods near town with Club Master Cofield, a member of the wealthy black family in Enfield. By learning to set up camp, cook, and gather supplies, he taught us self-sufficiency.

Mr. Cofield was also our Scoutmaster for the Boy Scouts of America. As such, he engaged us in many activities that included camping. All the while, he provided many lessons to instill the importance of citizenship, character, leadership, life skills, responsibility, and fitness.

"It's wrong to steal," said Scoutmaster Cofield. Our small troop sometimes consisted of only me and Morris; other times, was had as many as 10 boys. Many could not participate because families in our rural area lived far apart and lacked cars. During our activities, Scoutmaster Cofield reinforced the rules of good behavior. "Being a Boy Scout," he told us, "is all about upholding the good values that we teach you here."

Well, one day, my two brothers and I decided to defy that. We used a piece of hay wire (which was used to bind bales of hay) to open a lock on a room at Rosenwald School. Inside, we stole some of Mr. Washington's peanut butter candy called Nabs.

That night, after eating the stolen candy, I was tormented in my dreams by the terror of dogs chasing me. In the South, police used bloodhounds to catch criminals and prison escapees. Fortunately, our petty crime was never exposed, but I discovered that my conscience could not handle the guilt of rule-breaking. So, I committed to good behavior and honesty at all times.

Relationship with Father

My father was not affectionate, nor did he talk much to me or anyone else. Even when he spoke to my mother, it was all business, such as, "Miss Ida, what's for supper?" or "What do we have to do tomorrow?"

I don't remember him hugging me, or ever being friendly or joking. He was very quiet and stoic. His personality, at times, seemed as harsh as our living conditions.

My memories of him are especially vivid when I was in tenth and eleventh grade, living in yet another four-room house that was typical of sharecroppers' dwellings; I had been in seventh grade when we moved into this house. It sat about a quarter-mile back in the woods from the main road where my siblings and I caught a yellow school bus.

This last farm was owned by blacks: Mr. Goins and his son-in-law. However, we were still sharecroppers. Because my father was unable to work, and we had no recognizable, acknowledged head of household, we always lived near Harvey, who had to sign off for us. When we lived in the Goins House, Harvey lived in a house in front of ours.

This house, like all others during my childhood, lacked electricity and running water. We fetched water from a spring that was 150 yards from the wood-frame house. To bathe, we heated water on top of the wood stove and filled a metal tub. Later, we had a well in front of the house.

My parents never owned a car. Our single electronic item was a battery-run radio. We had no camera, so few photos exist of my childhood. I do have one sepia-toned picture of my father sitting in a white wicker chair. He's wearing a crisp white shirt and tie, a vest, trousers, black lace-up shoes, and an overcoat with buttons. His handsome face is solemn, his eyes joyless. In contrast, a black and white school portrait taken of me when I was 14 in 1951 reveals a strong physical resemblance. I'm smiling slightly, unlike my father's usual tight-lipped expression, and I'm wearing a white shirt and tie under a zip-up nylon coat.

This is my school photo when I was 14 years old.

We kept our clothes in the living room. My parents had a battery-operated radio; I remember rushing home to listen to a Joe Louis fight in 1947 or 1948. He and Jesse Owens made us proud, and they were respected by white people, especially when Joe Louis beat German boxer Max Schmeling.

On Saturday afternoons, the radio played three hours of black music. Otherwise, the programming was limited to country and western songs, along with *Amos 'n' Andy, The Lone Ranger,* and comedians such as Jack Benny on Sunday night. A few families had televisions. Sometimes we visited the home of Mr. and Mrs. Frank Adams to watch something historical about the President or Congress.

My two brothers and I slept in an unheated back room off the kitchen, whose wood stove provided warmth along with an abundance of quilts made from scraps of cloth. We boiled water to bathe. We hand-washed our clothes in large tubs with Clorox and scrub boards, and we used outhouses for the bathroom. In the morning before school, we had to walk through the kitchen to get washed up. Our mother was usually there, preparing breakfast for us. After eating, we exited the house by passing through the room where our parents slept in separate beds. Every morning, Pa would be lying there, watching to see that we were ready for school.

"Good morning," I'd say, walking past him toward the door.

"Good morning," he'd say. Other than that, Pa was very quiet.

I disappointed him once because I wanted a saxophone. I have always loved music, and I dreamed of playing the sax in school. That instrument was too expensive, so I chose the clarinet instead. My mother paid $108 by making payments over one year.

"I can't believe you did that," Pa said with an accusatory tone as if I had done something wrong. "Let your mom buy that old thing when she didn't have enough money."

Despite his disapproval, it delighted me beyond measure to play my clarinet; as I learned new songs at school, I would practice for hours until I perfected each one.

"Steve loved music, and he loved that clarinet," recalls my brother Floyd. "He used to talk about how his horn was his girlfriend."

While my father never mentioned the clarinet again, he did talk more openly with me as I got older. These talks occurred as he sat outside in the yard while I shaved him. Now nearly 90 years old, he was unable to shave himself. Pa often imparted words of wisdom that revealed his hopes for me to achieve far more in life than he ever had.

"Whatever you do, Stevie, you need to be at the top," he said.

I took his words to heart.

"Steve was All Business"

I lived in a house with electricity for the first time when I was in eleventh and twelfth grades, while staying with my brother Leslie and his wife Hattie. My brother Morris, my niece Yvonne, and I walked three blocks from his house to T.S. Inborden High School, named for a prominent black educator named Thomas Sewell Inborden. That school became my launch pad out of Enfield, thanks to educators who invested time and resources to prepare me for higher education and beyond.

I attended T.S. Inborden High School in Enfield, North Carolina. Because the school lacked an auditorium, my graduation ceremony in 1955 was held at Bricks School, a private school.

"Stevie, you have to go to college and get a degree," said Mrs. Willa Cofield Johnson, our class advisor who taught English, Reading, Writing, and Speaking. I credit her with providing the guidance and instruction required for me to attend college. Not only did she assist with the search process to help me decide where to apply, but she also guided me on how to complete and submit the applications.

Our Principal, Mr. Aaron Wilder, also motivated me by saying, "Decide what you enjoy and work hard at it."

That I did, and I talked often with my siblings and nephews about how I wanted to become a lawyer and help people in the field of racial justice.

"Steve knew he wanted to be somebody," Floyd remembers. "That's why in high school, he already knew that he wanted to be a lawyer. He wanted to impact people. So, he came up with a plan to make it happen. Bullocks are determined individuals. Steve was always challenging and persevering. He was so determined; he thought if he couldn't do it, nobody could."

I believed that everything I wanted in life hinged on earning good grades, graduating from high school, and getting accepted in college.

"He liked getting good grades, and he got good grades," Floyd says. "My mother kept pressure on him to do that. If he got a B, she said, 'You can do better.'"

My nephew, Richmond "Al" DeCosta, 77, a retired New York City police officer who lives in Las Vegas, Nevada, says my determination inspired him to pursue a better life.

"Steve was the most prominent in my mind in regard to trying to figure out how to make a better living as opposed to sharecropping," he recalls. "He impressed me and I used to try to emulate him. He knew there was something better in life than what we were experiencing on the farm."

James shares this recollection: "In high school, Steve was all business. He did not play basketball or football. He played clarinet in the band. He had a drive that he was going to school and college." He says I wasted no time on activities that did not prepare me for a better future.

"There was very little time for playing," James remembers. "In high school, he was well dressed, well groomed, and there was no running around. He did have a girlfriend that I thought was the prettiest thing that ever walked. I don't remember him running to see her every day, and when he went, he had to use my daddy's car to go see the girl. The influence of Mrs. Cofield Johnson created in him a desire to go to college, and that's what he was focused on."

As a result, James says, "Steve was a pioneer of school-going."

Yet the odds were very much against me.

"This was not the normal way of thinking, because this was a poor family from a poor area," James adds. "He was expected to do farming for himself or for someone else." In fact, James said when he ordered our high school transcripts after graduation, both of ours said, "Not likely to succeed."

"I Got A Body Out Here"

When I was 16, I worked for the Cofield family in their funeral home, doing any task they assigned. My job included opening the mail to record payments for a "burial association" in which people paid monthly fees toward the burial cost when they died. I prepared the payments for deposit and gave the money to someone to take to the bank. One day, my job responsibility veered into an area that I didn't like.

"I got a body out here," the embalmer told me. "I need you to help me go get it."

It took three months for me to rid my mind of the haunting images of that dead body. That was not the first time I had seen a dead person. Back then, it was not uncommon for a person to die at home; their body remained in the house as opposed to being taken to a morgue or funeral home. Instead, the undertakers came to the house to wash and dress the body, and the funeral was held in the living room.

I witnessed that at the home of friends that my siblings and I passed en route to school one day. We went inside and saw a body in a casket. That, however, did not disturb me as much as the corpse encounter while working at the funeral home.

One of my more enjoyable jobs during high school occurred during my senior year, when I worked for Mr. Cofield, my former Scoutmaster, at his restaurant. I cooked hamburgers and hot dogs, made milkshakes, and assembled sandwiches.

Applying to College

Just before my senior year, on August 20, 1954, I registered for the Selective Service. I still have the card that says: "This is to certify that in accordance with the Selective Service Law: Stevie Delano Bullock." It lists my residence at Route 3, Box 48, Enfield (Halifax County), North Carolina. My signature in blue ink appears on the card along with the signature of the local draft board clerk.

Three of the 23 students who graduated from Inborden High School in 1955 were Bullocks: Morris, Yvonne, and me.

When my senior year began, Mrs. Cofield Johnson recommended that I apply to three Historically Black Colleges and Universities (HBCUs): Hampton University in Hampton, Virginia; Saint Augustine's University in Raleigh, North Carolina; and Virginia Union University in Richmond, Virginia.

Virginia Union offered me a $250 scholarship, and I decided to attend.

Meanwhile, I thrived during my senior year, serving as Vice President of Inborden High School's graduating Class of 1955. Our graduation photograph shows 23 students, three of whom were Bullocks: Morris, Yvonne, and me. When I graduated fifth in my high school class, my mother admonished: "That's what happens when you do just enough to get by. You have to work hard at everything you do and reach to the top."

Chapter 2

The First in My Family to Attend College

The Summer from Hell

Mrs. Cofield Johnson told me that teachers typically worked summer jobs at restaurants and hotels as maids or bellhops. She recommended that I do the same to earn money for college.

So, at age 18, I headed to the oceanside resort town of Virginia Beach, Virginia, in search of a summer job. Mrs. Cofield helped me and my friend, Curtis Wright, secure rooms in the home of the local NAACP president. He was a good guy, and we were grateful for the opportunity to stay with him. When we first arrived, I wanted to see the ocean.

"I've spent my whole life 100 miles from the ocean," I told Curtis, "but I've never seen it. Man, let's go jump in!"

We ran through an alley, then stopped in our tracks. There before us was the bright blue Atlantic Ocean, stretching to the horizon as waves crashed on the white sand beach. We were in awe, and wanted to get closer. So, we ran onto the boardwalk.

"Boy, get outta here!" a police officer yelled. "You know you're not supposed to be on the boardwalk. If something happens, it's gonna be your fault!"

"No, sir, I didn't know," I responded.

"You can't go out there," a black man told me the next day, after I was hired as a bellhop at the Jefferson Hotel. "And you can't swim in the ocean here, either. You have to go to the colored beach, seven miles up the road. You have to take the bus."

I did, and the ocean looked exactly the same, minus a boardwalk.

"This is God's ocean," I announced over the crashing surf, hating that I lived in a world that banned me from going wherever I pleased, whenever I pleased. Unfortunately, the boardwalk incident was just the beginning of the indignities that I would suffer that summer.

To the white staff and guests of the Jefferson Hotel, my name was simply, "bellhop." No one ever called me Steve when I was carrying their suitcases, or doing dishes or mopping floors there. Nor did anyone pay me the respect of learning my name when I left the hotel and worked the evening shift at a bowling alley. Curtis was John One.

"Your name is John Two," the manager declared.

"My name is Steve," I corrected.

"Your name is John Two," he said, writing "John 2" on a brown envelope that held my cash wages. He did the same for Curtis, scrolling "John 1" on his envelope.

I needed that money, as well as my earnings at the hotel. So, I did not argue with the man who refused to acknowledge that my name is Steve Delano Bullock.

I hated that people treated me as less than human. At the time, "nigger" was used openly and unabashedly. Using water fountains, bathrooms, and public areas that were marked "colored" was a constant reminder of being treated in a subhuman manner in comparison to whites who were afforded all the privileges and luxuries that the world could offer.

Meanwhile, when I walked to work every day, I passed a young man working in the Florsheim shoe store. He was about my age, and always wore a white shirt with dark pants, standing with his arms folded. He appeared white, but my intuition told me that he was actually black and "passing" for white. That was not an uncommon practice among blacks whose skin color and hair texture appeared Caucasian; it enabled them to secure better jobs and even cross the color line entirely by marrying a white person and never looking back at their black roots. As for the shoe salesman, his refusal to look at me somewhat confirmed my suspicion.

My daily observance of him made me think about how I was washing dishes, scrubbing floors, bell hopping, and setting up pins in the bowling alley while he was standing there looking stylish in the relative comfort of a shoe store. All because I looked black and he did not.

Regardless of his race, his presence was yet another infuriating reminder that life was a struggle for people who were despised by the greater society for a physical trait with which they were born and which had absolutely no bearing on what kind of human being they were on the inside. As a result, anger boiled beneath my calm façade as I tended to my duties at both jobs.

Working at the bowling alley was physically painful. Curtis and I were tasked with setting the pins by hand. First, we had to press a foot pedal that made little pegs come up from the floor; we set a pin on each peg, then released the pegs back into the floor. We learned to work fast, because the bowlers were steadily chugging beer, and didn't care about our safety. By the time we set the pins and got the last pegs down, the ball was already at the head of the pins.

Bam!

Curtis and I got hit many times, and it hurt! We talked to the boss about it.

"They're bowling!" he snapped impatiently. "That's your job!"

Every indignity that summer bolstered my determination to become a lawyer and make the world a place where everyone was treated with equality and respect. But one day, I almost lost my cool, and I could have been killed as a result. One night when we left the bowling alley, a pickup truck rolled up carrying drunk guys who were sitting in the back with cases of beer.

"Oh, here come some niggers," they said. "We're gonna have some fun!"

Rage consumed me as never before. It was as if all the humiliation of the summer exploded inside me. I wanted to kill them all.

"I'm ready, Curtis. I'm gonna get one of them! They can do whatever they want to me. I'm tired of putting up with this every night!"

Curtis pulled me back. "No, you're not! We have more important things to do!"

We went home. Before I fell sleep, I remembered Sunday morning Bible study and prayer with my family back in Enfield.

"The Lord is my shepherd; I shall not want," my father had often said, citing Psalm 23.

"He maketh me to lie down in green pastures: he leadeth me beside the still waters. He restoreth my soul: he leadeth me in the paths of righteousness for his name's sake. Yea, though I walk through the valley of the shadow of death, I will fear no evil: for thou art with me; thy rod and thy staff they comfort me. Thou preparest a table before me in the presence of mine enemies: thou anointest my head with oil; my cup runneth over. Surely goodness and mercy shall follow me all the days of my life: and I will dwell in the house of the LORD for ever."

The Lord certainly had worked through Curtis to shepherd me away from danger and save my life that night.

The Slaughter of Emmett Till

My Summer from Hell in Virginia Beach concluded with horrific news that shocked the nation and the world. A 14-year-old black boy from Chicago had been beaten, murdered, and dumped in a river in Mississippi after allegedly whistling at a white woman. Her husband and another man were arrested.

What made the slaughter of Emmett Till different than the thousands of lynchings of black people across the South was that his mother, Mamie Till, demanded an open casket during his funeral, to show the world what had happened to her only son on August 28, 1955.

Seeing a photograph of his mutilated, unrecognizable face in the *Norfolk Journal & Guide* newspaper overwhelmed me with a rage and disgust that I had never experienced. The newspaper, as well as the *Baltimore Afro-American*, *Ebony*, and *Jet* – and media around the globe – showed that picture of him beside a handsome photo showing him when he was alive.

Emmett Till had been only four years younger than myself, and those white men had made an example of him to show what happens when a black male refused to obey their oppressive code of conduct that deemed personal contact with white women as an offense punishable by torture and death.

That the United States of America – allegedly the "home of the free and the land of the brave" – was allowing these racist vigilantes to wage their deadly domestic terrorism against blacks was incomprehensible to me. I wanted to divorce myself from all things American because this was not a place that granted me equal protection under the law. Again, this profound anger bolstered my determination to become a lawyer fighting for racial justice.

As I was heading to college, the two men accused of killing Emmett Till were going to trial for murder. I followed every detail of the case, because I wanted to attend law school, then work as a lawyer to help make a reality of those oft-spoken words in the Pledge of Allegiance, so that blacks, too, could live "with liberty and justice for all."

The First Bullock to Attend College

After spending the summer of 1955 working and suffering in Virginia Beach, I boarded a Trailways Bus with my two pieces of luggage. I traveled to Richmond, Virginia, where a taxi took me to the campus at 1500 North Lombardy Street, which would be my home for the next four years. This trip was the first time in my life that I had ever stepped onto the grounds of any college or university. For a moment, I was lost. *Where am I? Why am I here? Where am I going? Who is going to guide me?* Then it dawned on me, and I said, "Here I am, God. Guide me, lead me, and help me not to stray."

I now refer to this experience as "The Miracle on Lombardy Street" because it was truly a miracle that God's grace worked through the people around me to lift me up through education and opportunities to escape the hardship of sharecropping, and go to college.

As I walked into Virginia Union University to register for classes as an undergraduate, I felt an odd sense of excitement that this was a historic moment for the Bullock family, since I was the last born, and the first to attend college. Yet beyond encouraging me to get there, neither my parents, nor my brother William, or even Mrs. Cofield Johnson, had told me what to expect after I arrived on campus.

I had never visited a college campus until the day I arrived on the Virginia Union University campus to begin my freshman year.

And so, I tasked myself with the adventure of learning as much as I could about this place called college. It would provide the key to a golden doorway of opportunity that no one in my family had experienced; I was humbled and honored to become the first. No one on that campus knew me, nor did I know anyone. However, I soon learned that without knowing me, they all loved me, respected me, and valued me.

As I explored the 84-acre campus on Richmond's North Side – not far from the statues of Confederate war heroes on the city's famed Monument Avenue – I discovered a vibrant atmosphere where I was meeting people from around the world. Though VUU is an HBCU, the co-ed student body was racially mixed, with people from many countries. I shared a dormitory room with guys from Brooklyn, New York; Philadelphia, Pennsylvania; and Suffolk, Virginia.

"I knew it!" I exclaimed, recognizing the guy from Suffolk as the Florsheim shoe store salesman in Virginia Beach. The truth was revealed – he had been passing for white! We laughed about it, and I did not resent that he was taking advantage of an opportunity to do better for himself. Unfortunately, he did not apply that same commitment to college; he flunked out after one semester and got in trouble with a gun.

We were among 1,200 to 1,500 students on the campus that boasted the beautiful architecture of late-Victorian, Romanesque style on its seven main buildings constructed with Virginia granite. I was in awe of stately Pickford Hall (and the Old Pie Shop gathering place in the basement), the bell tower, and the Belgian Friendship Building, which was built as Belgium's exhibition hall during the World's Fair in New York City. It housed the library.

I was inspired to learn that VUU was founded in 1865 to educate some of four million newly freed slaves, most of whom were illiterate because learning to read and write during slavery was an offense punishable by violence, even death. Since then, notable alumni have included Virginia's first black governor, Douglas Wilder; NBA star Ben Wallace; and TransAfrica Founder Randall Robinson.

One of my first orders of business on campus was to declare a major. The university offered studies in business, education, psychology, the humanities and social sciences, mathematics, science and technology, and theology.

I selected history and sociology as a blended major, and was pressured by my counselor to take education classes as a fallback. At the time, I resented that because I had no desire to teach. Teaching was a noble calling, but it had been one of the few pursuits allowed to black people who wanted to do more than farming and domestic work.

Instead, I had a clear vision of studying history as a solid foundation for attending law school after graduation, and exploring the nation and the world. My history classes sparked many epiphanies that fostered clarity for my future and deepened my core beliefs and values.

One example of this occurred when studying Virginia native Thomas Jefferson, the lead author of the Declaration of Independence who became America's third president in 1801. Despite my disdain for some of Thomas Jefferson's activities – he was a slave owner – I appreciate his contributions, especially in the area of public education. Thomas Jefferson talked about and focused on the "diffusion of knowledge among the people, the masses." I am thoroughly committed to a democratic society, which requires participation of the people. Participation requires some level of knowledge and understanding.

I appreciate that he created a template for democracy that required a certain level of education. He was not talking about people who looked like me, but he created the framework. That's how I would later use it on the school board and as president of the school board. I fully endorse the belief that all levels of society – including the city, the county, the state, and the nation – all have a responsibility to provide a certain level of education if we expect democracy to work. That was absolutely a part of Thomas Jefferson's message that I affirm, having the objectivity to extract his positive contributions from the negativity surrounding the fact that he enslaved people of African descent and had children with one of them.

As a college student, this strong belief in democracy and education inspired me to participate in many campus activities. I joined the Student Government Association, where I would serve for most of my college experience. I sang in the choir, and played my clarinet in the orchestra marching band for the VUU Panthers, which had won the national football championship in 1948. I especially loved engaging new friends in spirited conversations between classes, and over meals in Martin E. Gray Hall. After dinner, we gathered outside in "the yard" to socialize and debate.

Dominating the headlines throughout September and October of my freshman year was the murder of Emmett Till and the trial of the two white men accused of killing him: Roy Bryant and J. W. Milam. The all-white jury deliberated one hour before returning with a "not guilty" verdict, despite overwhelming evidence that they were guilty.

NAACP Executive Secretary Roy Wilkins had declared the death a "lynching" and said that "the state of Mississippi has decided to maintain white supremacy by murdering children."

As people rallied and protested in several cities, newspaper editorials called for new federal legislation to protect black Americans' civil rights. At the time, things got worse for blacks in Mississippi, where a white man killed a black gas station attendant and was acquitted in the same courtroom as Emmett Till's murderers.

These events enraged me beyond words. The unfairness, the injustice, and the evil were shocking America and the world – and shaking my belief system to the core. How could a country based on democratic principles, the Declaration of Independence, and a Constitution that was supposed to protect the rights of everyone, allow this to happen? How could people literally get away with murder? Why didn't black lives matter?

I was so disturbed, I adopted a foreign identity.

"My name is Delano Korsakov," I told everyone I met, "and I'm from Money, Mississippi."

Taking the name of Russian musician Nikolai Rimsky-Korsakov enabled me to assume a foreign identity. Saying I was from the town where Emmett Till was lynched was my way of keeping that epicenter of racial injustice at the forefront of conversations, lest anyone forget what had happened to that 14-year-old boy from Chicago.

Black Mentors with Godlike Presence

College life exposed me to African American men whom I respected and revered with almost god-like status. Wearing suits and boasting multiple degrees and accomplishments, these men were unlike anyone I had met while growing up. I wanted to emulate their manner of speech, leadership, and ability to make a positive impact on the world, especially for oppressed people.

University President Samuel DeWitt Proctor ranked first on my list of men whom I admired. Dr. Proctor was young, with a heavy mustache, and though serious, he smiled often while dashing around campus with a gait so brisk that it seemed he was always everywhere.

He cultivated a family atmosphere on campus where everyone knew me, including the deans and the professors. They were always watching us and caring about us students, 24 hours a day, seven days a week, in ways that groomed our behavior and maturity. For example, one day I was hurrying across campus to class when Dr. Proctor stopped me.

"Stevie!" he exclaimed. "What is that on your face?"

"I'm growing a mustache," I said.

"Go back to the dorm and get that mess off your face!" he ordered.

"But I'll be late for class."

"Go back to the dorm," he said, "get that mess off your face, and go to class!"

I did as told.

Another time, a house mother from one of the dormitories stopped me, as did a dean. They both admonished: "Stevie, you need to polish your shoes!"

Attending this small liberal arts college provided far more than education; Virginia Union University taught me that the Historically Black College and University experience nurtures a student's entire being and helps to build character that lays a foundation for success in life, both personally and professionally.

Dr. Proctor cultivated this tradition at VUU. While I never took the theology classes that he taught, he engaged me in one-on-one conversations that honed a sharper vision for my life, as well as a strategy to achieve it. Most of our conversations occurred in his office in beautiful Pickford Hall, whose stately limestone façade and elegant turrets awed me every time I approached.

Dr. Proctor invited me on long drives to destinations throughout North Carolina where he would engage in fundraising for the university. During these excursions along two lane roads that began in the morning or the middle of the day, Dr. Proctor talked with me about life, and specifically, about human relations.

"We're going to make good time because I'm going to pay attention to what's ahead of me before I get to it," he would say, adding that he did not want to get stuck behind two or three trucks driving far more slowly than he desired. "While you're looking ahead, you can avoid whatever barrier or challenge may be in front of you. Stevie, you should apply that to your life as well. Pay attention to what's ahead of you. Prepare for it before you get there."

Dr. Proctor's words of wisdom sunk deep into my spirit, and I began to apply this strategy to my school work and other areas of my life. In fact, these talks were as valuable and useful as the lessons I learned in the classroom. Dr. Proctor inspired me to examine my life, starting with my upbringing, including the racial horrors of our time, and the impact that I wanted to have on the world to improve the human condition.

"The slaughter of Emmett Till," I told him during one of our many talks, "confirmed that I should become a lawyer working on racial justice."

"That's a noble calling," he responded. "We need more lawyers to dismantle a racist infrastructure that has been perpetuated for centuries. The power structure is not going down without a fight. You would make a fine lawyer, Stevie."

I paused to absorb his confidence in me. I appreciated that Dr. Proctor's advice and guidance was rooted in his strong Christian values. Years later, the school's theological training program would be called The Samuel DeWitt Proctor School of Theology at Virginia Union University.

"My goal," I confided, "is to improve my own condition and at the same time bring others along with me. By others, I mean my family and people outside my family."

"Stevie, where can you do the most good for yourself and others?" he asked. "Do you believe being a lawyer would enable you to accomplish that?"

Over the course of several discussions, I realized that my aspirations extended well beyond the practice of law.

"Dr. Proctor, you've helped me realize that my true desire is to change minds," I said. "I need to do something that will give me the opportunity to work with people in terms of their life's conditions beyond race."

"Very good," responded Dr. Proctor, a VUU alumnus who attended Yale Divinity School and would go on to pastor New York's prestigious Abyssinian Baptist Church and hold administrative positions with the Peace Corps in Nigeria and Washington, D.C.

"I want you to think big, Stevie," Dr. Proctor said. "Don't let anything limit your vision for who and what you can become. There's a whole world out there and you can choose to participate in any way you desire."

This broadened my perspective. "Dr. Proctor, you're right. I also want to learn more about the world, so I need to choose a path that will allow me to travel."

"Stevie, I'm certain that with more deliberation, you'll conceive a plan for your life that is beyond the imagination of many people you knew back on the farms of rural North Carolina," he said. "But I guarantee you this, whatever you choose will ultimately lift them up, too. I believe in you, Stevie."

I took this to heart, and it motivated me beyond measure.

Purpose, Preparation, Performance, Results

History class with Dr. Tinsley L. Spraggins convinced me that, through no fault of my own, I was extremely naïve about life and the world.

"I'm here to prepare you for success in life," he said. "You've got to know what it is that you're trying to accomplish. In other words, know your purpose. Then you have to prepare yourself to do it. When you get to the table, you have to perform. After that, you need to look back and evaluate the results."

I analyzed this concept, and committed it to both memory and application to every endeavor thereafter. It fascinated me to think that these four items could lay the foundation for success. So, I further defined them like this:

- PURPOSE is your personal and professional intent, mission, or long-term goals;

- PREPARATION enables you to take the necessary steps to ready yourself to achieve your purpose;

- PERFORMANCE is the action by which you achieve your purpose; and

- RESULTS provide quantifiable factors on which you can evaluate your performance, identify strengths, weaknesses, successes, and failures, and craft a strategy to improve where necessary to continue on an upward trajectory.

I began to apply this strategy of Purpose, Preparation, Performance, and Results when I served as chief justice of the Student Court. It simply meant that before I began working on the goal, I thought it through to the end, and decided what I would have to do to successfully achieve that goal. For example, if I determined that my Purpose was to earn an A on an exam, then my Preparation would be to pay attention in class, focus on reading assignments, complete homework, and study prior to the test. Then my Performance would need to be stellar. Upon receipt of my graded exam, I would review the Results in hindsight. If I earned the A as intended, then I would note what aspects of my Preparation and Performance had enabled me to excel. I would also ask, *What could I have done better?* This question would be especially important to answer with honesty and scrutiny if I had earned a grade below an A.

My method of Purpose, Preparation, Performance, and Results would prove invaluable as I progressed through college and into my career. While it was extremely helpful in academics and job-related tasks, this four-step success model can also be applied to personal relationships, health goals, and even planning a vacation. The key is forethought. Thinking things through before taking any action. It's like navigating a course on a map, or in today's world, looking at the route on which your GPS is going to take you. My observations of classmates and colleagues indicated that blindly embarking on a goal without a step-by-step strategy would yield poor results. It is a haphazard approach to school, work, and life.

Having such a structured, analytical approach to my goals endowed me with a feeling of control over circumstances that I had the power to mold through the application of my skills. In doing so, I discovered that Dr. Spraggins was actually giving me a formula to put into action The Parable of the Talents, and this propelled me to work even harder.

Dr. Spraggins, who was my advisor, taught us about the history of great empires, the impact of World War I and World War II, and the aftermath of slavery in the United States. His lectures exposed the problem of voting rights, and how we all needed to work to ensure that blacks were no longer tricked, intimidated, or blocked from exercising their constitutional right to vote.

I had witnessed that first hand in North Carolina, where blacks were led to believe they were not smart enough to vote. I needed to look no further than my own parents to understand the insidious cruelty of this racist practice that blocked blacks from the voting booth. My parents had tried to register to vote for years. But the law at the time required people to take a literacy test and pay a poll tax, neither of which black people were doing successfully. And if they did manage to pay the $2 or $5 poll tax, they would flunk the literacy test.

During my senior year of high school, I helped my father prepare for the test. When he arrived at the voter registration site, an administrator handed him and other prospective voters a written passage and said, "Read this and interpret it to my satisfaction." The administrator, mind you, was typically some uncouth guy chewing tobacco and spitting all over the place. The prospective black voters – who included my mother, my father, and my high school principal, Mr. Aaron Wilder – read and interpreted the selection.

"Wrong answer!" the administrator said. "You fail. You can't register to vote."

Neither my mother, my father, nor Mr. Wilder passed the "literacy test." While I had never visited the polling site, I trusted that the test was honest, and that black people were simply not intelligent enough to vote. But then I wondered, *How could a high school principal fail any such test?*

Suddenly, I woke up to reality. I understood that this was yet another way that the oppressive system was rigged to rob blacks of political power. Reflecting on this experience in Dr. Spraggins' class made me realize I had the power to change things.

"One of the greatest thinkers of our time, W.E.B. DuBois, calls you the 'Talented Tenth,'" Dr. Spraggins told my class. "That is the 10 percent of the black population in America that has the talent and opportunity and drive to make a difference for the remaining 90 percent. I urge you to do that in the area of voting rights, because as a collective community we can exercise our power in the voting booth by electing leadership that represents our best interests, and has the power to change things for everyone."

His words lit a fire in me. As part of the Talented Tenth, I had the power to help others. I was reminded of the Parables.

"It's a complicated problem that won't be easily fixed," Dr. Spraggins warned. "But each of you has the power to do something about it. You can, and you should."

I took action with other students. We promoted voter registration by passing out materials in the local black communities, instructing them on how to register to vote. When white people saw us doing that, they threw eggs.

Rosa Parks Inspires the Civil Rights Movement

Near the conclusion of my first semester in college, on December 1, 1955, Montgomery, Alabama seamstress Rosa Parks refused to forfeit her bus seat to a white man. She would later declare that her profound disgust over the lynching of Emmett Till, and countless others that never resulted in headlines or criminal charges, bolstered her courage to take a stand against injustice – by literally sitting down.

The law at the time required blacks to sit in the "colored" section at the back of the bus if the front seats were needed by whites. The courageous defiance of this soft-spoken woman helped spark the Civil Rights Movement that would, over the next decade, profoundly change American laws.

Mrs. Parks' appearance in the national spotlight also focused attention on the unknown minister at her side – Dr. Martin Luther King Jr. of the Dexter Avenue Baptist Church in Montgomery, Alabama. Four days later, the 26-year-old minister led the Montgomery Bus Boycott, which would span 381 days and result in desegregating the city's bus system. It also thrust Dr. King into the national spotlight.

I read the black newspapers and magazines with voracious curiosity to learn the latest news on the quickly evolving developments that filled me with hope that change was indeed on the horizon.

"Man, You Need to Change Your Name!"

Throughout first semester, my roommates mocked my name.

"Stevie, Stevie!" they taunted. This really started to bother me when I was attending choir practice to prepare for a trip to perform in Europe. "Stevie, Stevie!"

Around that time, a new roommate from Philadelphia was placed with us.

"Man," he said to me, "you need to change your name!"

"Why? My name is Stevie. That's what my mom calls me."

"Because you gotta put up from crap from those guys," our new roommate said.

During Christmas vacation, I went home to Enfield and told my mother, "I want to change my name to Steve."

"Why?"

"I want to smack these guys who are mocking me," I told her.

She agreed to take me to the courthouse, where I officially changed my name to Steve.

"You Cannot Pay Your Bills, But We are Going to Keep You"

While eagerly monitoring national news, I was oblivious to a very important detail about my status on campus. It resulted in a rude awakening at the start of second semester, when I returned to my dorm room to find a note that said: "Please see the Dean of the College."

I did, immediately.

"Stevie, when are you going to pay your bill?" asked Dr. Thomas A. Henderson, a caring but extremely serious man who rarely smiled.

Dumbfounded, I answered, "But I already paid."

"Yes, and you need to pay $1,000 for the second semester."

I had naïvely believed that $750 was the total cost of college, because no one had told me otherwise.

"You mean I have to pay again?" I asked.

"Yes, you pay twice each year," said Dean Henderson, who would become President of VUU shortly after my graduation. "Your tuition plus room and board are $1,000 per semester. That's $2,000 per year." He said that I owed $750 for the first semester, which was reduced by a $250 scholarship.

"I don't have any money," I confessed. Panic consumed me. Would I be kicked out of school? If I could not attend college, what would I do? Returning to life on the farm back home was not an option. But how in the world would I get the money to pay for college?

"I want you to come back and talk with Dr. Proctor tomorrow," Dean Henderson said.

I met with Dr. Proctor as instructed.

"Okay, Steve," Dr. Proctor said. "You cannot pay your bills, but we are going to keep you, and here is what you have to do."

"Thank you," I said, "but what do I have to do?"

"You have to pay your bill. You can have a campus job and work after school at another job."

"I can't work after school," I said. "I sing in the choir and I have to go to choir practice."

"In order to sing in the choir," Dr. Proctor said, "you have to be a student here. And if you don't pay your bill, you won't be a student here."

I sat there, stunned. I felt extremely naïve. Suddenly I remembered when my mother would read the Bible to me and my siblings on Sunday mornings. In particular, I recalled Corinthians Chapter 13, verse 11: "When I was a child, I talked like a child, I thought like a child, I reasoned like a child. When I became a man, I put the ways of childhood behind me."

That Bible passage referenced love and knowledge, and thankfully, I was getting a heavy dose of both from the two top leaders of Virginia Union University who could have just as easily told me to leave campus for being too ignorant to pay my tuition. I would have to work hard for what I wanted – and sacrifice something I really enjoyed.

"Okay," I said. "I understand."

"Work with Dean Henderson on the details," Dr. Proctor said.

After that, I began two jobs that I was fortunate to maintain for three-and-a-half years until graduation. The first, my campus job, required me to clean the four-story dormitory where I lived. I was one of a team of four guys whose duty every morning was to cleanse and sanitize the bathrooms, dust the halls, and wax the floors on the weekends. Sometimes I'd do the bathroom, but neglect the hallway.

"Mr. Bullock, did you do the hallways today?" asked Mrs. Brown, our dorm mother who supervised our team and checked for spotlessness by wiping a piece of white paper on the floor.

"Yes ma'am, Mrs. Brown," I responded.

"Mr. Bullock, did you clean the halls?" she demanded, crossing her arms and glaring at me. "You did not clean the halls! I'll check with paper again tomorrow. Now, no more kissing and more time cleaning up!"

I realized that by not doing my very best, I was violating two of my mother's oft-repeated admonitions.

"Stevie," she'd say, "if something is your responsibility, or it's in your space and you touch it, you must try to leave it better than you found it." She always challenged me to improve everything that I encountered or that came into my life.

Likewise, if my behavior were less than exemplary, my mother often said, "Don't you ever let me see you do that, or hear you say that, again!"

My initial response to myself, was: *Okay, she did not say, "Do not do it." She said, "Don't let me see or hear you do it."* But eventually, I grew up and realized that what my mother did not see or hear, God did, and so did I. So, I began to apply that discipline to both my personal and professional behavior. As a result, when the dormitory mother scolded my mediocre cleaning, I reminded myself to never let God witness such behavior again.

I applied this increasingly conscientious work ethic to my second job, for which I walked off-campus to Long Transfer Trucking Company. Each night when big trucks arrived, we unloaded cargo onto smaller trucks for delivery the next day. The downside was that I often worked until 11 p.m.; this robbed me of sufficient time for sleep and homework.

The benefit was that it paid well, enabling me to easily cover my $2,000 annual bill for tuition, room, and board. A bonus was that a co-worker there hired me to work on his home garden, and he would send me back to campus with food. By the way, I never returned to choir, although I did play clarinet in the orchestra and marching band throughout college.

While doing so, I earned an occasional $25 by selling my blood at the Medical College of Virginia. The hospital had an on-going arrangement with the college to solicit the purchase of blood from students. I needed the money, and participated in this arrangement, even though I knew this was something that I should not have been doing. In fact, it was outlawed, after Congress created the American Blood Commission and other organizations whose purpose was to clean up that aspect of health care. Selling one's blood was not and is not healthy, nor was it safe for the patient who might receive it, because it was not screened for contamination or communicable diseases as it is now.

Today I am stunned at the irony that I sold my blood for money! It's paramount to selling oneself, even selling one's soul. And that is just plain wrong.

Meeting Doris, My Wife and Partner for Life

One evening after dinner during my sophomore year, I was in "the yard" talking with friends, when I noticed a beautiful young lady.

"My name is Delano Korsakov," I told her, "and I'm from Money, Mississippi. I have 21 brothers and sisters."

"I know you're lying!" she exclaimed, staring straight in my eyes with a look that warned she would not be fooled. "Somebody else told me you were Steve."

I loved her confidence and sassy personality, and I couldn't wait to learn everything about her.

Doris Kelly and I met on campus, began dating, and dreamed about spending our lives together.

"I'm Doris Kelly, a freshman from Lawrenceville, Virginia." She shared her background as we enjoyed many conversations about our upbringings and future dreams. "I lived in Newport News, Virginia until I was 12 because my dad worked in the shipyard building war ships."

The oldest of four children, Doris was born on July 1, 1939. As the first grandchild in the Kelly clan, she says she was somewhat spoiled.

"My full name is Doris Louise Elizabeth Kelly." The proud way that she announced her name resonated deeply within me because here was a woman who shared my belief that our names are important and should be acknowledged, spoken respectfully, and honored.

"I do not use Louise or Elizabeth," Doris explained. "I've got so much name, because as the oldest grandchild, everybody wanted me to be named after them. My first name is from my oldest aunt. Louise comes from Della, my next oldest aunt. Elizabeth is my mother's and my grandmother's name. My mother is Clyde Elizabeth. My father is Needham Nicholas Kelly, Senior."

Doris made it clear that she did not want to return to the farm life that she experienced in Lawrenceville from age 12 until high school graduation.

"I didn't like living on a farm," she said. "I did not like dirt on my hands or between my toes. I had to do farm work. If you talk to my brothers, I didn't do anything, but I did everything. No plowing, but I did drop fertilizer, and did some hoeing. I picked cotton one or two times. I never got the hang of it. I sorted tobacco to get it ready to be put in the barn, then your hands are all gooey. That was not for me. The boys did the animals. When my youngest brother was born, I stayed home where I had to learn to cook and do the laundry."

I learned that Doris' life on a farm was far less harsh than mine.

"My family and my parents' friends were middle class," she said. "We were not struggling. During the war, we had to do the rations with those little coupon books for margarine and sugar. Milk was delivered, and a vegetable truck came around, and mom and the women would go buy the ration in the amount of food and vegetables they needed."

Doris grew up in this home in Lawrenceville, Virginia, where she lived with her family from age 12 until she left for college. Doris was born in her grandparents' home in Lawrenceville and her parents moved the family to Newport News, Virginia, shortly after her birth. Her father worked in the shipyard there during the early 1940's until the early 1950's, when they returned to Lawrenceville and built this home.

I got to know Doris as we attended church together, went to the movies, ate pie and drank Coca-Cola at the campus grill, and attended dances in "the rec" – an event space in the basement of her girls' dormitory.

The dorm mother who lived there was always peeking around corners to enforce strict rules about conduct between male and female students. She had even packed the bags of a girl who was caught returning to the dorm in the morning with a boy after they had apparently gone to breakfast or possibly spent the night away together.

"I have to get back before my curfew," Doris often told me. "I'm not going to do anything to jeopardize my chance to stay in college."

Doris revealed that her parents and teachers had encouraged her to attend college for as long as she could remember, and that she was at Virginia Union with the help of a $500 scholarship that covered $250 per semester; her father paid the remaining $1,500.

"When I was too young to understand, my mother told me, 'You're going to go to college,'" Doris shared with me. "My mother went to school up to seventh grade, and my father was 12 when they took him out of school to work on the farm."

Doris graduated from high school at age 16. "I finished early because back then, there was no eighth grade, so I left seventh grade and went directly to ninth grade. Four years later, I graduated from James Solomon Russell High School in Lawrenceville with a 3.8 GPA."

Doris dreamed of becoming a teacher, but her counselor was pushing her toward secretarial work.

"I have a vision of what I want in life," she said. "In Newport News, I saw all kinds of wealthy people. And I saw the kind of car I wanted. A red Corvette. We had a coal heater in the house, and I used to sit behind it and put my feet on the legs of the heater and drive my Corvette." She burst into laughter, eyes sparkling with excitement.

I was absolutely falling in love with Doris Kelly's fun personality, easy laugh, and ability to envision a future far and beyond what she had experienced as a child.

"I was impressed by Steve's ambition," she recalls now. "He had a very clear idea of what he wanted in life."

I concluded that I wanted Doris with me as I pursued my life's goals. That Christmas, I went home with her to meet her parents and three brothers. Doris was the oldest, followed by Charles, Needham Jr., and Mark.

"Our parents grew immediately to love the man Steve Bullock," recalls Charles, 76, a retired pastor in Chesapeake, Virginia.

We dated through my sophomore and junior years, which were her freshman and sophomore years. During our second year together, we sat in front of Martin Hall, designing our home that we would live in when we got married.

Family and Finances

Back in North Carolina, my parents were growing old and sickly. I spent every Christmas vacation with them, and it was a joy to see Harvey and Selma Doris, my older siblings who had helped to parent me. Now, they and other nearby brothers and sisters cared for our parents, as did a nephew, Charles Edward, who died young.

During the summers, I always worked. One job took me to the oceanside resort town of Atlantic City, New Jersey, to work in the laundry department of a hotel. My nephew James joined me; we earned less than one dollar per hour and paid five dollars per week to rent a room.

"I've never seen a man who could stretch a dollar like he did, while doing the things we had to do – pay rent and eat," James recalls now. "We were making the same amount of money, but he was saving money and I was spending it. I don't know how he ate. I couldn't match it. I had one habit that he did not have: smoking. At the end of the season, when it was time to go back to school, he went to Virginia Union University without having to go to anyone for help. To this day, I don't know how he managed that!"

Sadly, as my elderly father suffered with terminal cancer, I reflected on his lifetime of struggles and sense of failure. I vowed to honor his legacy by achieving great things for myself and the Bullock name, while helping as many people as possible. Thankfully, Virginia Union University was preparing me to do that.

Learning from Giants

I pledged Alpha Phi Alpha Fraternity, Incorporated during the fall of 1956. This particular black fraternity impressed me because it develops leaders and promotes brotherhood and academic excellence, while providing service and advocacy for our communities.

Pledging involved all sorts of hijinks, which I endured with my roommate and fellow pledge, Karl Walkes.

"Steve was always demonstrating his leadership skills," Karl recalls, "including on 'Turnback Night,' when they took us into the woods and told us to find our way back to campus. He was instrumental in getting us back. We didn't have a compass or anything. He was able to use his instincts and directions to get us out." Karl, who spent three decades as an educator in New York City, also remembers me as "a very, very hard worker, and a very studious individual."

Another roommate was from Japan. He taught me a lot about Asian culture, and I promised to visit him there someday. He broadened my perspective and bolstered my belief that exploring the world was truly an attainable goal. In fact, God seemed to be bringing the world to me by assigning a roommate from the other side of the planet.

Knowing him just over a decade after our countries had been at war reinforced the idea that profound change on a national and global scale was possible, and that warring people could make peace and live together in harmony. That made me hopeful that the same could occur between blacks and whites right here in America.

Meanwhile, those at the helm of Virginia Union University introduced me to men and women who were courageously changing the racial terrain of American race relations by exemplifying the most extraordinary leadership in the face of violence and even death. Every Friday, we attended chapel for a presentation by Dr. Proctor, Dean Henderson, or a senior professor. They talked about our privileged positions as college students.

Though I never attended one of his theology courses, Dr. Proctor peppered his lectures with scripture such as Luke 12:48: "For unto whomsoever much is given, of him shall be much required: and to whom men have committed much, of him they will ask the more."

He would also tell us, "You have a responsibility to use your education to help our people and others in the world to rise above the oppressive circumstances of our day and follow your footsteps to greatness."

VUU invited many leaders such as lawyers, judges, business pioneers, and the clergy. They emphasized the importance of participating in extra-curricular activities and campus organizations to hone our leadership skills. I was particularly attracted to joining campus events hosted by the NAACP related to voting rights.

Dr. Proctor often invited me and other students to participate in small group conversations with the prominent black leaders who visited our campus. They included entertainers such as Duke Ellington, and VUU alumnus and Civil Rights Attorney Spottswood William Robinson III, who would become Dean of Howard University's Law School and the first African American appointed to the United States Court of Appeals for the District of Columbia Circuit. Another visitor was Civil Rights Attorney Oliver Hill from Richmond.

Meeting these men, and hearing them speak in small group discussions, provided highly motivational moments. We felt special that Dr. Proctor considered us worthy of personal time with these history-makers about whom we had read in the black and mainstream media.

Meeting Dr. Martin Luther King Jr.

In the spring of 1957, seven of us on my "Line of Pledges" were inducted into the Gamma Chapter of Alpha Phi Alpha Fraternity, Incorporated. I was so proud to receive the card that said: "This certifies that Steve D. Bullock is an active member of above named chapter…" and is signed by the General Secretary and General Treasurer. Oddly enough, at a solid 5 feet, 11 inches, I was the tallest member of my fellow pledges. That put me in the back of the line, where I was given responsibilities for directing our public activities.

During that time, Dr. King visited our campus. Our fraternity's leadership called a meeting for the pledges and told us: "You guys need to do something to welcome Dr. King to campus because he's an Alpha."

I took one of the two sheets off my bed, washed it, and used one to make a banner by writing, "Welcome Dr. Martin Luther King Jr."

I was enthralled by his speech, which reinforced what Dr. Proctor and other visitors were instilling in us. "Prepare yourself, be informed, decide what you believe in and what you're willing to stand up for," Dr. King told us. "Do it in a nonviolent way and always work for equal rights for everyone."

He also talked about the importance of working for voting rights for blacks, and he described how the Montgomery Bus Boycott had sparked similar protests across America that would surely help obliterate legal segregation. After his speech, I shook his hand. I was in absolute awe. At the time, I thought Dr. Proctor was almost god-like; now he had someone of even greater stature visiting with us!

I carried the motivating momentum of that evening into the classroom and into the social gathering places on campus, where I enjoyed robust discussions about social justice with students and professors about the change that I believed would someday be possible in America. This mission was emboldened in February of 1958, when my father died at age 93. I was certain that his spirit would help strengthen me to achieve things far beyond his wildest dreams.

Doris Is Gone
More heartache consumed me later that year, after working all summer and returning to campus in September of 1958. Doris was not there, and I had no way of knowing where she was or why she had not returned to college. Mind you, this was decades before the instant communications that we enjoy today via cell phones, text messages, and email. It was not until I received a handwritten letter from Doris – months later! – that I learned what had transpired.

"When are we going to Richmond?" she had asked her parents at the breakfast table as her bags sat packed for her junior year at Virginia Union University.

"You're not going to Richmond," her father said. "You can't go back." He explained that he needed to send her brother to college instead, because he would need to support a wife someday. "Doris, you can find a husband to take care of you."

Furious, Doris jumped up from the table.

"You *will* go back to college," her mother assured. But for the moment, Doris was sent to Washington, D.C. to live with an aunt and take care of her kids. Doris was outraged that she was pulled out of college and relegated to domestic work because she was female.

"I was just mad!" she recalls now. "I went buck wild! I went crazy, just running around with friends."

At one point, I visited her in Washington, and her boyfriend showed up. I realized that Doris needed time to purge the anger out of her system, but I wasn't sure if the rage was at her father, or at me for hoping to become the husband that her father wanted her to have. I coped with that situation by remembering my mother's recitation of Corinthians Chapter 13, Verses 4 through 7:

"Love is patient, love is kind. It does not envy, it does not boast, it is not proud. It does not dishonor others, it is not self-seeking, it is not easily angered, it keeps no record of wrongs. Love does not delight in evil but rejoices with the truth. It always protects, always trusts, always hopes, always perseveres." Still, losing Doris to these circumstances created a great void in my life during my senior year on campus. As a result, I channeled my attention into my class load, which included education courses and political science classes, as well as my two jobs.

I relished my leadership roles on campus. I served as President of the campus chapter of Alpha Phi Alpha, and during my senior year, I was elected Chief Justice of the Student Court. I participated in other campus activities as well, including playing in the first VUU marching and concert band. In addition, I devoted my time to our school's voter registration drive. Sometimes we were pelted with eggs, because many whites did not want blacks to exercise their power to vote and change the status quo.

At times when I faced blatant racism, I may have felt victimized, but I never allowed myself to become a victim – not intellectually, not emotionally, not spiritually. I never allowed myself to become defeated. During tough moments, I drew strength from the William Ernest Henley poem, *Invictus*, which I learned as a college sophomore and would use throughout my life to help me through difficult experiences. Here is the poem:

Invictus

Out of the night that covers me.
Black as the Pit from pole to pole.
I thank whatever gods may be
For my unconquerable soul.

In the fell clutch of circumstance
I have not winced nor cried aloud.
Under the bludgeonings of chance
My head is bloody, but unbowed.

Beyond this place of wrath and tears
Looms but the Horror of the shade.
And yet the menace of the years
Finds, and shall find, me unafraid.

It matters not how strait the gate.
How charged with punishments the scroll.
I am the master of my fate,
I am the captain of my soul.

While I value the poem, I believe the last two lines are a lie. I am neither "the master of my fate," nor the "captain of my soul." God is both of those in my life. So, after much nudging from my wife, I add, "With God's help," before the line, "I am the master of my fate and I am the captain of my soul."

An Education Better Than An A-Plus

In June of 1959, I graduated on time, completing my degree in four years, with hours and credits to spare. Given more time to study, I could have earned better than a B-minus grade point average.

However, the education I received about life was better than an A-plus, because I learned to live and thrive in an environment rife with challenges. It taught me that I was strong and that with the help of caring individuals such as Sam Proctor and Tom Henderson guiding my way, anything was possible.

Later in life, I saw Dr. Proctor several times, and he referred to me as one of his "boys." I thank him and God for giving me the opportunity to be one of his "boys."

I left campus with just one tie, some values, and a vision. But I didn't go home to Enfield, and this disappointed my mother, whose health was failing.

"I thought after going to college," she said, "you would come back here and take care of me like Mr. Willie Williams did for his mother. He didn't walk away from her." In fact, he had spent the bulk of his lifetime teaching school in North Carolina, where teachers were making $2,700 per year. He was 55 years old when his mother passed away.

I had absolutely no desire to stay in my hometown; the world was beckoning me. My mother did not want to hear this. So, I explained that while returning to Enfield as a public-school teacher was a noble profession, it was not what I wanted to do. Nor was it the greatest good I could do for myself and others, including her. Rather, my siblings and I established a plan to take care of our mother together.

In addition, I lovingly told her that I intended to do what she had encouraged me to do: make something of myself while exploring the world and seeking big opportunities to help myself, my family, and as many people as possible. With that mission, I left Enfield on a quest to find the best path and purpose for Steve Delano Bullock to pursue in the world.

Chapter 3

Joining the U.S. Army and Getting Married

Despite determination to make my mark on the world after graduating from Virginia Union University, I was uncertain about how to transition into the next phase of my life. In search of guidance, I engaged Dr. Proctor in many spirited conversations that inspired my decision against attending law school.

"You should consider a graduate degree in social work," Dr. Proctor advised. "I'm going to refer you to talk with one of my friends, Mr. Whitney M. Young Jr."

A social worker, Mr. Young was Dean of the Whitney M. Young School of Social Work at Atlanta University, and later became Executive Director of the National Urban League. Grateful for the referral, I was excited about the possibility of having Whitney Young as a supporter, and maybe even as a mentor. But I was not convinced that I wanted a degree in social work, and was unsure about where to seek development and preparation for the world of work.

One thing was for sure. I would never go to New York City. The Big Apple's allure had wrenched most of my siblings away from me during childhood. In my young opinion, their departure from Enfield was a detriment to their future success because it had robbed them of the opportunity to graduate from high school on time. Earning GEDs in New York resolved that problem for Floyd and Margaret. They went to college; she studied business and became a sales person.

However, neither my older brother Estee nor my sister Lillie ever returned to school. Lillie worked as a housekeeper, while Estee's septic tank business in Port Chester was quite successful. Paul owned a thriving trucking business.

I wanted to excel in my career far and above anything that my family members had achieved. As I contemplated how to accomplish that, I took a job as a stock boy with a company that supplied electrical fixtures to construction sites that included an apartment complex. For the first time, I worked only one job, and it provided a glimpse into the corporate world. The job paid well and the work was not bad, but I could not embrace the company's core values.

"Steve, we need you to come to the office," I was told one day. There, I was informed that my position had been vacated by a man who was drafted into the U.S. Army, but was now discharged and returning to his job. That was a common occurrence back then.

As the company proceeded to transfer me to various jobs, I was introduced to the expression, "You're over-qualified for that position." All the while, I remained confident that I would find my place in the world, and it would not be at the lighting company.

As summer became fall, I often thought of Doris. We had not spoken since my senior year. She was working at a school in a Virginia town a few counties away from her parents' home.

Meanwhile, my brothers Floyd and Morris had both joined the military after high school. Floyd served four years in the U.S. Air Force, during which time he was stationed in Okinawa, Japan. Morris' three years in the U.S. Army enabled him to experience Europe. Both clearly benefited from traveling overseas.

Joining the U.S. Army and Getting Married

My service in the U.S. Army provided invaluable lessons about discipline and human relations that laid a foundation for success and leadership.

At that time, the military draft obligated all men to serve – if they were 18 or older and met the requirements. That obligation could be waived by being enrolled in college or having someone who could pull strings. I wanted to satisfy the obligation; perhaps the Armed Forces would enable me to travel the world as I so deeply desired.

My hope spiked in early October, when Harvey forwarded my draft notice from Uncle Sam, inviting me to serve in the U.S. Army. I gave notice to the company and worked until the week before I was supposed to report.

I was inducted into the U.S. Army on November 9, 1959. At the induction center in Halifax, North Carolina, while my fellow recruits sat nervously in silence, I asked the people in charge a lot of questions about what was happening and what we could expect during the coming days, as well as during the next three months of Basic Combat Training. Meanwhile, my brief conversations with the other recruits revealed that few had welcomed the draft as I had. Next, still wearing street clothes, I was lined up and sworn in with about 20 young black and white men, including one of my high school classmates.

"Bullock, you're in charge of those black boys," an Army official said. He then turned to a white inductee and said, "You're in charge of those white boys."

I don't know why they picked me for my first military experience in leadership. Perhaps it was because I had asked questions for clarification about what was happening. As a result, I became responsible for overseeing my fellow black recruits as we traveled to Raleigh, the state capital, to complete another set of induction activities, before heading off the same day on a train to Basic Training in Fort Jackson, South Carolina, near the state capital of Columbia.

Before we departed early in the morning, I was given a food voucher for our meals when we stopped to eat, first in North Carolina, then in South Carolina. My job was to order our food, which was handed to us through the hole-like window in the back wall of the restaurant where – inside – our white peers were being served and eating at a table. Likewise, the Jim Crow laws of the South also relegated the black recruits to one train car while the white recruits were in a much nicer one.

At midnight, we arrived at Fort Jackson, where we were processed, issued clothing and equipment, and given instructions. We were told that we ranked at the lowest possible level in the Army: as a private PVT or Private E-1, compared to the next higher classifications of a Private E-2 and E-3.

The next morning, we reported to our basic training unit, where we all ate the same food, served by the same people at the same picnic-style table. Later, we were waiting for a bus that would transport us to various locations to continue our induction. A drill sergeant approached and ordered: "Pick up this trash and the cigarette butts on the ground."

This lesson began to orient us to life dictated by the Army's strict protocols and rigid power structure: it was imperative to obey orders from the superiors to whom one is assigned, and always make oneself useful. The drill sergeants were constantly giving orders and correcting everything we did.

The atmosphere was quite nerve-racking, because failure to perform in a way that pleased the drill sergeant could result in push-ups or assignment to an unpleasant detail or duty. We were expected to stare straight ahead while in line, lest we risked the drill sergeant barking an angry, "Don't look at me, boy!"

Exacerbating my anxiety was the humiliating and infuriating racial climate. For example, the drill sergeant would call each man's name, and he was supposed to respond by saying, "Negroid" or "Caucasian." I was having a hard time with this; I often felt so flustered that it was difficult to speak.

"Bullock!" the drill sergeant called.

"Caucasian!" I responded. "I mean, Negro!"

Nobody laughed. Everybody stood with their mouths shut, looking forward. Embarrassment burned through me, but I maintained a stiff face.

These experiences honed the emotional discipline that I had begun to develop during the 1955 Virginia Beach Summer from Hell. Then, as now, failure to do so could have dire consequences. As a result, I steeled my emotions to stop the Army leaders from intimidating me. My mental and physical survival in this environment required performing as they demanded: dressing correctly, stepping lively and quickly, moving when given an order, and never stuttering or saying, "What did you say?" The more I committed myself, the better I did.

I was assigned to Company C of an Infantry Unit where I quickly became a leader whose responsibilities included carrying the banner for my platoon and later for the company. The platoons and companies competed with each other in many activities, including full pack drills. These drills involved running long distances while carrying all equipment and competing with other units.

"We never leave anyone behind!" our Army leaders drilled into us. We wanted to honor this core value at all times, but an overweight, physically unfit member of our platoon posed a challenge. During a drill, I was up front, carrying my own equipment and the banner. The unfit solider was holding us back. So, I went to the rear of the platoon, took his pack, and added it to mine.

"Keep up!" I ordered.

I returned to my position, proceeding to crawl under barbed wire with fire overhead. Our victory helped leadership achieve its goal of proving that we were the best in the battalion by going the extra mile, even while carrying a heavier load. By the way, the overweight soldier improved significantly and was able to carry his own weight.

After three months of a mentally, physically, and emotionally grueling indoctrination into Army culture, we graduated. Each soldier received a Military Occupational Specialty or MOS. I was selected to work in Communications, an assignment that would endure for my entire 27 months of service in the military and in the reserve.

It began in Fort Gordon, Georgia, where I began specialty school from February until April of 1960. I graduated from the Communications Program with an MOS in Teletype and Morse Code, which I used on a two-way radio.

After a transfer to the headquarters of a missile site at Fort Niagara, New York, I was promoted to E-4. My Army portrait taken at this time shows me in uniform with a big A on my left shoulder. That meant I was part of the First Army Unit. Below that was my rank, which was Specialist E-4. Military rankings are very important because first, they provide a clear-cut explanation of one's duty, and second, they allow one to measure progressive ascent up through the ranks.

Thus far, my Army experience was all domestic; I had asked to go overseas, but was told to stay in the United States at least through the summer of 1960. Meanwhile, my friend who was a soldier from Texas remarked that I had mentioned Doris several times.

"Why don't you try to reach Doris?" he asked.

"Why?"

"You keep talking about her," he said, in a way that made me feel like he was my therapist.

I wrote a letter to Doris at Route 2 in Lawrenceville, Virginia.

"I'm coming home for Christmas," I told her, "and I'd like to visit you."

She received the letter and agreed. As I drove the 40 miles to her hometown, I marveled that we had grown up in such close proximity without knowing each other.

"Doris, will you marry me?" I asked.

"I'll think about it," she said.

I waited with patience, and ultimately, she said yes. We planned a June wedding.

"I met Steve when he came to our home in Lawrenceville, Virginia, from Virginia Union in pursuit of my sister Doris," recalls Charles Kelley, 76, a pastor in Chesapeake, Virginia. "He was a proud African American man who brought with him the power of being an Alpha man. We did not understand what was going on with him, but the way he carried himself with dignity, grace, and purpose was impressive and made us want to be a part of what it was that made him an exceptional man. I marveled at who he was. He had joined the Alphas; we didn't even know what an Alpha man was. We liked what we saw in him as a person who had dreams and ambitions, and was focused on his dreams and ambitions."

Charles says that I inspired him and his brothers to see the world in a bigger, broader way than their surroundings.

"We were farmers," he says. "We lived back in the woods. We didn't see people who were educated. Steve was a distinguished man and we needed someone else to emulate. He began a tradition in our family that wherever possible, the Kelly men following after him would be proud Alpha men also. I and my two brothers ultimately became Alphas because of Steve Bullock. We discovered that the same quiet determination displayed by our brother Steve could be ours also if we just tried to follow in his huge footsteps. We worked to be like him. We strived for excellence in the way we lived our lives."

Doris' youngest brother, retired U.S. Army Colonel Mark Kelly, 65, who now works in real estate with his wife, Valerie, in Clarksville, Tennessee, adds, "I went to college because of Steve Bullock. He showed us that you can have a greater life than the one you're leading."

Shortly after visiting Doris and her family, I was put on a list of Army reserve specialists who would be transferred to Fort Drum, New York.

"I can't do that," I told my company commander. "I'm going home to get married in June."

"Now if I say you can't go home to get married," he responded, "because you have to go on this assignment, then some years later you'll thank me that you didn't get married."

I was thinking, *I want to get married.*

Thankfully, they pulled me off that list.

Marrying Doris

Our wedding was scheduled for 4:00 p.m. on June 24, 1961 at Poplar Mount Baptist Church in Lawrenceville, Virginia. But while driving there during a leave from the Army, I got lost.

When I finally arrived, 25 family members and friends greeted me. Doris was absolutely beautiful in a short white dress, small veil, and white gloves. Her aunt Dorothy Kelly was the matron of honor in a blue chiffon dress, and John Robinson was the best man in place of Robert Harvey, who was unable to travel from Enfield. We also had a flower girl and a ring bearer.

"Given in marriage by her father, the bride wore a ballerina length dress of silk organdy," says a short article published in the local newspaper under the headline "Bullock-Kelly Vows Are Spoken." The news clipping, which we keep in a photo album, also says, "Her veil was attached to a matching lace hat. She carried a white prayer book centered with a white orchid."

Doris and I married on June 24, 1961 in Lawrenceville, Virginia at Poplar Mount Baptist Church, where Doris was baptized at age eight.

Four black and white photographs in our family album show me in a dark suit and bowtie, standing with Doris at the altar as we exchange rings.

Our joy was not reflected on my mother's face. She was disappointed that I was getting married. With her health ailing after cancer surgery, she reminded me of her wish for me to return to Enfield to serve as her caretaker. As a result, she was cold toward me on our wedding day, though she loved Doris. Over time, as she remained in a house in North Carolina near Harvey and his family, her bitter feelings sweetened.

"Everybody was happy they were married," says Doris' youngest brother, Mark. "My family has come to appreciate that Doris made quite the catch."

After the ceremony, Doris and I took a Greyhound bus to Enfield and spent the night in a rooming house, the closest thing to a motel one could find in the small country town. Thrilled to be married, we envisioned the type of bountiful life that's described in the Bible. We simply wanted a comfortable life for ourselves and the two children we hoped to have someday.

The day after the wedding, Doris returned to Lawrenceville and I went back to Fort Niagara. I left her with a sepia-toned photograph of me in my Army uniform. In blue ink, I wrote on the photo: "Always yours, Stevie."

I was supposed to be discharged from active duty six months later, in November, after serving my two years. But the Bay of Pigs Invasion of Cuba in April of 1961, as well as the Berlin Crisis from June until November, prompted President John F. Kennedy to place a moratorium on discharges and retirements for an indefinite period. He required that all soldiers be ready to go to war. My security clearances were not high enough for me to know exactly what was happening between Europe, the United States, and Cuba.

"We don't know how long you'll have to stay here," my Chief Operating Officer said. "If you want to bring your wife up here, you can."

We made plans to do that, only to learn that none of the available housing outside the post in Youngstown, New York, would rent to black soldiers and their families. Qualifying for housing on the Army post required one to rank as E-5. I was still an E-4.

"Nobody will rent for you," my COO said, "so we'll make you eligible for housing on the post."

Doris and I lived together for the first time as husband and wife in a nice little apartment on the post.

Leaving the Army

In mid-January, I received notice that I would be discharged into the Reserves as an E-5 in communications on February 2, 1962. We cleared the apartment, and Doris returned to her parents' home in Virginia.

Meanwhile, I was contemplating my next career move. The Army had failed to satisfy my voracious appetite for global travel; I craved new work opportunities that would introduce me to foreign lands, especially Japan. All the while, I explored many opportunities, including a job opening at the Boys Club in New York City. They led me to believe that I would be hired.

I shared this with very few people, because it contradicted my declaration to avoid New York. While contemplating my future as the first in our family to attend and complete college, I was determined to do something fulfilling that would significantly elevate my financial station in life for myself, Doris, and our future children. At the same time, I wanted a career that would excite me, expose me to the world, and provide leadership opportunities.

"Do you still want to travel overseas?" asked the civilian who was conducting my exit interview for the Army.

"Yes, I still want to do that," I answered, "and I want to be in a human service organization."

"Why don't you consider the Red Cross?" he asked.

I had little knowledge of the American National Red Cross outside of its blood drives and assistance for victims of natural disasters such as hurricanes.

The recruiter explained that the non-profit humanitarian organization, whose headquarters were in Washington, D.C., provided emergency assistance after fires, hurricanes, tornadoes, floods, and other catastrophes. It also: collected and distributed blood products; facilitated communication between military service members and their families; and educated people about health and safety.

Most importantly for me, the Red Cross met the two top criteria for my next job. I applied, and was interviewed in the Eastern Regional Office in Alexandria, Virginia.

"I don't want this job unless you'll allow me to go overseas," I told the interviewer. "And I want to go to Japan."

"Oh, sure you can go to Japan," they said. "You'll probably have to go to Korea first and serve a year, then serve two years in Japan."

"That sounds exciting," I responded. My plan was to have an overseas experience, then return to the U.S. and work for another organization or company while deciding what kind of graduate study to pursue.

After 27 months of service, I was discharged from the U.S. Army on February 2, 1962, and reported to work at the American Red Cross the following month.

CHAPTER 4

Beginning a Career with the American Red Cross

ADJUSTING FROM MILITARY SERVICE to my first assignment with the American National Red Cross was quite easy, because it began at a United States Army installation in Fairfax County, Virginia. There I spent four months at Fort Belvoir, which was housed in a large brick building whose white-columned façade reflects its history as Belvoir Plantation.

I trained with several other new hires to serve as social workers for military service men and women. This required me to draw upon my collegiate study of sociology and re-ignited my fascination with human relations.

During this training, I observed that the Red Cross' historic role in supporting the Armed Forces in combat zones during World War I and World War II had inspired the organization to emulate military culture; this afforded me a smooth transition in dress, demeanor, and workplace protocol. Quite frankly, this was one example of how the Red Cross struck me as a sleepy follower as opposed to an innovative leader that could implement changes to vastly improve the organization's efficiency and impact.

As such, the Red Cross, which operated within military bases, mimicked the Armed Forces' policies and procedures. One example was the Red Cross' use of the military's "Permanent Change of Station (PCS)" concept, which officially relocated an employee and his or her nuclear family members to work at another military or office location. That assignment would remain in effect until another PCS order required relocation.

For me, this occurred in May of 1962 at Fort Monmouth when I began working as an Assistant Field Director in Service at Military Installations, serving military persons and families, for the American National Red Cross in Fort Monmouth, New Jersey. Doris and I lived on the Jersey Shore in Asbury Park, New Jersey.

Each morning, I rode a bus to Fort Monmouth, where I passed through a gate and stopped at a check-in point. One morning, I encountered a problem during this routine, because the Red Cross required me and other employees in the Service to Armed Forces sector to wear attire that resembled military uniforms.

"You're AWOL from the Air Force!" an Army guard accused.

"I work for the Red Cross," I insisted.

The soldiers eyed me suspiciously while scrutinizing my dark blue cargo pants, pocketed shirt with sleeves rolled above the elbows, and black lace-up boots. My Red Cross uniform was quite similar to the attire worn by U.S. Air Force personnel. They refused to acknowledge or believe the authenticity of the red and white Red Cross patch on my shoulder and at the front of the baseball-style cap.

"You guys are harassing me," I said, showing my Red Cross identification card.

They called someone from the Military Police station, who finally escorted me to the Red Cross' offices on the base. There, I proceeded with my daily routine, reporting to the Field Director, who often sent me and several other colleagues on temporary assignments to Fort Dix, New Jersey, and McGuire Air Force Base, both of which were huge.

At each location, I was a social worker who counseled military personnel and their families. Whether the service men and women were working domestically or abroad, I coordinated communications and solutions to their social and financial problems with their families in their home towns. I also worked closely with the Catholic and Protestant chaplains on each base. Though many Jewish service members were present on each military installation, I often wondered why the Department of Defense did not provide rabbis.

Each day, I reported to the Communications Center on the base, where my daily responsibilities utilized the communications training that I received from the Army. We used the telephone as well as U.S. mail to reach and correspond with service members and their families.

In addition, well before email and text messages, the military and Red Cross used Teletype or TTY. It's an electromechanical typewriter that sends and receives typed messages from a location to one or several places via a variety of communications networks.

"We have three messages for you, sir," the receptionist said, handing me six Teletype print-outs. "They're all emergencies that require your immediate attention."

I looked through the messages. First was a "Health and Welfare Report" requested by a soldier's mother.

"I haven't heard from Leonard in a month," she wrote. "Can you please let me know that he's ok?"

My job was to locate Leonard at the Army base where he was stationed in Europe, confirm that he was doing fine, and relay that message back to his mother through the same communications system. In addition, I assured her, "He's been encouraged to stay in touch with his family." Sometimes the service personnel complied; other times they did not.

My next Teletype message said: "The family of Officer Jones is requesting emergency leave because his mother is critically ill." I contacted the military unit and presented the information to the commanding officer.

"You can let him know," the commanding officer said, so I arranged to meet with Officer Jones to discuss his departure. After that, the commanding officer worked out the arrangements to approve his emergency leave, which was only granted for the illness or death of immediate family members, not including grandparents.

Likewise, my third Teletype message was extremely common: a serviceman who had married immediately prior to deployment in another state or country would receive a letter from the Red Cross back home. It would cite family issues that required the serviceperson's attention and that he should be granted "compassionate leave" to come home to resolve the family problems. The serviceman would have an emotional breakdown, and would need to either go home to save his marriage, or receive counseling to cope with the loss. Death, divorce of parents, and illness were other common problems that I helped mitigate.

Ironically, I was doing social work – the very vocation that I had chosen not to do. However, it was fulfilling to help people, and I enjoyed my work. However, I longed to implement changes that I believed would improve the efficiency and impact of the Red Cross' policies and procedures.

"I really wish that I could be in charge of the organization," I often told my colleagues, "so I could decide the policy and make things better."

"You don't need to do that," they said. "Just get in a position to impact policy in this organization."

I was determined to become a leader in the Red Cross, and worked hard to lay a solid foundation to do that.

Racism Hinders Progress in Workplace and Community

Despite my ambition and hard work, I was confronted with blatantly racist behavior that reflected society's bigotry. First, Red Cross leadership was all white; none of the chapters had a black leader.

And not unlike most organizations during the early 1960s, the Red Cross was infected by the status quo of American racism. It tainted workplace culture in ways that hindered both my personal progress and the organization's ability to include black communities in its outreach and disaster services. For example, I noticed that the majority of the organization's black employees were relegated to Service to Military Installation Persons and Families, where I worked.

"Service to Military Installations is the right place for you guys to be," my boss' boss told me. "You have the manual, so you don't have to be able to think." He was implying that blacks lacked the intellectual capacity to excel in other areas of the organization as creative contributors and as leaders. Adding insult to injury, his tone of voice implied that I and the other black employees understood and agreed with this prevalent mindset.

Instead, I interpreted his statement as a common brainwashing tactic by the larger society that was motivated by the belief, "If I can demean you and detract from you enough, I'll convince you that you have no value."

This belief was manifest in the organization's compliance with society's racist practice of segregation in public accommodations. For example, I could not attend a conference in Charlottesville, Virginia, because the Red Cross did not challenge the Southern practice of banning blacks at hotels. Instead, our organization sent black employees to training in Brooklyn, New York, while white staff members went to Charlottesville.

I often questioned why the Red Cross chose to follow society's dehumanizing traditions when it could have stepped out as a leader to demand equality for its employees and the people we served.

If you're not part of the solution, you're part of the problem. Our mission was to help people, yet we were perpetuating injustice. Why was the Red Cross a sleepy follower rather than a leader in the realm of social issues that impacted our ability to serve people of every race, everywhere? If the organization was not addressing this with its own employees, how could it do so with the general public that we served?

These questions deeply troubled me as I thrived in my new position.

Going Global and Becoming a Father

Doris and I moved to Fort Monmouth, New Jersey, where we received news that we would be blessed with a baby in July of 1963.

"Steve, we'd like to send you to Korea," my supervisor said, believing that I would be excited to finally satisfy my lifelong desire for international travel.

"I don't want to go," I responded, "because my wife is expecting a baby."

A short time later, my employer said, "Steve, we've got another opportunity for you to take an assignment in Korea."

"I have to decline right now," I said, "because our baby is on the way."

"We can send you to Germany instead," my boss persisted.

"I don't want to do that either," I said, "because the baby is still not born."

"Eventually," my employer retorted, "you'll have to take this assignment, or you will no longer work for the Red Cross. Or we'll send you to Korea without your family."

"OK," I conceded. "I'll go to Europe."

I was never a person who wallowed in a "woe is me" attitude or who succumbed to victimhood. I did not resent that my employer was sending me on this assignment, nor was I angry that I would depart in July, the same month that our baby was due. Instead, I honored my responsibility to the Red Cross, which was granting my wish to travel. Leaving the country on the eve of our child's birth presented the intersection of three of the four pillars of my life: God, family, and the Red Cross. And it was the fourth pillar, Virginia Union University, that had in fact provided the education that enabled me to embark on a professional career that led me to this opportunity to travel.

To reiterate the importance of these four pillars and their meanings, the following chart defines them in detail.

The Four Pillars and Significance

1. The Church

God is first and foremost in my life. He is the guiding force of my every thought and action, and my relationship with Him has been honed through the Christian Church, and more specifically, the Missionary Baptist Church.

As the Bible says in Jeremiah 1:5, "Before I formed you in the womb I knew you, before you were born I set you apart; I appointed you as a prophet to the nations."

Believing that God has been orchestrating every step of my life before I came into being, my unwavering faith has endowed me with trust that God always makes a way out of seemingly impossible circumstances, and provides ideas and opportunities that lift us into positions to help ourselves, our families, our communities, and our world.

2. Family

Were it not for my parents, I would not have come into this world. And were it not for their nurturance of my physical, emotional, spiritual, and educational needs, I would not have survived. Their love and encouragement molded me into a conscientious citizen intent on making a positive contribution. Marrying and having children, then grandchildren, has been my greatest source of joy. The family unit is the building block of a stable society; it is where we learn our values and tenets of appropriate behavior. My life has been fueled by the need to provide for my family and nurture responsible children and grandchildren into adulthood so that they can share their talents to improve the world.

3. Virginia Union University

This educational institution and its caring leaders developed me far above and beyond the classroom instruction required to earn a degree. This HBCU shaped and molded me with invaluable life lessons that bolstered my character, challenged me to become my best, and prepared me for a life of leadership that has helped people around the world. VUU would also enable me to continue this work on a broad scale through my participation on the Board of Trustees in later years. This empowered me to help make important decisions about the school's finances and selection of a new president.

4. The American Red Cross

My nearly 40-year career with this global humanitarian organization enabled me to work to improve the human condition for myself, my family, and all others within my reach, which ultimately extended around the world. Through my work with the ARC, I have forged lifelong friendships and made lasting changes, such as designing and building the offices for the Cleveland chapter. And as an African American leader, I cultivated diversity and inclusion within the organization and within the communities that we served, both through specific programs designed to do that and by showing an example that a black person could serve with excellence in leadership capacities.

Pardon me for skipping forward in the above grid, but it's important to illustrate the breadth and depth of these pillars as the foundation of my personal and professional life.

As such, they enabled me to process the prospect of leaving my pregnant wife in order to take my assignment in Germany. My deep faith convinced me that these pillars were synchronizing to create a positive outcome for me, my family, my career, and all of the people whose lives I might improve as a result. With that belief, I left Doris in the care of my mother and her older brother, who stayed with her for six weeks.

In Germany, the Red Cross sent me on temporary assignments to acclimate me to its operations. I spent significant time at a military airbase near Toul, France, as well as Pirmasens, Germany, which was centrally located near the French border. I still have my white plastic "Officers' & Civilians' Open Mess" card that gave me entrée to the mess hall, or military dining room. My work was the same as what I had done at Fort Monmouth. This time, however, I relied more heavily on Teletype messages without telephones or the U.S. mail.

It was through a Teletype message that I received news that Eric Delano Bullock was born – a month later than expected – on August 20, 1963. My heart soared, but sunk when I learned of Doris' ordeal during the birth.

"They did not treat me with respect," she recalls. "I was petite, and they thought I was a 15-year-old black girl, having a baby by herself, with no father. They did not give me the same quality of care that was given to the other patients. Fortunately, my brother stayed with me, and Steve's brother and mother arrived after the baby was born."

Again, I did not embrace a victim mentality when she described what happened. I simply longed to comfort Doris, and I was grateful that our baby was healthy. All I could do was dream about seeing him and holding him. Doctors would not allow Eric to fly until he was three months old, so Doris sent me a lot of photographs, and I was overjoyed. Finally, during mid-November, my wife and our son joined me in Germany, and I was absolutely enamored with our baby boy. I looked forward to the day when Eric could actually hold a conversation with me, as opposed to crying.

"Stop crying," I would whisper. "Stop crying. Just be quiet."

Never did I hold my son closer than on November 22, 1963, the day that President Kennedy was assassinated. Extremely disturbed that someone would kill the President of the United States, I prayed for the safety of all Americans and the world. His death shattered Americans' sense of security and highlighted the perilous world in which we lived.

At the time, we were awaiting placement in housing on the military installation. In the interim, we lived in an apartment building, where we learned that Germans generally do not use much heat. One morning, the building manager entered our apartment and flung open a window. Then she placed the bed beside it.

"What are you doing?" Doris demanded, holding our infant son as cold air gusted toward them. "It's already too cold in here!"

The German woman shook her head dismissively and said, "This is what we do every day, to freshen the linens and the bed."

The single heater in our studio apartment was no match for this frigid tradition. And because Eric liked to kick off the blankets while sleeping, he became very ill with diarrhea. We took him to the military hospital, where we waited hours to see a doctor. Eric became even more sick as we waited. When we finally saw the doctor, he scolded Doris:

"Why did you wait so long to come to the doctor? You have allowed your baby to become dehydrated."

"Look!" Doris responded. "I've been sitting in your lobby waiting room for hours, and the whole time I was out there, he was having diarrhea."

Eric spent the night in the hospital, and we feared he might die. My heart ached as I watched him lay listless and quiet; I recalled his crying prior to getting sick, and wished he would look and sound that robust again.

"Boy, you can make any noise you can make," I said.

Thankfully, Eric recovered quickly, and we made certain to keep him well hydrated and warm in our cold apartment. Meanwhile, Doris was hardly impressed with the military hospital system.

"I decided, 'I am *not* getting pregnant over here!'" she recalls. "That is just not going to happen.'"

A short time later, things improved significantly after we moved onto the military installation; Doris and I delighted in watching Eric take his first steps there.

"I'll be really happy when you and I can have a conversation," I would tell him, feeling like that day might never come. But when it did, he talked nonstop. Then I'd say playfully, "Okay, we've had enough conversation!"

I loved that we had a comfortable home where all our needs were nicely met. Our life often inspired me to reflect on the harshness of life when I was a boy in Enfield, North Carolina. And I would think, *This is a long way from those days of walking barefoot behind a plow.*

Work Offers Opportunities for Friendship and Travel

My work in Europe involved collaboration with the chaplain and eight other Assistant Field Directors. We were all case workers, and we were all men, handling the same types of situations that I had mastered at Fort Monmouth.

A short time after arriving in Germany in 1963, I befriended Lieutenant Horace Montgomery, along with his wife, Jane, and their son. Horace and I shared night duty and weekend duty, which required a commissioned officer and a non-commissioned officer to work simultaneously. In those instances, he was the contact person when I was handling messages about emergencies in the United States.

"I would dial Steve's number in the middle of the night," Horace recalls with a laugh when telling the story to friends now, "then put the phone down and let it ring. In those days, phones didn't hang up. So, I let it ring until I'd wake him up."

I don't remember that happening. When I was on duty, I was fully awake and available to respond to phone calls at any hour. However, Horace's humorous recollection is always a delight. To this day, Doris and I enjoy our friendship with the Montgomery family. After serving in Europe, Horace would go on to serve in the U.S. Army for more than two decades before retiring as a Colonel and moving to Virginia. Our families often got together to socialize after we moved back to the States and lived in Virginia.

As our friendship deepened in Germany, and I counseled servicemen and women through distressing situations, I suffered a personal tragedy of my own. My brother Morris, who was 31, died during surgery for a heart problem; he never woke up. Being far away from my family and unable to attend his funeral made the grief all the more difficult. However, it deepened my capacity for empathy and sympathy while helping individuals to resolve family problems, serious emotional issues and the loss of loved ones.

The Holocaust was a Taboo Topic Among Germans

While I was learning how to look forward, I also wanted to glimpse back to comprehend the history of the nation where I was living and working. Specifically, I was determined to engage at least one German person in a conversation about the Holocaust. Now 20 years after that horrific event in world history, I wanted to hear from them about how that could have occurred without anyone stopping it.

Since many Germans worked on the base in the dining hall, restaurants and clubs, my daily contact with them afforded countless opportunities for what I hoped would be enlightening and poignant conversations.

No such luck. Not a single German person would engage me in a conversation about the Hitler era. They all claimed ignorance about what had been happening at the time. Many of these individuals were in their fifties; I was convinced that they were not as open as Americans are, as if they had taken some collective oath of secrecy to never speak to outsiders about how their country had committed one of the worst atrocities against humanity.

Likewise, when these same individuals expressed great sadness after President Kennedy's assassination, their condolences had felt insincere.

My desire for answers became even more acute after Doris and I visited two concentration camps in southern Germany. One place allowed us to write a note and leave it. I wrote: "I pray this can never, ever happen again, anywhere."

During this time, Doris and I visited the world headquarters of the International Committee of the Red Cross in Geneva, Switzerland. Housed in an impressive, chateau-style building, the organization executes its mission worldwide: "To protect the lives and dignity of victims of armed conflict and violence and to provide them with assistance."

Doris and I came away from each trip with a deeper appreciation and understanding of the international scope of this organization whose neutral presence in combat zones is honored by its mission to protect humanity. We were awed by the far-reaching impact that the Red Cross can make to save lives when war, famine, natural disasters, and other catastrophes threaten the lives of men, women, and children.

We also learned that the International Committee of the Red Cross maintains its neutrality by being entirely comprised of Swiss people. Its website says, "The ICRC is an independent, neutral organization ensuring humanitarian protection and assistance for victims of armed conflict and other situations of violence. It takes action in response to emergencies and at the same time promotes respect for international humanitarian law and its implementation in national law." Among the many endeavors of the International Red Cross, it responds to disasters and refugee situations, and helps prisoners of war.

Fulfilling My Dream to Travel the Globe

While growing up in North Carolina, attending college, and beginning my career, I longed to travel the world. Now, Doris and I were blessed with the opportunity to do that, so we decided to get a car during the late spring or early summer of 1964. We purchased our British-made Tanus Ford from an enlisted serviceman who had been a client. His dilemma was that he was being discharged, but could not afford to pay for his wife – a German woman whom he had met while serving in Europe – to return to the United States with him.

Though I appealed to the Red Cross to finance his spouse's airplane ticket, I was not successful. I advised him to go home, get a job, and send back for his wife. Meanwhile, he was trying to give away or sell his car. I bought it for $500 and purchased two new tires for it.

I did not expect the car to last long, and I was right. Doris and I drove it for a month, until we took our first trip north on the Autobahn to visit our good friends Horace Montgomery and wife Jane, north of Frankfurt. Smoke suddenly started pouring out of my car. It stopped. We pulled over to the side, where we encountered a farmer on a tractor. He was kind enough to tow the car into his place and fix it, but the car died anyway. Horace drove down and picked us up. Unable to salvage any value on the vehicle, including the two new tires, I junked the car. I don't regret the purchase; I did the right thing to help a serviceman in need and I knew what I was getting into.

Later that year, we bought a new vehicle, a little Volkswagen station wagon. We drove that car all over Europe and would later take it back home to the States where we ultimately sold it.

That Volkswagen took us on vacations to Brussels, then Amsterdam and the Netherlands. A book that we purchased called "How to See Europe on $5 a Day" enabled us to afford the trip, which included staying in a bed and breakfast.

At one point, I got a parking ticket and went to pay it.

"You have to go before a judge," I was told.

"This is very complicated," I said. "Maybe I won't get back to Germany."

When I appeared in court, the judge had fun with us.

"Since this is the first time you've been here," he said, "maybe you didn't understand what you were doing, but what you did was illegal. I'm going to have to fine you." He spoke in a way that made me feel that he was insulting my country. I decided not to get in a fight with this judge.

"I'm going to fine you fifty cents," he said.

"Oh, how much is fifty cents?" I asked, thinking this guy was trying to trick me. Then he said:

"And I know a black man would not get away with this kind of thing in the United States."

I kept my mouth shut.

He laughed, shook my hand, and I paid 50 cents.

Thankfully, that was the only such glitch during our frequent travel during my three-year assignment in Europe. We ventured throughout Germany, France, Austria, Northern Italy, Switzerland, and our favorite place, Amsterdam. While we did visit Paris and Rome, we did not go to Berlin or London. One excursion included a cruise around the boot of Italy to Greece and Southern France, all the way to Spain.

I chuckle with every recollection of a trip to the French Riviera in 1965, when women sunbathed topless on the beach. In 2005, Doris and I returned, also visiting Nice and Marseilles. Doris was tired and wanted to rest, so I walked the beach, where I saw a topless, old woman. I chuckled, thinking, *That's the same woman I saw in 1965, but things have kind of moved on her body.*

Career Progress and Civil Rights Spark Culture Shock

When we returned to the United States in 1966, I visited a shopping center in Virginia. As was my habit, I wore a shirt and tie, because being well groomed and neatly attired always conveyed an air of integrity; it also garnered greater respect and better treatment. This habit is not about skin color; it's about presentation, and it's something I practice to this day.

Back then, as I proceeded to shop, a white store clerk approached and asked, "May I help you, sir?"

Startled, I looked around, thinking, *She can't be talking to me!*

But she was.

I stood in stunned silence, reeling with culture shock. After all, I was in the same state that had inflicted the Summer from Hell, when I had been so outraged by relentlessly racist treatment that I was willing to risk my life by lashing back.

Now, as this white woman treated me with dignity and respect, I was awed by how dramatically the racial climate in the United States had changed since our departure for Europe. Because the 1964 Civil Rights Act had banned segregation in public accommodations, Doris and I and other blacks were permitted to stay at hotels that previously had closed their doors to us.

While our nation was changing, I was considering a career change. I was not sure if I would remain with the Red Cross or seek employment elsewhere. The Red Cross resolved that question by promoting me to Field Director, assigned to Fort Belvoir, Virginia, a critical location in the heart of Red Cross activities.

Doris and I and Eric lived on the post at Fort Belvoir, in Fairfax County, Virginia, where the Red Cross owned a building that reminded me of a church rectory. Living there made me feel as if I were a church pastor. The home was free, and it was a nice experience, as our family life was joyous. Doris and I were so proud that three-year-old Eric returned from Europe speaking both English and German.

"My earliest memory is from Fort Belvoir," recalls Eric, now 54, a security officer married to Cathy and father to 19-year-old Elizabeth. "We'd sit in the little family room and watch TV together. I remember watching the Kent State shootings on the news as it happened. We also had fun at the Fourth of July celebrations on the base."

During that time, we learned that Eric had a little brother on the way.

"I got pregnant as soon as we returned to the United States," Doris recalls. We were blessed with the birth of Brian Dennis Bullock on August 11, 1967 at the New Alexandria Hospital.

Our apartment was connected to my five-room office suite in the rectory-like building. Servicemen and women who were walking past often saw the Red Cross sign outside, knocked on the door, and entered, seeking help. Sometimes they would speak with the individual on duty whose job was to respond to emergencies. Other times, they spoke with me. As a result, I felt that I was always working.

We assisted many young couples who needed financial assistance for a down payment on an apartment. Other times, we helped them cope with illness and death of loved ones back home. And we visited some real tough guys in the military prison who were awaiting a court martial or who were AWOL, the acronym for "absent without leave."

Meanwhile, my eight-member staff was all female except for one male. Their light workload made me uneasy; it left too much time for chatter.

"An idle mind is the devil's workshop," my mother used to say. And I felt that I wasn't doing my job if we were not accomplishing something. So, I became quite creative with ideas to motivate productivity; one such project was to rearrange and reorganize our office.

Vietnam: "I Could Have Been Killed Anytime"

In 1967, shortly after Brian was born, Red Cross leadership told me that I was being assigned to a war zone.

"Steve, we're sending you to Vietnam," they said. "You'll spend six months in a combat area and six months in a noncombat area."

I knew better; Vietnam was *all* combat area. This was a dangerous assignment; the war would ultimately claim the lives of five American Red Cross staff members and injure many others, according to the organization's website.

I was acutely aware of the deadly risks as I spent the first seven months in Vietnam in what the Red Cross classified as my combat zone duty with the Ninth Infantry Division. Every night, rockets and mortar rounds were fired at our post on the Makong River – a battle zone of the Viet Cong and the North Vietnam Army.

It was impossible to know the difference between the VC and a Vietnamese person who was working on the U.S. Army base. This added a terrifying dimension to the already hazardous environment because the enemy lurked behind the seemingly innocent faces of the people around us.

Every day, I prayed that I would return safely to Doris, Eric, and Brian, who stayed with Doris' parents in Lawrenceville, Virginia, while I was in Vietnam.

The blurred lines between malicious people and innocent people reflected the amorphous nature of the Vietnam conflict. In a nutshell, the United States was working with the government of South Vietnam to stop the southward progression of Russian Communism. North Vietnam was Communist, and the Viet Cong used traditional combat and guerilla tactics to stop the anti-Communist forces, which included the United States, from blocking Communism from advancing throughout Asia.

For me, being unable to identify the enemy in plain sight created an extremely tense environment; I was aware that I could get killed anytime, anywhere. For example, Vietnamese men worked in the dry cleaners where we took our uniforms, shirts, and other clothing, as well as in the cafeteria and barber shop. A constant sense of danger permeated my daily life. Were any of the Vietnamese men who worked at the base by day, plotting to kill us at night?

Meanwhile, I served in the same communications and counseling capacity as I had in Europe and the United States. Every month, chapter staff and field directors like myself helped about 27,800 servicemen with personal and family problems. Illicit drugs played a prominent role in the problems that many of them experienced.

As for communications to service members' families back in the States, we did not use the phone. We used Teletype messaging through the local Red Cross chapters. I handled some of the 2,168,000-plus emergency communications that the Red Cross facilitated between servicemen and their families during the Vietnam War, according to the Red Cross.

"Serving our men on the battlefields here in Vietnam, the American Red Cross is a hotline to the folks back home, an oasis in the heat of battle, and a comfort during hospitalization," wrote General William Westmoreland, then commander of the U.S. forces in Southeast Asia, to Red Cross national headquarters in 1968.

Many military leaders praised our work to help soldiers and military staff cope with the horrific realities of Vietnam. At the height of the war, 500 Red Cross field personnel were working in field stations throughout Southeast Asia.

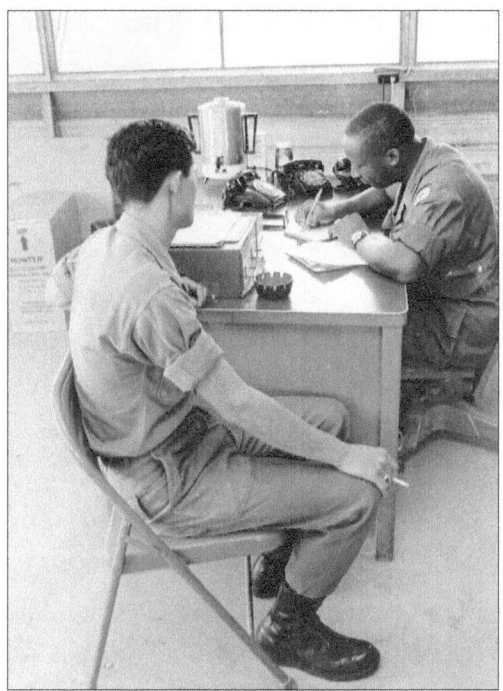

The American Red Cross sent me to Vietnam to serve on two different military bases. My job was to facilitate emergency communications between servicemen and their families. This assignment was an extremely dangerous because the enemy literally worked among us on the Army base.
Photo Credit: American Red Cross

Several black and white photographs capture me in Vietnam, wearing the same Air Force-like uniform emblazoned with the Red Cross insignia on my arm. One picture shows me sitting at a desk, using an ink pen to complete forms for the young soldier who's sitting in a chair facing me. Three rotary-dial phones, as well as a coffee maker, sit on the desk.

Another photo shows me standing outside on the base beside sandbags piled well over my head, as I grasp a clipboard and talk with a young solider. This time, I'm wearing the dark blue baseball cap that displays the Red Cross patch. Yet another picture captures me clasping that large clipboard while walking past a tank and a wall of sandbags, while soldiers stand guard on a truck behind me.

For the second half of my Vietnam duty, the Red Cross transferred me to Second Field, near the United States Army Vietnam Headquarters, or USAV, at Long Binh Post. Located not far from Saigon – now called Hồ Chí Minh City – the bustling and sprawling base also known as "Long Binh Junction" was like a city, and would ultimately house 60,000 personnel in 1969.

There, my Vietnamese barber confirmed my worst fears about the enemy among us. This man would routinely cut my hair, shave me with a straight razor at my throat, and massage my shoulders. I'd feel great, then leave. I later learned that he and other enemy fighters were caught at the "ammo dump" – a highly explosive storage bunker packed with ammunition. The ammo dump was a dangerous place. During World War I, black soldiers, who were often relegated to the most undesirable work, were ordered to guard the ammo dump.

The Viet Cong, however, was so bold that the barber and his fellow soldiers were caught attempting to blow up the ammo dump; they could have easily set off an explosion to destroy a huge amount of American ammunition. In fact, that had occurred the year before. In the case of my barber and his fellow soldiers, however, American soldiers shot and killed them before any damage was done. For me, the discovery of his true identity was especially chilling. This man could have killed me or others instantly on many occasions. Likewise, suicide bombers were not uncommon. Viet Cong fighters would strap explosives to their bodies, ride a bicycle into a crowded area, and detonate the bombs.

This atmosphere intensified my determination to exercise self-discipline at all times. I was extremely cautious about the people with whom I associated, where I went, and what was happening around me. As a Red Cross employee, I carried two identification cards that said I was "non-combatant." I was instructed to show the cards if I were ever captured. If my captors abided by the Geneva Conventions, they would do me no harm and I would do them no harm. I had one such experience, and it did not bother me; I knew that I was going into a dangerous area and I would not legally have any means of protecting myself.

All the while, I continued to advance within the Red Cross, being promoted to a Field Director 3, the highest rank of that position. I enjoyed supervising people at military installations. Each opportunity enabled me to learn quickly and effectively how to lead people and how to keep them focused on our purpose and the task at hand.

As I helped individuals through difficult times, my desire to improve the organization through a leadership position inspired me to take a few non-classified military trainings and workshops to learn how to become a more effective leader.

Moving Up in the Red Cross
Thankfully, I returned safely to the United States in October of 1968 and was immediately promoted to Assistant Area Director for Service at Military Installation in Alexandria, Virginia. I was one of three people who worked with staff at military installations in 14 states between Virginia and Maine. My job was to supervise those locations, where I was providing counseling sessions and constantly pushing myself to become a better supervisor.

The following year, on August 17, 1969, Hurricane Camille devastated the Mississippi Gulf Coast, killing 259 people and causing $9.16 billion (in today's dollars) in damages in the coastal states.

The catastrophic aftermath of Camille shined a spotlight on the Red Cross' longtime practice of providing disaster relief to white communities – while ignoring blacks and other racial and ethnic minorities. This made ugly headlines during the fall of 1969, when the NAACP, the Urban League, and black doctors from Chicago lambasted the Red Cross in the U.S. Congress. The groups had filed a complaint against the organization for specifically ignoring black residents in Louisiana and Mississippi.

This resulted in a consent decree on racial discrimination that required the Red Cross to implement policies and plans to ensure outreach and inclusion for blacks across America. The United States Department of Health, Education, and Welfare monitored the Red Cross' progress, and two or three members of Congress visited the Red Cross to discuss the problem.

I was hopeful that this scrutiny and public pressure would force the Red Cross to change its culture of racial exclusion both within the organization and in the communities that we served.

Meanwhile, Doris and I were living at Bailey's Crossroads in Fairfax County. My annual salary was close to $10,000, the equivalent of about $65,000 today. Doris and I had two cars, a Volkswagen and a really nice Mercury Cougar. To earn extra income, I moonlighted in the men's department at Two Guys, a discount store. I kept this a secret because some of my co-workers had been reprimanded for having part-time jobs. About two weeks before Christmas of 1969, the deputy manager of the Red Cross headquarters called me.

"I need you to come see me first thing in the morning," Sheldon Williams said.

I panicked, thinking, *Oh, my God. I'm being fired. They found out I have a part-time job.*

"Steve," he said, "we want you to be part of a team that we're going to assign to travel with Ross Perot on behalf of Vietnam American prisoners of war."

Overwhelmed with relief that my employer had not discovered my moonlighting, I then learned the next morning that Dallas businessman H. Ross Perot had requested Red Cross personnel to travel with his team to Hanoi, Vietnam, to deliver health and welfare items, to provide support and communication to the POWs, and to bring home injured prisoners.

My gut instinct told me that declining this opportunity was not an option. This was a classic *kairos* moment. That Greek word means "opportune moment for decision or action." My belief was, when the door opens for a new opportunity, you walk through eagerly. Declining an international mission was not an option. I concluded, *OK, I have to do this.*

"No!" Doris declared. "It's Christmas."

How could I simultaneously accommodate both my career and my wife? Extensive discussions resulted in our agreement that I would go, while Doris would take our sons home to her parents for the Christmas holidays. She was quite unhappy about my departure.

Leadership Lessons from Ross Perot

Ross Perot led our six-member team into the most volatile region of the world as if he were the president of a country. At times, I was convinced that he was actually President Richard Nixon.

His determination was relentless, even when Vietnamese leaders in Hanoi threatened to shoot us down if we attempted to land our two 707 jets that were loaded with health-related supplies (but no medications) as well as clothes and pajamas. Nor did they want us to bring home injured soldiers.

Perot insisted that he had permission from the U.S. government and President Nixon. His confidence and tenacity despite life-threatening obstacles – all for the sake of executing his self-styled, self-funded humanitarian mission – provided an extremely valuable lesson on leadership. He was a visionary who wanted to achieve a goal that others might deem impossible, and he persisted until he got results, even if that took years and monumental effort far above and beyond the average person's quitting point.

Every step of the way, I studied Perot's bold leadership style as he interacted with the media, government leaders, and our team. As the Communications Director, I had the distinction of being the only team member who had served in Vietnam. My responsibility was to gather all the details and report them back to national headquarters, as well as to deliver any change in instructions back to the team. It included: a French-speaking representative for Red Cross International; the head of disaster services; another individual who had some training and experience with prisoners of war; the director of the Red Cross in Dallas; a physician; and a male nurse.

After stopping for more supplies in San Francisco, we took off for Hanoi in North Vietnam. Our first stop was Hawaii, followed by: the Philippines; Tokyo, Japan; then Hong Kong. All the while, we were in continuous negotiation with Hanoi, which was telling us we could not travel there.

"If you try to land in Hanoi," we were warned, "it will be considered an attack, and you will be shot down!"

Perot never downplayed the danger of our mission.

"Anybody who wants to get off can get off here," he told us.

My determinism and desire to help kept me on the team. I had just spent 11 months in Vietnam, and the Lord had carried me through that. I expected Him to protect me through this journey as well. I did not relay the dangerous nature of this mission to Doris during the single phone call that we enjoyed during those weeks.

Prohibited from landing in Hanoi, we returned to Bangkok. On occasion, we'd have a staff meeting or press conference on the plane or in the hotel.

"Why are you doing this?" reporters asked Perot.

"I've met with wives of POWs," he responded, "and I've taken several groups of them to France to negotiate a release of some or all of the prisoners with the North Vietnamese." Perot was adamant: "We need to bring the POWs home. We don't leave anyone behind. That's why we're here. To take some relief and aid to Vietnam, and to bring back ill and wounded soldiers."

Perot refused to take no for an answer.

"There's always another way," he repeatedly said.

Perot's undaunted pursuit of his goals, as well as his motivation for the trip, impressed me profoundly. As a former Naval Academy phenom, his military service inspired him to help soldiers.

During those weeks, Perot was approachable and freely shared his philosophies. He believed that he was blessed beyond measure by the huge financial success of his company, Electronic Data Systems or EDS, which earned Perot the status of "fastest, richest Texan" on the cover of *Fortune* magazine in 1968 and later made him a billionaire. Now, he explained that he wanted to use his wealth to help others.

He was also inspired by his Christian values, and he gifted each of us with a Bible; I still have mine. Everything about him reinforced my desire to improve my own condition and help others along the way.

At one point, Ross Perot inquired about who I was and what I was doing. We talked about his being a military veteran, and how he appreciated the opportunity to serve his country. He would attempt to do that in the highest capacity, when running for president of the United States in 1992 and 1996.

Meanwhile, undaunted by Hanoi's threats to shoot down our aircraft, he rented a small plane and with a French steward went to Hanoi, where he landed and spoke with the authorities.

"You need to leave the country," they told him. "You are not going to bring your supplies and you most certainly will not take anybody out of the country with you."

They said he could take the supplies to Russia and ship them back to Hanoi from Russia, but not from the U.S.

"I'll try again," he said upon return to Bangkok. "I will never quit until the day comes when I have no option. And there will always be another option."

That last sentence has always stuck with me.

We went to Laos, a small country with one hotel where we spent Christmas day, while Ross Perot negotiated with Hanoi and Moscow.

Also, while in Laos, we visited a POW camp for North Vietnamese. Technically, we weren't supposed to be there. We were trampling on the neutral jurisdiction of the International Red Cross. Yet we were granted entry because Ross Perot told the Laotians that he wanted to tell the North Vietnamese prisoners that we were there to take Americans home. And he wanted assurance that they were receiving adequate care.

The Laotians granted us entry, along with the media. Things got tense when an aggressive cameraman stepped on my ankle and knocked me down as he pushed close enough to photograph the prisoners. They were Vietnamese – held in a grass-floor hut where they slept on blankets. Fortunately, they were not cold in the warm, humid climate.

After that, Perot decided that we would take the supplies to Moscow. First, we flew to Anchorage, Alaska, touching down on a very light December night. I arranged to have Red Cross volunteers unpack our huge, bulk items, then repackage them into smaller boxes, and re-load the plane according to instructions from Hanoi officials.

As we headed toward Russia, authorities in Moscow said, "Don't come here, either."

We went to Copenhagen, Denmark, before returning to Washington, D.C., on New Year's Day, 1970. Ross Perot took the supplies to Dallas and gave them to an agency.

Still, we considered the trip a success, because we opened the door for discussion. Upon our return, Perot lobbied the Department of Defense and others to negotiate with Hanoi to release prisoners on behalf of the wives. Within the year, the Vietnamese began to release POWs, including future U.S. Senator and presidential candidate John McCain.

A few years later, while living in Atlanta, I was walking through the airport, bound for a national Red Cross meeting in Chicago with a group of colleagues.

"Wow," I said. "There's Ross Perot carrying his own luggage. I need to stop and say hello."

One of my colleagues quipped: "You don't know Ross Perot."

I simply replied: "You don't know me," and proceeded to stop and chat briefly with Ross Perot, who of course remembered me, as we had communicated by letter for a short while after our trip. I just wanted my friends to meet a billionaire who was traveling commercial and carrying his own luggage, which was another humble trait that I admired about him.

"Serving and Involving the Entire Community"

While I was in Southeast Asia with Ross Perot, the Red Cross appointed a new president, George McKee Elsey. His mission included promoting a culture of racial and ethnic inclusion for the organization across America. The California native had studied at Princeton University and Harvard University before becoming a U.S. Navy commander who advised Presidents Franklin D. Roosevelt and Harry S. Truman during World War II.

When he took the helm of the Red Cross in early 1970, George Elsey emphasized excellence in our disaster relief, preparedness, and response. He also initiated a new conversation at the Red Cross about racial inclusion, which he had addressed at the railroad company where he worked prior to this post.

As a result, during his first year of leadership, the Red Cross created a program called "Serving and Involving the Entire Community," which we called SAITEC. Its mission was to enable the Red Cross to start serving black people and Latinos. Five Red Cross employees were chosen to oversee SAITEC in the Northeast, Southeast, Midwest, and West Coast regions of the Red Cross.

I was selected to promote the SAITEC initiative in the southeastern United States, which included hurricane-ravaged Louisiana and Mississippi. Though I was on the national Red Cross' Service to Chapters staff, this position required me to move to Atlanta with Doris, three-year-old Brian, and seven-year-old Eric.

We lived on Mercury Drive near the small airport on the southwest side of Atlanta, where Eric attended G.A. Towns Elementary School. I took the expressway to work at the Southern Regional Office on the north side of the city off Route 85.

The SAITEC supervisor at national headquarters was Terry Townsend, a bright, sensitive, committed guy who was highly respected both at the national headquarters where he worked in Washington, D.C., and among the chapters under his supervision.

Shortly after he began, George Elsey invited Terry and the four SAITEC representatives to discuss our objectives in his office at the Red Cross headquarters in Washington, D.C. Three of us were black; one was white – a longhaired hippie from California who never wore socks or a tie. I entered the meeting full of hope and enthusiasm that our new president would make aggressive changes to foster racial inclusion both within and outside of the organization.

"Let's get started by introducing ourselves," Mr. Elsey said, never looking directly at us, but instead looking down or up and away. It quickly became apparent that George Elsey was not comfortable talking with black people. "I just wanted to take this opportunity to rap with you guys."

The word "rap" echoed in my head, as I and my black colleagues sat in stunned silence, masking our dismay, dislike – and downright insult – of his colloquial word selection. Here we were in a professional business meeting with the president of the American Red Cross, and he was attempting to cross the unspoken racial divide that is always present in workplace dynamics, by using a word that neither I nor my colleagues would ever speak, especially in the workplace.

It was clear that – with his Ivy League education, military background, and work alongside presidents – George Elsey was someone who had obviously never used the word "rap" before. Someone must have told him, "You need to speak their language." Some of the people around him were not prepared to help him. This is a case where the leader has blind spots and someone needed to help him. No matter how experienced or well-trained we are, if you're the leader of a complex organization or situation, there's the potential to have blind spots, just some things you don't know. The leader needs to know where his or her blind spots are and surround himself or herself with people who can identify them.

Rather than become angry or offended, I concluded that we needed to help him feel comfortable in working with us. The situation inspired me to draw upon my ongoing study of "human relations," which would later be known as Emotional Intelligence. It emphasized knowing who you are, how you affect other people, and how to formulate an understanding of how people are receiving you.

This concept enabled me to step outside of myself and take a bird's eye view of our meeting. I saw Mr. Elsey, who sincerely wanted to help but was hindered by a discomfort with black professionals. I saw Terry and my three SAITEC colleagues, eager to excel in our roles to execute our new president's vision for fostering outreach and inclusion of racial and ethnic minorities.

How could I facilitate a more comfortable and effective atmosphere for achieving our mutual goals? First, I refrained from allowing the situation to push any emotional hot buttons that might cause a negative reaction and sabotage the meeting and the mission. I did not say, "Mr. Elsey, you don't need to 'rap' with us."

Instead, I met with him later in private, and let him know that we spoke his language – the proverbial King's English. "Mr. Elsey," I told him, "while we're happy to 'rap' with you, we're also happy to meet and talk with you." The conversation that followed between us laid a foundation of openness and comfort where he relaxed, made eye contact, and began to build an important, lifelong relationship with me.

However, an air of awkwardness hung over the meeting with Terry, me, and the three other SAITEC representatives. It began to dissipate when our new president described a new, progressive era for the American Red Cross.

"We have to prepare for a new century," Mr. Elsey told us. "We have to avoid some crises and cope with those that do occur."

As he spoke, I became – for the first time! – encouraged that Red Cross leadership was willing to address some of the serious issues such as racism and exclusion.

George Elsey filled me with hope that the Red Cross was finally taking action to change its racist-by-conformity culture. He struck me as a man of vision, courage, and commitment as he immediately set out to revitalize and energize the organization in every aspect of our work, domestically and abroad. From the start, he was on a mission to reconnect us with the rest of the Red Cross world. As he spoke, I had a feeling that he could see around corners and over mountains.

From then on, I had many opportunities to spend time with George Elsey, and our conversations and interactions became more natural and relaxed. We spoke man to man, and he became more comfortable, looking me in the eye while speaking words that sounded normal.

Successful leaders are generally also successful followers and vice versa. Both are inclined to stay focused on the corporate purpose and goals. Both are more concerned about service and service outcomes than they are about status. In all aspects of my life, I put *service* above *status* as a goal. While status should be a goal, especially in the life of a leader or potential leader, service is my purpose (improving the human condition), so that is my first goal. I have found that when I am effective in my service efforts, status eventually follows.

Inclusion was Easier Said than Done

While encouraged that George Elsey had implemented the SAITEC initiative, my experience was tough. I served in the regional office, known as the "area office," which had jurisdiction over 10 southern states: Alabama, Arkansas, Florida, Georgia, Kentucky, Louisiana, Mississippi, North Carolina, South Carolina, and Tennessee.

Every Monday morning, I boarded an airplane to one of these states, where I would remain until Thursday. If I were heading to a natural disaster such as a hurricane or tornado, I would be away from home indefinitely.

This was difficult for Doris, who was alone with the children in a state where staunch segregationist Lester Maddox had served as governor. Atlanta offered little opportunity for blacks to socialize in public. Gatherings occurred in private homes, yet Doris found the town to be cliquish and therefore our social circle was limited to two black couples that included Charlie and Janet Fincher, whom we had known in Germany when Horace served in the Army and I was in the Red Cross.

Making matters worse for Doris was that Brian was quite rambunctious. One Sunday, after I had departed on a flight for a national Red Cross meeting in Chicago, Brian ran into our large Grundig record player from Germany. Thankfully, the couple we had met there drove Doris and the boys to the hospital where Brian received stitches. Doris was so upset, she fainted during the procedure. And I did not learn of the ordeal until I called that evening from Chicago. After that, my mother stayed with us for a short while.

Meanwhile, I was a one-man operation for SAITEC, as my administrative assistant remained in the Red Cross offices in Atlanta.

Traveling alone through the South put me at risk of physical danger. Every time I went to Jackson, Mississippi, I was given the same room in the same hotel. The scariest part about being in "the black room," as I called it, was that every Klansman in the state knew exactly where I was. How? Klansmen on the Red Cross staff quietly made themselves known to certain people. The youth director told me three names of active KKK members, and one was a prominent leader in the organization. My colleague told me that sometimes at the end of the day, they would say, "We're going hunting tonight," which meant they were going out looking for black folks to hurt or kill.

In moments like this, I drew upon my faith and specifically meditated on Romans 5:1-5:

"Therefore, having been justified by faith, we have[a] peace with God through our Lord Jesus Christ, through whom also we have access by faith into this grace in which we stand, and rejoice in hope of the glory of God. And not only that, but we also glory in tribulations, knowing that tribulation produces perseverance; and perseverance, character; and character, hope. Now hope does not disappoint, because the love of God has been poured out in our hearts by the Holy Spirit who was given to us."

I chose to "glory in tribulations" because perseverance was a character trait that I admired and wanted to cultivate within myself. I had to look no further than the Civil Rights Movement to see that the perseverance of Dr. King, Rosa Parks, Thurgood Marshall, and many others had resulted in the 1964 Civil Rights Act and other efforts to eradicate institutional racism in America. Perseverance produces character, which creates hope, which does not fail.

However, at times I felt my tribulations were many, as I dealt with racist attitudes and behaviors, yet I tried to do my best.

Attempting to perform my professional duties in an environment where I felt the very real threat of danger inspired profound reflection about my moral beliefs and behavior. As human beings in a civilized society, we are expected – and I believe – *required* to love humanity, and to love one another. However, there are several aspects of love, including trust, respect, and value. So, I often asked myself, *Can I be trusted, respected, and valued?*

As a husband, I knew with absolute certainty that I could be trusted, and I had no doubt that Doris respected and valued me. As a Red Cross employee, I asked the same question. I concluded that yes, the organization could trust me to execute my duties and responsibilities to the best of my ability, and I believed that my employer would respect and value me as a result.

Faith that God would protect me and empower me to persevere enabled me to achieve my two-fold assignment. It was my responsibility to support disaster preparedness and relief, as well as work with chapters to help them reach out to underserved or unserved segments of their communities to make certain they were being served. At the same time, they were to take steps to ensure that these communities were being involved in the work of the local Red Cross. This included serving on the board as well as participating as volunteers, donors, and employees.

I worked only with chapters that invited me to visit and offer help in nine of the ten states. With each chapter, I would meet with the chapter manager, staff, and the board, talking with them about the value of involving the people that they wanted to serve. I explained how they could welcome people from the black and Hispanic communities to serve on the boards, as volunteers, as donors and even as employees.

Sometimes I did this work in partnership with my Red Cross colleague Ernie Rose, who was white. One evening, he and I arrived at the Red Cross chapter board meeting in Greenville, South Carolina. After I delivered a rousing speech about the tenets of SAITEC, a white man approached me.

"I really appreciate you coming to do this," he said, "and I appreciate what you had to say, but when you came in, I thought you were Ernie's driver."

Rather than get upset, I understood the climate in which I was working. I viewed his statement as progress that this man learned to appreciate seeing a black man in a professional position who was adding value to society at large.

Another incident that involved driving, racism, and Steve Bullock keeping his cool occurred when Doris and I were taking a weekend trip to Pensacola, Florida, with her brother Charles and his wife.

"We were stopped by the police of LaGrange, Georgia," Charles recalls, "because my sister and my wife were sporting the Afro hair styles that looked a lot like the kind that the fugitive Angela Davis wore. She was reported to be traveling towards Montgomery, Alabama, in a car which had Atlanta license plates on it. Steve did not lose his cool with all of their guns pointed at us, but he let the officers know that he did not appreciate the harassment and he would not tolerate it. I now marvel at his restraint and his daring. Although he lived in Atlanta, but was passing through rural Georgia, we discovered that being a black man in rural Georgia and standing up for your rights and dignity was still a dangerous proposition, but Steve stood up and out as a man."

I applied the same resolve during my travels when I led workshops to help chapter leaders develop strategies to implement the tenets of SAITEC. In addition, I always coordinated meetings for chapter leadership to meet church leaders as well as representatives from the local Urban League chapters. National Urban League regional director Clarence Coleman, based out of Atlanta, became a trusted ally, confidant, and mentor. I also collaborated with the civil rights leader Fannie Lou Hamer, who connected me with members of the labor organizations such as the AFL-CIO and Communication Workers of America.

Shortly after moving to Atlanta, I was blessed to meet Dr. Charles Orr, a retired college professor who became one of my confidants and mentors in the Red Cross. A longtime volunteer, he often recounted his experience of being nominated and elected to the board of the Red Cross chapter in the small community near Durham, North Carolina. When he attended his first board meeting, he took a seat at the table.

"You can't sit at the table," the meeting leader told him. "Take a chair by the wall."

Dr. Orr got up and started to leave, but then decided, *No, I am going to stay and change this.* Here he was exhibiting the perseverance cited in Romans 4:5. He stayed, and eventually took his seat at the table, became a member of the Red Cross South East Area Advisory Committee, and was finally elected to the National Red Cross Board of Governors. At the end of his service, he was awarded the American Red Cross Harriman Award, the highest award presented to BOG members.

"Steve, I'm telling you this story," said Dr. Orr said, "because I need to inspire you and motivate you to never give up. Stay focused on your guiding principles and core values. Always do what you believe is right and fair and pray that you make more people happy than you make sad."

I sought the counsel of Dr. Orr when discouraged by my racist work environment. I was humbled and honored to speak at his memorial service during the fall of 1999.

All the while, I was helping very much with improving race relations, convincing people that everyone had value and although we're different, black people and Latinos can bring value to the work of the Red Cross, as much as anyone else.

The Rotary Club's "4-Way Test" assisted me in making the best, most ethical decisions for SAITEC. For every opportunity to promote inclusion,

I asked, *Is it the truth? Is it fair to all concerned? Will it build goodwill and better friendship? Will it be beneficial to all concerned?* I needed a "yes" for each question before I would proceed.

I continued studying ways to improve my abilities as a leader, both now and in the future. I studied leadership principles that would, three decades later, be called Emotional Intelligence, the title of a 1995 book by Daniel Goleman. I was familiar with the concept; back in the sixties, it was known as "human relations."

We learned about the importance of applying empathy, objectivity, and adaptability to interactions with others. More specifically, the instructor explained that could be achieved by gauging other people's emotions, and adapting your speech and behavior in ways that made the other individual comfortably engaged with you. This cultivates understanding of how you impact others and how to process how they affect you. I also became adept at anticipating problems.

Comprehending and applying this concept bolstered my ability to counsel people more effectively. I gained a broader vision to see around corners and over hills, which provided insight about what to expect and how to manage it when it occurred.

Disaster Preparation for Everyone

At the same time, it was my responsibility to help the chapters prepare for disasters. Hurricanes typically struck during late summer and early fall, while spring and summer comprised tornado season. The Red Cross was responsible for the immediate response, providing shelter and food, as well as supporting the other activities like hospitals and emergency responders – police, fire, and EMS – to make sure we knew where all the people were, so we could feed, house and support in other ways.

The key was to establish a plan before a disaster struck. That was difficult in the environment I was working in.

If 500 people were suddenly displaced from their homes, where would they be sheltered? Jackson, Mississippi, which was vulnerable to hurricanes and tornadoes, had two major shelters: the Jefferson Hotel, where the white people were housed, and Jackson State University, where African Americans stayed in dormitories. However, the dorms had to be vacated at the end of the summer to allow college students to move in. Where would black people sleep?

That question resulted in a disturbing answer as I surveyed communities to learn where the black people lived, and what kinds of housing accommodations were available. The black disaster victims were housed at a military base which was used by the Army Reserve. It gives me a sense of satisfaction to say I saw this situation improve over time. However, my team also discovered that black people were living with the animals in barns on a plantation in Mississippi.

"Get off my plantation," the owner told us. "My Negroes are fine."

While this was very discouraging, I was equally encouraged by Louisville, Kentucky, which had one of the most positive chapters in the 10 states under my jurisdiction. Well-known and respected in the black community, the chapter's executive director had a strong board and black volunteers in all of the different areas, including health and safety training, and disaster planning preparedness and response.

Those volunteers were trained to respond to house fires, which typically occurred in the middle of the night. The Red Cross would arrive to find a family outside with only the clothes they wore while escaping the burning home. The Red Cross's job was to transport them to a hotel where arrangements were already made, then give them vouchers to buy clothes the following day.

Other cities that cultivated strong SAITEC programs were Birmingham, Alabama, and Durham, North Carolina.

As one of nine members of the management staff in the Area Office, I attended meetings that required giving a report about my activity. Then, during the general discussion, I would try to join in.

"This is not your area," another leader would snap at me. "You don't need to think about this."

Another time, while we were discussing efforts to teach first aid and CPR in the black community, one of my colleagues quipped: "I think we need to do a presentation in black English so they can get it."

I objected.

"We can teach a monkey," my colleague said, "so I know we can teach black folks."

"It's not black English," said Billy Newsome of the Safety Service Department. A white man with a Southern twang, he spoke with great conviction and confidence, unconcerned about what others thought. "It's Southern English. Blacks speak the same language as we do."

I was surprised when Billy spoke up, because he was a fairly quiet individual. I thanked God for putting him in that room that day. That moment supported Dr. Orr's guidance to stay focused on our goals and be guided by core values and guiding principles. It also underscored the importance of finding people who will collaborate and partner with you. Billy Newsome was a quiet supporter.

His behavior reminded me of my mother's edict to leave everything I encounter better than I found it. Billy, apparently, was practicing the same philosophy, in a quite courageous manner for the times. For that, I deeply respected and appreciated him.

This incident also brought to mind one of my core beliefs about human relations and especially race relations. We are often encouraged to employ a measure of tolerance toward those who may be different from us in some way. While I understand the intention, tolerance is not good enough; I cannot sustain it. Instead, I believe that every person has value, so I pinpoint each person's value and respect him or her for that.

It was reassuring to have an ally in Billy Newsome. When he spoke, it was from the power position inherent with being a white man; that would have more leverage and impact on enlightening ignorance among our peers.

Despite that, after the meeting, I was so outraged, I called Dr. Orr in North Carolina for counsel. As a member of the Red Cross' National Board of Governors, he talked with my boss and others in Atlanta and D.C. to address the issue. He also told me, "Steve, you've got to say something to somebody in this organization before you lose it."

So, I spoke with a Red Cross leader, Don Northey, who helped change the structure of the regional management team. I also found support in regional manager Jack Evans, who came to my defense when he stood up in a division managers' meeting and warned: "You guys better be nice to Steve, because he may be your boss one day!"

It was encouraging when the organization was responsive to complaints, but at times I felt the environment in our Atlanta offices was unbearable.

Fostering Inclusion While Being Excluded

Ironically, while my job was to lead a campaign for inclusion, my boss was practicing segregation. It played out when he routinely took the management team to lunch at an all-white country club. As a management team member, I was also the only black professional on the 200-person staff; the other blacks in the building were file clerks and the two maintenance men.

The area manager, who was my boss and known as PMM, conspired with other leaders to exclude me.

"PMM is taking us to lunch today," regional manager Jack Evans would say loudly while walking down the aisle past our cubicles. "I've got two cars, let's go." Our entire group then went to Morrison's Cafeteria, where we enjoyed camaraderie, fried chicken and peach pie, and conversations about work.

Other days, Jack approached only my white colleagues and whispered. They would all leave for lunch. I was not included. I instinctively knew that something was going on that did not feel right. So, one day when they left, I got in my car and followed them. Their destination was the all-white country club that welcomed neither blacks nor Jews.

I was furious!

I called Red Cross headquarters, which confirmed that the Red Cross was paying for the Atlanta office's membership to the country club. I demanded that the organization stop supporting a racist institution that was enabling our leadership to exclude me.

The next morning, I sat by PMM's door.

"Oh, he looks like he's waiting for the principal!" Jack taunted.

"I guess I am," I said.

"The boss is busy. Talk to his deputy."

I did; he responded, "You know, I don't believe I've seen any black people there." Then he told PMM I was upset and that I had called the national office.

"I don't think the club is segregated," the deputy manager said.

My thought was, *He's lying to me and thinks I'll believe it.*

"We don't need to continue this discussion," I said. "I'll wait until PMM has time and I'll share with him why this bothers me and why I don't think it should continue."

When I finally got a meeting with PMM, he was angry with me.

"What PMM does is PMM's business," he admonished. "It is not *your* business! The Red Cross pays for the membership, but when I use it, I pay my way."

That was not true either. I was told that the membership was cancelled, although I could not verify that. I learned during those years that it is important to stay focused on your long-term goals and not be distracted by a short-term solution. Ultimately, the Red Cross canceled the membership.

But in the midst of my campaign to stop this discriminatory practice, I thought, *I can't take this anymore.* The racism was not unique to the Red Cross; it reflected attitudes and behaviors in society in general. Thus, I was forced to follow leaders who were, at best, followers.

Sometimes it pushed me to a breaking point.

"I Can't Take This Anymore! I'm Out of Here!"
I was so frustrated, I told Jack Evans that I was going to leave the Red Cross. Talk about a kairos moment; this negative one inspired me to meet with Clarence Coleman.

"I've had it!" I declared. "It's time to go!"

"Where are you going?" he demanded. "Are you running away from something, or are you running to something? What makes you think you won't find the same thing somewhere else? Are you going to the Catholic Church? There's racism there, too. You need to stay and deal with things where you are. If you run away, you've given up!"

I also demanded that others see my value. This requirement in my personal belief system was especially important during this very difficult experience. By making my colleagues see my value, I believed that would inspire them to respect me, and support at least some of my efforts. As I put this plan into action, I channeled my anger and frustration into hard work that transformed my whole experience in ways that would open the doors to major leadership positions. It bolstered my ambition; I set my sights on leading a Red Cross chapter in a major city.

Learning and Growing in New Assignments
In 1971, I was asked to head up the Quad State Project to teach home health care to black people in Mississippi, Louisiana, Arkansas, and Tennessee. My job was to lead a team that would train black people in poor, rural areas about how to be self-sufficient in taking care of their health by learning first aid and by using a midwife to facilitate childbirths (as opposed to the usual high-risk situation of having no health care professional on hand when a woman delivered a baby).

This assignment was an opportunity to help people, cultivate inclusion for people of color, and create visibility and recognition for me and my team on a national level.

But as a black leader in a white power structure, I struggled with some individuals who wanted to block my success. This happened as I was assembling my team with the help of bosses in the Southeastern offices. When I rejected one individual who was not a good fit for the team, I was summoned to one manager's hotel room, where he was eating peanuts and throwing shells on the floor, while five other men sat around the room.

"I don't know who you think you are," he said, "but you don't make decisions about who works where."

"Okay," I said. "You're the boss."

Then I returned to PMM, who was my boss and this guy's boss, to state that I did not want the individual in question on my team.

I would not be bullied, nor would I allow racism to hinder the best possible outcome for my assignment. I took great pride in selecting a team in this instance, and every other occasion throughout my career when I was given the responsibility to choose the best individuals whose talents and temperaments could help achieve a goal. When there is a clear choice of inclusion or exclusion, if it is not criminal or evil, I will almost always choose inclusion. Generally, it makes me, the team, the organization, and the outcome better.

With the team that we had selected, we proceeded to work with the University of Mississippi School of Nursing, a team of nurses and health care professionals who were assigned to help us execute this project. A young white couple, both nurses, taught midwifery. Our goal was to train midwives in every community.

But our campaign was not always welcomed. Especially at one plantation in rural Mississippi, where we stated that we wanted to teach the black workers about health and the importance of using a midwife during home births to promote wellness among the mothers and their infants.

On Assignment in Africa as "Mr. American Red Cross"

The success of the Quad State Project inspired the Red Cross to send me to Africa to share the program during the Spring of 1972. I was reluctant to leave Doris in Atlanta, because we were expecting our third child within weeks of my trip.

We had been through this before, with a positive outcome for Eric's birth while I was in Germany. So, I departed, first reporting to the International Red Cross headquarters in Geneva, Switzerland, where our team convened for several days. During that time, we received instructions on how to lead workshops and training exercises at The University of Ghana in Accra, the capital of Ghana. There we met representatives from seven English-speaking countries that had obtained independence from the British. They were: Botswana, Cameroon, Gambia, Ghana, Liberia, Nigeria, and Sierra Leone.

"Mr. American Red Cross" became my nickname among the African participants.

For three weeks, we trained Red Cross representatives on the midwifery program. We also worked with a group of professors from the University of Ghana about the programs that interested them. All were interested in midwifery. We did not meet with mothers, but we did instruct volunteers who would help disseminate this information.

I shared material and information we'd been using in Mississippi to help them develop a training program for their own country. It was ironic that I came from the most advanced nation on earth, where we had yet to finish teaching these skills to Americans, and now we were bringing the information to Africa. It was also interesting to learn how to work with people from the African diaspora; we were simultaneously so similar and different.

We stressed the importance of having doctors present during childbirth. However, we were teaching midwifery as an alternative when doctors were not available. We also emphasized the necessity for prenatal care and postnatal care, exactly what Doris was receiving at home in Atlanta.

When I returned from Africa, our daughter, Kelly Alicia Bullock, was born on April 11, 1972. I called her my Georgia Peach, and continue to do so now. Likewise, Doris, who was still not loving the city, will tell you to this day that Kelly was the best thing we brought out of Atlanta.

"The other Red Cross wives were very kind to me," Doris recalls. "Because Steve was gone so much, they threw a beautiful baby shower for me. Even the boss' wife was very nice. Once she called me about a party that the Red Cross was hosting. I had surmised by the invitation that it was formal, so I bought a long dress. During the call, she said in a tone like I couldn't read, 'You know we're supposed to wear a long skirt.' So, I went and bought black velvet fabric, asked my neighbor who was a seamstress to make me hot pants, which I wore with a one-piece red top and high heeled boots. When I walked into the party with my hot pants, Steve said, 'You're gonna get me fired!' They never said anything. When I got older, I wouldn't do anything like that for fear they might try to fire him."

I made it a priority to balance quality family time with my busy work schedule. This included spending time with my mother during the period that she lived with us. I also enjoyed evenings when Doris and I helped Eric and Brian with their academics, enabling them to thrive in elementary school. At the same time, Doris and I made it a priority to enjoy "date nights" that ensured time to cherish each other and keep our holy union strong. This set a positive example for our children to witness a successful marriage.

"Dad set extremely high standards for himself and for us," recalls Brian, 50, a filmmaker and television producer who is married to Patricia Hopewell Bullock. They live in Upper Marlboro, Maryland. Their children are: Marcus Delano Bullock, 21; Brianna Clyde Bullock, 16; and Brandon Hopewell, 32. "He would always stress working hard, and he would show us."

Brian adds that I was quite similar to my mother. "My grandmother was a disciplinarian. She didn't play. She was such a stickler for good manners. One time we were eating at McDonald's, and I had finished my milkshake, when she asked, 'May I have the rest of your milkshake, please?' That's how she spoke and expected us to speak. When we were with Grandma, we had to watch our P's and Q's. I remember thinking, 'Don't mess up. Don't get in trouble.' My dad was a lot like her."

Doris and I expected our children to perform well in school.

"If we brought home a C or a D," Brian says, "Mom would say, 'Why did you get a C? You've got to do better and you can do better.'"

I often shared stories of the struggles that I endured while growing up in North Carolina, and I wanted to provide the best for our children.

"Dad would always ask, 'Are you hungry? Do you want more? Get more food if you're hungry,'" Brian recalls.

On Sundays after church, I would ask the kids, "Do you want to stop and get some lunch?"

"Yes, I want a hot dog!" Kelly always said.

But her brothers countered, "Be quiet! We might get something better than a hot dog!"

Brian adds, "Dad always made sure we ate enough. He wanted to make sure that we never experienced the kinds of things he experienced."

Fostering Inclusion in a Northern Town
When I returned to work with SAITEC, Hurricane Agnes caused widespread damage throughout the eastern United States. I was sent to Harrisburg, Pennsylvania, to assist with disaster recovery.

Unfortunately, the Red Cross chapter there had failed to help the town's poor, black community. Our job was to help them clean up the mess. Yet when I met with the head of the Harrisburg Red Cross, her attitude was as vicious as those I had encountered in some southern towns. She refused to help the black neighborhoods, declaring:

"I'm not going over the railroad tracks! Those people rioted when Martin Luther King was killed!"

Our solution was to engage volunteers to help us distribute supplies to the black community. We even had two people transporting mops, brooms, cleaning materials, paint, et cetera. Unfortunately, I received a report that the volunteers were stealing just as much as they were delivering. Critics within the Red Cross immediately pointed fingers, saying I should not have trusted these individuals to transport our goods.

I met with the volunteers, and said, "Look man, I know what's going on. You have to stop this."

They were a little sheepish, because we had incriminating evidence against them. They were dismissed, and we never saw them again. It was disturbing that some of my colleagues used this as an argument against the SAITEC mission, but I defended the program whenever I heard grumblings of that sort.

A Help or a Hindrance? Dealing with Paternal Racism

Despite our disagreements, PMM wanted to help me achieve my career objectives. Unfortunately, he was guilty of paternal racism; he treated me like he was my dad.

For example, I told him that my goal was to take a leadership position within the Red Cross as head of a chapter in a major city. The largest of these chapters were called "The Big 12" because they provided major funding for the organization. I would be the first black Executive Director in a large chapter. At the time, the highest ranking African American in the Red Cross was Executive Director of a small community chapter in New Jersey.

"Steve, I'm trying to protect your feelings from getting hurt," PMM said. "A white community is not going to accept you as head of a Red Cross chapter because you're black."

"I don't need that kind of protection," I said.

I did not want to continue serving as an executive at the national level. I always compared it to a bank where everybody is the vice president. Banks have a lot of vice presidents and they do great work, but – like my position at the Red Cross – they are focusing on a limited area, not leading the organization. I wanted to get beyond my area.

"I'm telling you, Steve, you need to stay with the national organization," he warned. "Blacks won't be accepted in the local community."

"I'm big and bold enough to try it!" I declared. "So, tell me, what does it take for me to be seriously considered as a candidate for leading a local Red Cross unit?"

Despite his cynicism, PMM introduced me to a senior vice president from national headquarters, who invited me to lunch.

"I'm being interviewed," I told Doris, "but I'm not being told I'm being interviewed. However, I'm ready for it."

This gentleman asked all kinds of questions, which I answered in a straightforward manner.

"You're really solid," he said.

I just looked at him, as I processed his underhanded compliment spoken as if he were surprised at my ability to articulate my work ethic, accomplishments, and goals. Still, like many black professionals, I have mastered the skill of masking my true feelings, suppressing anger and insult, and proceeding with a professional façade in facial expression, body language, and tone of voice.

In doing so, I suppressed the urge to say, "Define 'solid' for me." Instead I said, "If I can't be head of a Red Cross chapter, then it's time for me to move on."

He was very supportive of my ambition, as was PMM.

"The only way you can do this is to serve as an intern with somebody," PMM told me. He put out the word to match me as an intern with a chapter leader. Several offers poured in.

"I want Steve to serve as an intern with me, and he can start Monday," said Buck Willocks, head of the Jacksonville, Florida, chapter, who introduced himself as "the ugliest man in the Red Cross." He was a really nice guy who was accustomed to being rejected and alienated.

The following week, I drove to Jacksonville and served for five weeks. I came home to Doris and the boys and baby Kelly a few weekends.

After that, I continued to do SAITEC work in Nashville, Tennessee, then Miami, Florida, where William "Mike" Miracle served to mostly the white communities in each city. So, I shared my SAITEC strategies to reach out to Miami's Cuban, black, and other ethnic communities. Then he transferred to become CEO of the local chapter in Washington, D.C. Half the city was black; it was not all friendly territory.

"Steve, when you finish your internship," Mike said during a phone call in late 1972, "I want you to come here and consider serving as an Assistant CEO with me. But you've got to compete for it."

"Okay," I replied. "I'm ready."

I returned to Atlanta for a few months before receiving the call: "Steve, come for an interview and bring your spouse."

If selected for this position, it would, for the first time, move me from the national staff into chapter work where I preferred to go. In Washington, the board interviewed three people. By the grace of God and my perseverance to do my best against the odds, I was chosen as Assistant Chapter Executive for the Washington, D.C. chapter.

Achieving a Major Goal

I was elated to finally achieve my goal of rising into the Red Cross Chapter Sector. I vowed to invest my absolute best effort in my new position so that I could reach my next goal: becoming Executive Director of a Red Cross chapter in a major city.

For now, I was in the perfect place to learn and grow in preparation for that. The Greater Washington Chapter was one of six local chapters around the capitol: Arlington; Alexandria; Prince George's County; Northern Virginia; Montgomery County, Maryland; and Prince Williams. Three D.C. branch offices reported to me.

As Doris, the children, and I settled into our home in Greenbelt, Maryland, in early 1973, I spent long hours at work and in the community.

No matter how early I arrived at the office, Mike Miracle, was already there.

"Steve, join me for coffee," he said every morning at 8:30 when he took a break. We talked about what we'd do that day or what we had done the day before. After that, he would go through the morning mail.

"Take care of this," he said, after coming through the executive assistant's workspace separating his office and mine. After entering through the side door, he'd put the mail on my desk. Then he might separate a letter or document from the pile and hold it up. "Here's something to pay special attention to."

I took the paper.

"Steve, if I put too much weight on you," Mike said, "you need to yell. I figure you've got it covered."

Though it was a challenge to keep my head above the daily flood of paper, I never yelled or asked, "What do you want me to do with this?" Instead, I worked diligently at a brisk pace. Handling these details of the chapter's Executive Director's work, I considered myself on a crash course for learning everything necessary to someday lead a large chapter on my own.

Mike would return to my office at noon and ask, "Want to go to lunch?"

We always joined his friends at the Watergate complex. As they talked, I listened and learned information that would enable me to lead a large Red Cross chapter on my own.

For the time being, my job involved service delivery: disaster planning preparedness response; health and safety training and education; the nurse aid program; and outreach.

My work with SAITEC proved invaluable as I executed my duties in this new position. First, I was also tasked with establishing two additional branch offices: one in the mostly black, historic neighborhood of Anacostia in Washington, D.C.; and the other in the Hispanic community known as the Adams Morgan area north of the White House and near the Red Cross headquarters.

Second, it was my responsibility to create an advisory group of people from the community. I invited other organizations to collaborate so that we could better help those areas with disaster assistance and other services.

Innovation was also key, as we implemented nontraditional programs such as a tax preparation course. We also purchased sewing machines at the request of a woman who wanted to teach this valuable skill that had enabled my mother to make clothing and other home goods for our family. These innovations attracted people from the community to participate in the Red Cross and helped us introduce our programs to them.

After three years, I talked with Mike about applying to the vacant chapter CEO position in Richmond, Virginia. I thought it would be nice to "go home" to Virginia Union University to lead a Red Cross chapter there. I sent my letter to the area officers in Alexandria who oversaw 14 states.

"They won't interview a black person," the HR Director informed me. "They want you to apply to Jersey City, New Jersey."

"I'm not going there," I answered. "That chapter is a zero. I have no interest in going someplace that's already dead."

Still, I was disappointed.

"Why are you upset?" Mike asked. "You can do better than either one of those."

I was not thinking big enough. Not long after that, I received a call from the past chair of the St. Paul, Minnesota, chapter who was on the Board of Governors.

"I heard good things about you," he said, "and I'd like to interview you."

He took me and Doris to dinner, then invited us to St. Paul for an interview, which led to a job offer to lead the St. Paul Area Chapter. This was another pivotal moment for me to walk through that door of opportunity to achieve a major goal. In 1976, Doris and I and the children moved to St. Paul.

I was overjoyed and immeasurably grateful that God had blessed me with this privilege of becoming Executive Director of the St. Paul Area Chapter and Manager of the Minnesota-Wisconsin Division. As such, I was the first African American to lead a major chapter – as well as the first to serve as a Division Manager for the American Red Cross.

CHAPTER 5

Becoming CEO of the St. Paul Chapter

IN JANUARY OF 1976, I moved to St. Paul, the capital of Minnesota. Doris remained in Maryland while the children completed the school year. Meanwhile, I was invigorated about assuming responsibility for revitalizing this 130-person field office that was housed in a new building.

The St. Paul chapter worked in tandem with the Minneapolis office. I was assuming a concurrent leadership role, serving double duty as Manager of the ARC's Minnesota-Wisconsin Division. My goal in that position was to renew relationships between field offices and initiate cooperative programs and services. The division manager position elevated me into a select group which included leaders from the Big 12 Red Cross units – the largest in the American Red Cross. This was an extremely exciting and fulfilling opportunity because I was finally in a position where I could impact the organization's vision, programs, and policies. Clearly, I was stepping into a very high-profile position with tremendous breadth, and I wanted to demonstrate my mother's oft-repeated advice to leave everything I touch better than when I found it.

As it pertained to the St. Paul chapter of the American Red Cross, that edict encompassed nearly every service that our humanitarian organization provided: emergency assistance; disaster relief and education; communications services and comfort for military service and family members; the collection, processing, and distribution of blood and blood products; and educational programs on preparedness, health, and safety. To accomplish this, I embarked on an ambitious agenda with the goals of:

- Strengthening our Board of Directors;

- Hiring outstanding professionals;

- Boosting morale and productivity by cultivating a positive workplace culture;

- Introducing new community support and human service programs;

- Implementing innovative ideas to improve the Red Cross' impact on helping people and saving lives;

- Negotiating local government funding;

- Expanding outreach efforts;

- Heightening the organization's visibility, stature, and performance; and

- Furthering my commitment to preparation by beginning work on earning my Master's in Business Administration (MBA).

As I embarked on this long-awaited leadership opportunity, I revisited my personal formula for success that hinges on Purpose, Preparation, Performance, and Results. I spent quiet time alone, reflecting and strategizing on how to lead with distinction and improving the St. Paul chapter of the American Red Cross. In the context of our organization's work, that could be measured by bolstering community outreach, responding above and beyond the call of duty during disasters, implementing innovative programs, cultivating positive relationships with citizens that inspire them to utilize our services as well as volunteer with us to help others, and maintaining a fiscally sound organization with a balanced budget.

Furthermore, as one of few African American leaders in the entire organization, it was extremely important that I set an outstanding example for everyone from the president to our volunteers to see that a black man was leading our chapter with impeccable integrity and excellence on every level.

All the above objectives comprised my Purpose. My Preparation was rooted in the years of service that I had provided to the American Red Cross, as well as the U.S. Army. In addition, my fascination with and subsequent study of leadership and human relations, starting in college, equipped me with effective tools for interpersonal interaction that encouraged people to be their best.

With that, now was the time for Performance. I committed to taking action every day to achieve short- and long-term goals that would enable me and the chapter to achieve our Purpose. While doing so, I evaluated my Results every time I led a meeting, assembled a committee, spearheaded a new initiative, visited headquarters in Washington, or led a team to respond to a disaster. Each time, I critiqued my Performance by identifying successes and failures, with the goal of improving my efforts next time.

Very importantly, the Four Pillars were an integral part of my work as CEO. God had provided this opportunity. My Family was my support system that would benefit from my advancement, while this new position helped me provide a comfortable life for them. My involvement in the Church provided spiritual sustenance. And of course, my service to the American Red Cross represented the fusion of these pillars.

"We Can Do This!"
Hiring an All-Star Team

My first order of business was to hire the professionals who could enable me to achieve the goals that we had established for the chapter. Getting the word out about the services that the Red Cross provides to the community is always a top priority, and I needed an excellent Public Relations Director to achieve that.

I hired David Therkelsen, who remained with me for six years, laying the foundation for his 28-year Red Cross career that culminated with him serving as CEO of the St. Paul office. David is an excellent example of a key tenet of leadership success: selecting good people because their experience and expertise make you better than you are.

Smart leaders know they are ignorant in some areas, and that they have blind spots that could prove detrimental to their leadership. When I took the helm of the St. Paul chapter, I knew I was not a marketing aficionado. If promotions and public relations were my blind spot, then hiring David ensured our success in those areas. Marketing is a tremendously important aspect of our work; it promotes our services to the community and enables us to recruit volunteers who are in some ways the lifeblood of the organization.

Hiring David underscored the reality that an all-star team is imperative to the positive impact of an organization or company. Even a Heisman-trophy-winning quarterback cannot win a Super Bowl by himself. Nor can a great pitcher win the World Series alone. They both need their entire teams, because every person plays a crucial role in each quarter, inning, game, and championship. That said, leaders should play to win for his or her own organization's employees and the people they serve. This requires acknowledgement that no one person can do everything.

I kept this in mind as I hired my team, and I took the necessary steps to compensate for the fact that I did not know everything – and never would. The businessman and *Forbes* magazine founder Malcolm Forbes once said, "The dumbest people I know are those who know it all."

That is an extremely dangerous trait for leaders. As is status-seeking.

In all aspects of my life, I always try to make certain that I put service above status as a goal. While status should be a goal, especially in the life of a leader or potential leader, service is my purpose (improving the human condition), so that is my first goal. I have found that when I am effective in my service efforts, status eventually follows.

Therefore, I suggest when assembling a team, a leader should cultivate the humility required to admit that he or she has weaknesses or blind spots.

One of the greatest business minds in American history, Henry Ford, understood this. Once, when the founder of Ford Motor Company was being cross-examined in court by a condescending lawyer, the automobile magnate famously responded: "If I should really WANT to answer the foolish question you have just asked, or any of the other questions you have been asking me, let me remind you that I have a row of electric push-buttons on my desk, and by pushing the right button, I can summon to my aid men who can answer ANY question I desire to ask concerning the business to which I am devoting most of my efforts. Now, will you kindly tell me, WHY I should clutter up my mind with general knowledge, for the purpose of being able to answer questions, when I have men around me who can supply any knowledge I require?"

Of course, he said that nearly a century ago before women (and people of color, for that matter) were afforded opportunities in the workplace, and prior to the advent of computers and other technology. His point, however, emphasizes the powerful truth that good leaders cover themselves by empowering the team with a diverse array of talent and expertise. Good leaders know their weaknesses and recruit accordingly.

"Leadership is the first word that comes to mind when I think of Steve Bullock," Dave Therkelsen says now. "I was inspired by him and modeled my own management leadership style after what I learned from him."

Specifically, Dave recalls several tenets of leadership that I cultivated in this position:

Give people space to do their jobs and trust that they will succeed.
"Steve involved everybody and got the best out of everybody," Dave recalls. "His motto was, 'We have the capacity. We have the will. We have great people. We have a great board. We can do great things.' Steve always demanded that I and everyone else be prepared, and give their best advice. At the same time, he always conveyed belief that, 'You can do this!' In fact, as I advised and counseled younger managers, I relayed the same encouragement and it created a much better staff."

Assume the best in people until evidence proves otherwise.
"Steve had so much belief in humanity and capabilities of every human being that anybody could fool him once," Dave says. "If an expert said something was true, he would believe it. He had this great mind, but nobody could fool him twice."

Break the rule when the mission is more important.
It's important to respect rules, people, and institutions, but some circumstances merit breaking rules to accomplish a greater mission.

"Steve demonstrated this," Dave recalls, "when he wanted to hire me above the upper limits of the Human Resources Department's established salary range. He did this to the great dismay of the HR director, who said, 'You never do that! You never violate the salary ranges.' It was entertaining for me and others on the senior staff. The accountant was also rules-bound. I learned that good executives see beyond the rules and see when it's time to break the rule in favor of the mission. Steve always responded by saying, 'We're trying to help people in this community, and sometimes we will break a rule to do that.' That was a central theme of his leadership."

Keeping People Warm: The Interagency Coalition of St. Paul
Another example of putting the mission before the rules involved the life-or-death issue of keeping people's heat on during Minnesota's notoriously cold, snowy winters when temperatures routinely plunge well below zero.

The rules said that the energy company would shut off the heat in any home where the occupant or owner failed to pay the bill. But unfortunately, for many low-income people, paying the heating bill was impossible.

Our mission at the American Red Cross was to keep people safe. In a northern climate, having heat is a safety issue. So, here, we had to put the mission before the rules. We took action that exemplified my belief that large goals could be accomplished. I convened the "Interagency Coalition of St. Paul," which united numerous social service agencies with the area's main energy supplier. The coalition decided that we would not shut off people's heat during the winter. Instead, we created ways for residents to catch up on payments between March and thereafter.

"Steve was the convener who brought groups together to figure out what started as local rules and evolved into a state law that exists today," Dave says. "That's another example of his innovation. There was certainly nothing in Red Cross lore that said the St. Paul Red Cross had to take the lead in solving this community problem. Steve himself said the St. Paul Red Cross would take the lead, and he personally chaired this group."

Dave adds, "That was an example for me later as a leader and top executive that you can aspire to large goals. They don't necessarily have to be in the job description. If there's a large community need, you can go ahead and meet it. I gained confidence in that premise from Steve."

Twin Cities Teamwork Makes the Dream Work
St. Paul and Minneapolis are known as the Twin Cities. Today the chapters are combined as the Twin Cities Chapter. Back then, they were separate and my counterpart in Minneapolis was Robert Bender, Executive Director

of the Minneapolis chapter, whom I had met during brief encounters while doing Red Cross work in the 1960s.

"I was in meetings with the two of them," Dave remembers, "and they were kind of tense because their styles were so different. Bob was a very direct, I'm-going-to-tell-you-what-to-do kind of executive director. Whereas Steve rarely gave directives or 'thou shalts.' He just let the people who worked for him and with him know, 'We can do this!'"

Despite our differences in personalities and management styles, Bob and I became lifelong friends, as did our wives.

"I'm the gunfighter," Bob says now from his retirement home in Maine. "Steve is the peacemaker. That is another very impressive thing about Steve. He knows he can take fire for a lot of things. He doesn't flinch. His style is not confrontational and that works well for him."

Bob appreciated that I developed this style while enduring what he calls "latent prejudices" during my early years with the Red Cross in the South.

"Steve had to overcome barriers that were subtle and real," Bob says. "The country was undergoing changes that coincided with a lot of civil rights activity. In his own way, Steve began to open the Red Cross to the possibility of people of color being engaged at higher and higher levels. He did that without challenging or confronting people, but instead made change through excellent work, careful coaching, and living with situations that people learned to respect. Thanks to his personal style, he made an extraordinarily big difference in terms of how quickly he brought change to the organization. Steve's ascent into leadership roles enabled him to apply a non-work agenda about acceptance and as such was a leader for minorities. He did it in a thoughtful, quiet way that was extraordinarily impressive. All the people who worked for him either liked him or loved him."

Bob and I became friends, and often socialized together with our wives.

"In St. Paul," Bob recalls, "we and our wives went to dinner one night. It was obvious that the hostess was making us wait. People who had later reservations than us were going ahead of us. It took a long while. Steve was very patient and kept Doris calm. I got angry and went up and blasted the hostess, threatening to report this to the Civil Rights Commission. And we got seated. Steve was very patient and a little embarrassed. His style came right through."

Bob adds that in the Red Cross, the support of my wide circle of friends enabled me to make a difference.

"Steve always preached 'team,'" Bob says. "Being civil to people. Trying to work with people and helping to build their own skills."

Bob and I deepened our friendship while working on the Big 12 leadership team, where we got to know James Krueger. His larger-than-life personality was endearing to most whom he encountered. I had met Krueger when I was assistant manager of the Washington, D.C. chapter and he was the executive director of the Baltimore regional chapter.

Strategic and long-term relationships are a critical area of consideration for successful leaders. We need to identify and develop relationships with others where there is a potential for mutual benefit. Personal relationships cultivate greater love and respect for others. My mother always said that it will be hard to love and respect others until you are able to love and respect yourself.

"Another reason we became good friends," Krueger says, "is that Steve believed in a team concept and really setting the stage to have input from all levels of the organization. As peers, we really began sharing ideas about how to do things better and push the organization into more of a planning mode. The Red Cross, being a response organization, had a very difficult time with planning ahead."

It was during this time at one of the Big 12 leadership meetings that I met one of the few other African Americans at the Red Cross.

"Steve was the dean of big city Red Cross chapter executives," says Harold Brooks, who would become CEO of the San Francisco Chapter and later senior vice president of International Operations. "Steve was always in the center of it, the one with the most gravity, the person to whom everyone looked for good, solid leadership and guidance. All the respect and leadership that you could muster was to be found in Steve."

Harold recalls how the Big 12 group met regularly to provide "thought leadership for the rest of the organization. The senior management folks at national headquarters, and the chapter folks throughout the land, would look to them to forge the future for the Red Cross. Again, Steve was always in the forefront of that group and made it go. A group of chapter executives joined him in doing activities there. We carried out what the leader came up with for fundraising, volunteerism, and other activities. He provided energy and inspiration. We would provide manpower and resources to make it happen."

As two of only a few African American leaders in our organization, our colleagues routinely greeted Harold as Steve, and mistook me for Harold. While this exemplified the stereotypical phenomenon that all black people look alike, we reacted with humor, putting it in perspective. We were working daily to quietly promote diversity and inclusion within the organization. And we were serving as positive examples of African American professionals. So, we had fun with it.

"Hi Steve," I said whenever I saw Harold.

"Hi Harold," he said, rousing a chuckle in us both.

"Making Some Dust" with the Chair of the Board of Directors

As an African American leader of a large Red Cross chapter, and the first in St. Paul, I was an anomaly. As was the chairwoman of our Board of Directors. Barbara Scherek had the ultimate responsibility for the chapter, which included a highly-regarded blood program servicing the University of Minnesota Hospital, the Mayo Clinic, and many outlying hospitals in Minnesota and Wisconsin.

Together we shouldered a tremendous responsibility. Adding extra pressure to our situation was the fact that – whether spoken or not – African Americans and women in leadership positions "represent" our respective race and gender; people are watching and judging, and using our performance to evaluate the abilities of other people of color and women.

Knowing this, Barb and I wanted to do an extraordinary and exemplary job. Our goal was to demonstrate to the Red Cross, our community, and the world at large that a black man and a woman were capable of excellence in leadership.

"Steve, we're both minorities," Barbara declared. "Let's show them!"

I chuckled and said, "Okay, I guess you're right."

Barbara was a nurse and her husband was a physician. She had served on the search committee that selected me for the position. She and I embarked on a plan that I, as an assistant manager in Washington, and my colleagues had suggested: getting to know our board members to foster cohesion, enthusiasm, and teamwork. We made a short list of questions, then interviewed each board member at their place of business or in their home. After sharing the responsibilities of a board member, we asked:

"How and why did you become involved in Red Cross?"

"How much time can you give?"

"What committee would you like to be on?"

This process enabled us to get to know our Board members and their capabilities, while the interaction imparted a sense of ownership for them.

"To Steve's credit," Barbara says, "at the end of my two-year term – one of the old-time board members said he had never seen so much board involvement and chapter accomplishments."

Another major priority that Barb and I tackled was a long-range plan for the chapter. Shortly after I arrived, we established a Long-Range Planning Committee, as well as a Needs Assessment Study, and a Program Planning and Evaluation Committee. We used surveys to pinpoint specific dynamics and demographics within St. Paul's changing population. This information was important to assess future Red Cross programs in St. Paul. Each Red Cross service volunteer chairman and director received this data, and embarked upon a planning phase to help the Red Cross address our community's changing needs. All of this flowed into a five-year, Long-Range Plan.

"Steve almost immediately made contact with people and organizations in the community," Barbara recalls.

I did this by applying the principles of SAITEC, such as setting up meetings with community groups, churches and the greater faith community, city leadership, corporate leaders, small businesses, schools and universities, organizations, and citizens. Our staff also visited community centers, the largest of which was the Hallie Q. Brown Community Center.

This community outreach enabled me to reconnect with a friend from Virginia Union University, Cornell Moore, an attorney who lived in Minneapolis and who was a prominent and active leader in the business and civic communities. Cornell introduced me to many local leaders; this helped me build relationships that benefited the St. Paul chapter.

Our job was to make sure that we provided service to every member of the entire community. Minnesota is a very liberal state, and the population is quite diverse. This included several refugees from Laos in Southeast Asia, whom we met while attending Pilgrim Baptist Church, where Rev. Dr. Earl F. Miller was a VUU alumnus.

This outreach enabled me to introduce myself and share the goals of the Red Cross, as well as how working together with health education, blood drives, and safety programs, we could create win-win relationships for our organizations and the residents of our region.

While doing that, Barbara and I and our team implemented innovations that were unlike anything the Red Cross had done in the past. For example, during a strategy session, we learned that many people in the community that we served could not get basic health services because they lacked transportation. So, we applied for a grant and received federal funding through a state program to provide free transportation with Red Cross vehicles and volunteer drivers. We took people to doctor visits and other necessary appointments.

As we introduced these new programs and services, we never lost sight of the American Red Cross' mission to respond to disasters, collect blood donations, and provide classes for first aid, safety, and CPR.

Our community outreach endeavor was rooted in the basic Biblical truth that when you give, you receive. By showing a positive presence in the community, and providing a service that did not directly relate to the mission of the Red Cross, we fostered trust and familiarity with residents. That would make them more open to learning more about our services, so that they may become blood donors, volunteers, and participants in our education programs for first aid, disaster preparedness and disaster response, health and safety, water safety, boating safety, CPR, and nurse aid health programs which taught people how to be more self-sufficient in taking care of themselves and to better cope with minor health situations like injuries and fevers.

"Steve became a well-liked and a highly-respected leader in the non-profit community," Barbara says. "He gradually developed an awareness that people really did want to know what he thought and that what he had to say made a difference. He was thoughtful, caring, and fair, and had integrity."

Like several of my closest colleagues, Barbara became a family friend. "My association with Steve and Doris," she says after serving many years in that position, "still brings a smile to my face. I feel we both did some growing up together. I have a high regard for him – for what he has accomplished, but mainly as a sensitive caring person."

Sadly, Barbara passed away shortly before the publication of this book.

Identifying a Need to Save Lives: *The National Bone Marrow Donor Program and the Tissue Donor Match Program*

Barbara and I cultivated a culture of innovation and creativity for our programs. This inspired our team to present and execute new ideas that helped the community in unprecedented ways.

The most dramatic examples of this were our National Bone Marrow Donor Program and our Tissue Donor Match Program. Dr. Jeff McCullough, who was head of Biomedical Services and an innovator who was leading research in the blood program, conceived the idea after I talked with him about the need to expand our services to include bone marrow donations and tissue donations. Smart and visionary, he was the scientist and the trailblazer in this matter, because he brought this opportunity to the American Red Cross and me. Our ability to implement it was extremely beneficial for the community we served. I must credit Dr. McCullough for bringing the science to the marrow program, which led to many technological advancements that improved the safety and impact of our services.

As a result, we became the first Red Cross entity in the United States to implement a national bone marrow donor registry program and a tissue transplant service. These initiatives were fully embraced in St. Paul and we tried to promote them throughout the Red Cross on a national level.

Now allow me to explain how these pioneering programs came into being. First, I concluded that the Red Cross could play a life-saving role in matching blood marrow donors with patients who suffered from diseases such as leukemia that could possibly be cured by bone marrow transplants from donors who had a genetic match with the patient. During those treatments, the sickly bone marrow is removed and replaced with healthy bone marrow from a donor.

Finding genetic matches was difficult, as was recruiting donors who were willing to undergo the discomfort and risk of allowing their bone marrow to be harvested. As for tissue donation, it is like organ donation; a donor signs up to donate upon his or her death. An example of a tissue donation could be using healthy skin from a donor to replace skin on a burn patient.

Before I go further, it's important to understand the Red Cross' role concerning blood services. Human blood cannot be manufactured; it can only be collected from donors. It's used to help people who need blood due to car accidents, surgeries, cancer, other illnesses, disasters, and many other reasons.

One of the American Red Cross' major functions involves its Biomedical Services, which, according to RedCrossBlood.org, "plays a critical role in our nation's health care system. It is the largest single supplier of blood and blood products in the United States, collecting and processing approximately 40 percent of the blood supply and distributing it to about 2,600 hospitals and transfusion centers nationwide."

The website also says that, "Providing life-saving blood and blood products to patients is a key component of the Red Cross mission to help people in times of emergency and disasters."

The Red Cross collects that blood through donations. Even though about 38 percent of the American population are eligible to donate blood, fewer than 10 percent of Americans actually do. The number is even lower among African Americans and other people of color, who have been traditionally less likely to donate blood than whites for a variety of reasons. To ensure the collection and distribution of adequate supplies of blood, the Red Cross engages in extensive efforts to educate people about the importance of blood donation.

Today, the Red Cross collects 13.6 million units of whole blood and red blood cells every year.

In St. Paul, our Blood Donor Recruitment Department worked aggressively to educate people and host blood drives in schools, offices, factories, community events, churches and other faith institutions, and many more venues. Our chapter provided blood and blood products for hospitals throughout our region; that included the world-renowned Mayo Clinic in Rochester, Minnesota.

During our regular blood operations and outreach, I identified a serious gap between our biomedical services, our field chapter operations, and our programing. These schisms were nothing new between our biomedical division and the rest of the institution. But I found that unacceptable. We needed cohesion between all departments to deliver the most effective and efficient services to the people who needed our help.

So, here was where I set out to solve this problem by seeking the scientific assistance of Dr. Jeff McCullough. He brought the science to the marrow program, which led to many technological advancements that improved the safety and impact of our services.

I am not a STEM person. But I know how to put the meaning of numbers and scientific information into words. Also, I am not afraid to surround myself with people who are smarter than I am in some areas; that is a key tenet to successful leadership. As a result, we stayed focused on our goal.

A bit of background is necessary here. When I first joined the Red Cross, we distributed units of whole blood in a pint bottle that contained all blood components: platelets, white cells, and red cells. We had to collect, type, and process blood. Blood is really a transplant. It has many components that are utilized for different purposes. For example, platelets are used for treating cancer, and red cells can be effective in other ways.

However, back then, we were not separating the blood components. Later, the entire procedure changed. We collected blood in plastic bags, and in a laboratory, the blood components such as red blood cells and platelets, were separated and used for different purposes.

Our blood donation model served as a template for creating the marrow donor program registry and the tissue donor registry. The goal of creating the marrow program and the tissue program was to build the donor registries. We embarked on a campaign to find people who were willing to be on a donor list.

While the race or ethnicity of a blood donor and recipient does not have to match, it is sometimes easier to find a genetic match between bone marrow donors of the same race. The problem was that very few African Americans lived in the St. Paul and Minneapolis region. As a matter of fact, we lived in West St. Paul, which according to the 1980 U.S. Census had 17 black residents, and five of them lived in our house!

Finding a genetic match between donors and recipients can be extremely difficult. It becomes even more so among African Americans and other ethnic minority groups, which tended to be less apt to donate blood and tissue. On top of that, the American Red Cross had not effectively targeted the African American population for recruitment.

Therefore, we had to educate people to first understand the importance of blood and tissue donation. Then we had to encourage them to sign up and be available. In addition, we had to promote the benefits of saving lives by submitting to the bone marrow donation procedure that involves discomfort. (Years later, after I retired, a member of our congregation who had leukemia needed a transplant. Two people agreed to donate, but then backed out).

To raise awareness in the African American community, our Blood Donor Recruitment Department identified specific parts of the population, and engaged in aggressive outreach at schools, colleges, employee groups, General Motors plants, Ford Motor Company plants, and other companies with large numbers of employees. Our team then went on-site to promote blood tissue and marrow donor education.

Donor education was the strength of the program and promotion. We did that in the St. Paul-Minneapolis area while encouraging other chapters and regions to get involved as well. In time, the registries became successful.

Crisis Management: Never Tell a Lie

Throughout my career, I have understood the importance of cultivating good relationships with my colleagues. Establishing a good rapport with people lays a foundation for trust and productivity.

This proved especially true during my first experience with crisis management, after a Planned Parenthood center in St. Paul was burned. The director came to us and asked permission for the organization to temporarily use our space to teach its health education programs for women about how to take care of themselves.

I consulted with my leadership team, and we agreed to allow Planned Parenthood to use the space. During that time, two of our staff members – one who worked in health services and the other who helped clean up the classrooms – called the Catholic Diocese and told them that we were "doing abortions at the Red Cross." In fact, one woman said she observed the procedure on a table at the Red Cross. The Catholic Church called the United Way, which helps to fund the Red Cross; then someone from the United Way phoned me.

Meanwhile, the local TV news reported on the story and we talked with the press.

This story had the potential to create a major public relations disaster for the Red Cross and for me as CEO of the St. Paul chapter. This was my first experience with a crisis and how to manage information around it. The situation could have blown up in a negative way, and it had the power to taint or even jeopardize our chapter's relationship with both the Catholic Church and the United Way.

I did not want that. Nor did I want to lecture the two women.

At the same time, I remembered something that my mother said: "You want to be better today than you were yesterday, and better tomorrow than you are today. Knowing what your purpose is helps you to lean towards being pure. It's your North Star that will guide you."

This enabled me to apply my strategy of Purpose, Preparation, Performance, and Results. My Purpose was to prevent both a public relations problem and a financial hardship that could result from losing funding from the United Way. My Preparation was to examine the situation from every angle, and decide how to proceed. In doing so, I recalled the lessons on crisis communication during my studies and training on leadership; this is a topic that is crucial for all leaders to understand because it will inevitably be required at some point in any leadership career. My understanding was that the organization and its spokesperson should:

Tell it all. Tell it first. And never, ever tell a lie.

However, blurting out the truth is not always necessary. The story and circumstances can change quickly, so it's better to reveal only what is required. In this instance, I concluded that we needed to tell the truth. We had to tell our story, and all of it. And if a problem arose, we needed to make sure we were in the process of fixing it.

The best solution was to be totally transparent to show that we were doing nothing wrong. When representatives from the Catholic Church and the United Way called me, we opened our doors to allow them to see for themselves that no wrongdoing was occurring at the St. Paul chapter of the American Red Cross. During the visit, we showed them the Planned Parenthood curriculum and what was happening in our classrooms. We also had them speak with the Planned Parenthood people on the site while I was present. Barbara stood side by side with me and was also interviewed by the media.

This underscores the importance of cultivating good relationships with your peers. All the people involved already knew me; now during a crisis and potential conflict, they were looking at and speaking with the same Steve Bullock and Barbara Scherek that they had been looking at and speaking with before. As a result, the folks from the church and the United Way did not believe the two women's comments that we had changed for the worst.

Thankfully, the media, the church, and the United Way moved on, and the story was over. We told the truth, and the problem was resolved.

"Never ever tell a lie," I told my staff. "It's not always necessary to blurt out the truth, but don't lie. Be transparent. Knowing your purpose helps you lean toward being pure. In an organization that's serving the public, you want to be perceived as transparent and truthful."

I strongly recommend that your organization and its leaders receive some crisis communication training so that you will be prepared before an incident occurs. This will enable you to protect and preserve a positive image for your organization. You will also ensure the best possible outcome for anything that may occur.

In the end, my first experience with crisis management was an excellent learning experience. I reviewed my Results, and quietly celebrated that I and my team had achieved our Purpose. The "story" went away. No harm was done. Instead, it reinforced my major life principle to be honest at all times, especially during times of crisis. This situation also demonstrated the fact that, as a leader, you must know what's going on at every level of the organization, because ultimately you are accountable.

Cultivating Win-Win Relationships

No man is an island, and achieving big goals requires collaborations with like-minded people and organizations. That's why, early on as head of the St. Paul Red Cross, I met with the city's Mayor, George Latimer.

One key to connecting with people is to find common ground, but what grounds me is my Purpose to improve the human condition and leave society better than I found it. That goal is foremost in my mind when I encounter new people; I am eager to identify how our partnership can facilitate positive change for our communities. This was definitely the case with Mayor Latimer, who was well-connected in St. Paul. A short time after meeting him, I took a few of my Red Cross team members to meet with Mayor Latimer. He listened intently as I described our early goals:

1. Strengthening and diversifying leadership on the Board among our professional staff; and

2. Ensuring that the Red Cross had solid programs that would help to attract new volunteers and staff members.

Mayor Lattimer helped us recruit people. He also introduced me to public officials in Ramsey County and the Minnesota House of Representatives. Our relationship flourished during my six years in St. Paul, until I announced that I was moving to Ohio.

At the time, I had no intention of leaving St. Paul. However, CEO positions in Cleveland and Philadelphia became available, and I contemplated the benefits of moving to another chapter. Living in Philadelphia did not appeal to me. Cleveland was an even larger chapter than St. Paul, and I was intrigued about the possibility of applying all that I had learned throughout my career to remedy some of the challenges facing the Cleveland chapter. So, I interviewed in Cleveland, praying throughout the process for guidance on making the best decision. They offered me the position. By now, Doris was tired of moving, so I promised her:

"The next time we move, I'll retire from the Red Cross. They won't move us again."

When I told George Latimer about the move, he said lightheartedly, "I don't know why you're going to Cleveland, but since you're going, I have a friend there I want you to meet. His name is George Voinovich." I promised to call him.

My relationship with George exemplified the many positive working relationships that have developed into long-term friendships that prove mutually beneficial for not only ourselves as leaders within the Red Cross, but for the countless people we serve.

Cherishing Family Life in St. Paul
In St. Paul, and throughout my life, I have kept the Four Pillars foremost in my mind to ensure that I remain grounded in them. This created a sort of four-point circuit of thoughts as I first praise God for blessing me with our Church life to cultivate my relationship with Him.

While in Church, of course, I was surrounded by the second pillar, Family. As spiritual nurturance was poured into me, Doris, and our three children, we strengthened our relationships with God and with each other. At the same time, I was cognizant and grateful that my education at Virginia Union University, as the third pillar, had laid the foundation for me to embark on a career that had brought me to this leadership position with the American Red Cross, the fourth pillar. As my thoughts progressed from one pillar to the next, I maintained a strong determination to show our children an example for them to emulate our God-based lifestyle and values as adults.

When we moved to Minnesota, Eric was 13, Brian was nine, and Kelly was five. We lived in a spacious, split-level home at 12 West Logan Avenue, in West St. Paul. I did not spend a lot of time at home, because I typically worked seven days a week. However, nurturing and celebrating my family was a top priority. So, I often took the children to the office with me. That gave Doris a break and ensured that I invested quality time with Eric, Brian, and Kelly. They would walk around the office, and people gave them sweets.

"I used to love going to work with my dad," Brian says. "We would walk in and it was so cool that my dad was the boss and was so well-respected. He was in a suit, and I was there with him all day. We sat in his office while he held meetings. He had a cool office with people coming in and out, asking him questions. You could tell he was important, the leader, but he was not pretentious. He had the same humility about him that he has today. I wish he had beat his chest a little more and said, 'Hey, look I'm the man!' At one point in my life, I wanted to be what he was, the leader."

Brian had a best friend whose parents were educators. They saw me being interviewed on the television news.

"We were the only black kids in the school district," Brian recalls, "and they saw my dad in this leadership position. There was no direct conversation, but they asked me, 'What does your dad do?' and I said, 'He's director of the St. Paul Red Cross,' and they said, 'Oh, wow, very cool.'"

Later, Brian volunteered in the Blood Donation Center.

"Dad took me to lunch and I had fried shrimp for the first time," he says. "It was my favorite thing."

I also made special time with Doris. Despite my long working hours and the children's extracurricular activities, I also reserved Friday evenings as "date night." Doris and I went out to dinner, socialized with friends, and attended cultural events such as theatrical productions and concerts. We took family vacations every summer, and always ate dinner together as a family.

"We loved having cook-outs," recalls Kelly. "Holidays were extra special, when Dad told us about Christmas when he was younger. Every year at Thanksgiving dinner, our parents taught us about gratitude; we had a tradition to go around the table and everyone had to say at least one thing that we're thankful for. At the time, as kids, we protested and said, 'Can't we just eat, please?' And our parents said, 'No, you have to go around and say one thing.'"

Eric chuckles at the memory. "Oh, my gosh, I hated to do that as kids, but now I understand that my parents were trying to get us to appreciate all our blessings."

Kelly agrees: "I was thankful for my brothers and things that were easy to say, like health. This became more meaningful as an adult, and now I practice this tradition with my own children."

While Brian really enjoyed our life in Minnesota, Eric disliked the climate and missed his friends that he had left in Maryland.

"I had to recreate myself every time I changed schools," he says. "I started school in Atlanta, then Maryland, then St. Paul, then Cleveland. I was the chameleon. But it's been a great experience. I don't regret anything. My dad was a great example. He taught us how to be adults before we were adults."

Eric, who studied political science, married Cathleen on April 23, 1993. Their daughter, Elizabeth, is a sophomore studying music therapy at Cleveland State University.

Making All the Children's Sports Events

Despite my intense work schedule, which often took me out of town to oversee disaster response teams, I attended our children's sporting events and school activities.

"Dad was always traveling," Brian recalls, "and would get home late at times, but I remember him being at all of my basketball games, football games, and baseball games. He would be cheering."

Once Brian scored five touchdowns during one game. He was a very good football player, and he was named All Region. Likewise, Eric enjoyed playing on the school hockey team. While it's a very expensive sport, it enabled him to travel to away games and tournaments with the team. He also ran track.

Thankfully, Doris managed our home and our children's schedules.

"I don't know how our mother did it," says Brian, a filmmaker and television producer who earned a master's degree in film from American University, and specializes in historical and social issue documentaries. His wife, Patricia, is an account manager at Verizon.

"Our mother schlepped us around to sports practice and Boy Scouts, and she cooked," Brian says.

Doris vividly remembers juggling everyone's schedules while making family time a top priority.

"The girls' basketball team was the last team to practice," Doris recalls. "I would be making dinner for my family and I had to stop cooking and go to school to pick up Kelly from practice that ended at eight o'clock. Kelly was fast; the coach wanted her on the team. But I asked the coach, 'Why do the girls have to be the last ones to practice? You wouldn't want your daughter out here on a dark campus at night trying to get home. It's not safe for either one of us.'"

The coach refused to change the schedule, so Doris pulled Kelly from basketball. After that, Kelly ran track, and Doris carpooled with the other mothers to pick up the girls from practice after school.

Doris also took the kids to restaurants, museums, and the theater. "I didn't expect Kelly to become a prima ballerina," she says. "I just wanted to expose them to things that I never saw while growing up in a country school."

All of our children learned to play music; we had a rule that if we bought an instrument, they had to play it. Eric chose clarinet and drums; Brian preferred the trumpet; and Kelly played piano, performing at concerts and winning awards. She also ran and played basketball. Doris took her to get her hair done every Friday, but her Saturday morning practices would just mess it up, so Doris stopped taking her.

Family Vacations

We took family vacations every summer. We would pack the car and spend one or two weeks on driving trips to Montana, North and South Dakota, Yellowstone Park, and Mount Rushmore. We even went to a rodeo.

"Dad would get a AAA map and navigate the entire trip with hotels and everything," Eric says. "He always made sure we experienced things together. Our trip to Yellowstone National Park and Grand Teton National Park was one of the best experiences that we've ever had."

On that trip, we saw the Old Faithful geyser and the kids loved the animals.

Doris and I also took the children to our hometowns, so they could see the stark reality of how and where we grew up. Eric vividly remembers visiting Enfield, North Carolina.

"I didn't know peanuts came from the ground," he recalls. "Dad had to show me. We also visited the one-room schools that he attended and my mom attended. My dad talked about working near the Virginia Beach boardwalk. I could not imagine. The racism they had to endure was rough. But these lessons are another gift that he's given us, to show that life is never easy."

Kelly remembers that our activities had purpose. "Dad always wanted us to do things that had value, that we could learn from. He was very stern and focused, but we did fun things, too, like going to the pool."

I always used time with our children to have conversations about character and values.

"Be the best that you can be in everything you do," I told them repeatedly. And, as my mother often told me, I said, "Whatever you're going to do, do your very best. You are not average. You are better than average, so don't settle. And you must get an education."

The Role of Church in Our Lives

Our family joined Pilgrim Baptist Church, where I shared a special connection with Pastor Earl Miller because he was a graduate of Virginia Union University. With him, I served as a church leader by becoming a trustee.

"We went every Sunday and loved it," Brian recalls. "We were friends with Pastor Miller's kids, who were our age, and we visited their house. Our parents said we are going to go to church no matter what. Dad is a believer. He is a praying man and he encourages all of us to be the same way, and I am. The church plays an enormous role in his life, and always has."

We emphasized the importance of having a relationship with God. All three of our children attended Sunday school, were baptized, and joined the church. At home, we always prayed together and said a prayer over meals, but we did not read scripture and pray like my mom and dad did.

Kelly remembers how Doris and I taught our children about delayed gratification and appreciation.

"I remember him taking us to McDonald's after church before we went home," she says. "It was a great treat, and I was so excited. So, every week, I would ask, 'Are we going to get to go this Sunday?' And he would say no. He had high expectations of us, and he wanted us to learn how to appreciate a treat. I didn't understand that at an early age. I just thought, 'Ugh, no McDonald's! Maybe next week.'"

Blazing A Trail for Educating Red Cross Leaders

My personal commitment to becoming better every day inspired me to pursue a Master's degree in Business Administration so that I could improve my leadership and management skills. I believed that an MBA would maximize my ability to run the business side of the organization.

So, I enrolled in the MBA program at the University of St. Thomas in St. Paul. Then I asked for support from the American Red Cross, whose Education Incentive Plan pays for its leaders to earn degrees in social work. I was told the degree I was seeking had no value for work in the Red Cross.

I disagreed, and paid my own tuition, attending class while working full time as CEO of the St. Paul chapter, balancing time with my family, attending church on Sundays, and serving as a trustee.

"Steve worked so hard!" recalls Dave Therkelsen. "He was in his office at lunchtime reading books. I said to myself, 'If somebody as smart as Steve is working so hard, how can I possibly successfully earn this degree?'" Dave chuckles at the memory: "He always scared me away from it, but after Steve left in 1982 to go to Cleveland, I started earning my MBA."

During the final year of my MBA program, the Red Cross' national director of training called me to say that the organization was going to assist me through the balance of the program.

"Thank you," I said, quietly celebrating the change that President George Elsey was making in the organization. He was a visionary who understood that educating Red Cross leaders would prepare the organization to deliver better service in the new century.

"When Steve earned his MBA in St. Paul," recalls Bob Bender, "it was a feat. He was working full time and always trying to find ways to educate himself and to find new ways to do things that would equip him for the next job that he had. He did very well with that."

The MBA transformed me into a business executive and a better leader. It took me out of operations and put me more into leading the organization by focusing on the people, their needs, and satisfactions.

Very simply, leadership is about relationships: making people feel valued, confident, and involved in the planning and implementation of plans. The MBA program underscored my belief in the importance of team-building, and how our work impacts each person. As I put this into practice, I watched individuals who were negative about the organization transform into more positive, productive employees.

A Dream Deferred: Doris Earns Her College Degree

As you may recall, Doris was forced to leave Virginia Union University after her sophomore year because her father decided to pay for her brother's college tuition rather than hers. Beyond her understandable anger, she resolved to someday earn her college degree. Thankfully, when we lived in St. Paul and the children were in school full time, Doris began taking morning classes at the College of St. Catherine.

After two-and-a-half years, she earned her bachelor's degree in Elementary Education, focusing on pre-Kindergarten to eighth grade. On Sunday, May 24, 1981, I was overwhelmed with pride as she walked across the O'Shaughnessy Auditorium stage to receive the diploma that she had dreamed about earning decades before. After the ceremony, Doris stood on the college grounds in her cap and gown, posing for pictures with our children and me, beaming with great joy. The local newspapers even ran stories listing Doris' name among the graduates.

One of our family's proudest moments was watching Doris receive her college diploma from the College of St. Catherine in St. Paul. Her bachelor's degree in Elementary Education enabled her to begin teaching fifth grade in St. Paul.

Her dream had been deferred, but to reference the poem by Harlem Renaissance Poet Langston Hughes, it did not "dry up like a raisin in the sun." Thanks to her hard work and determination, Doris' dream was realized, and put to good use to help others. Doris began teaching fifth graders in St. Paul, and her schedule was ideal because it facilitated her presence at home after school to help Eric, Brian, and Kelly with homework and their activities.

When Eric graduated from high school, he attended St. Cloud State University for two years, then transferred to Kent State University in Ohio. After that, he joined the Marines and spent four years in the reserves.

I am extremely proud that everyone in our family has embraced the Pillars of God, family, education, and a purposeful career as the foundation for creating a fulfilling, meaningful life.

CHAPTER 6

Serving as CEO of the Greater Cleveland Chapter

AS ONE OF THE largest Red Cross chapters in America, the Greater Cleveland Chapter was one of the Big 12. When I became CEO, I took on the responsibility for full strategic planning, as well as finances, operations, and programming. I became the leader of more than 400 employees and 3,000 volunteers, and I managed a $25 million annual budget. My jurisdiction included Cuyahoga and Geauga counties, and I was the Coordinating Chapter Manager for the state of Ohio. I had become a Big 12 leader and state coordinating manager.

From the first day, I applied my strategy of Purpose, Preparation, Performance, and Results to everything I did. My Purpose remained to improve the human condition, and I now had the largest platform ever in my career to do that. Preparation included not only meeting with colleagues and people in the community, but also making certain that I maintained a solid personal foundation by nurturing my Four Pillars. I also set priorities to get adequate rest, spiritual sustenance, and family support.

As I embarked on my mission with the American Red Cross in Cleveland, my first conversation with chapter leadership directed my attention toward a major overhaul in three major areas:

- Relocating to another facility or constructing a new building because our current offices were literally crumbling and were too small to accommodate our needs;

- Dramatically improving our fundraising; and

- Upgrading professional staffing and workplace culture.

I was also challenged to lead an aggressive turnaround and revitalization of the organization by addressing immediate needs for programs and community outreach. I also set the goals of creating a new infrastructure, recruiting talented management and staff, and leading the organization through growth and expansion to build it into one of the most successful American Red Cross operations in the nation.

How would I achieve this? I wanted to transform the organization from its rather dormant state into a highly visible community partner. I would do that by building outstanding relationships with the top leaders in business, industry, banking, community affairs, and human services.

This challenged me to lead an aggressive turnaround and revitalization of the organization.

"The Building that Bullock Built"

When I arrived as CEO of the Cleveland chapter, the building was in such poor condition that the basement walls were riddled with holes. The chapter had also outgrown the building, forcing us to move the Blood Services Center to a different location. We faced the decision of either finding a new facility or constructing one to meet our needs.

I consulted with the chapter's Board, which included my first chairman David Ludwick and Marshall Wright, vice president for government affairs at Eaton Corporation. The Albert M. Higley Company evaluated the building; they determined that it was beyond repair. As a result, we spent a year searching for a building that we could renovate. It was imperative that we find a space that could house under one roof our blood services, chapter operations, and a laboratory that met the standards of the Food and Drug Administration, as well as other parameters. We found no such building.

As a result, we needed to design and construct a new building. So, we assembled a team of outstanding individuals who could create a state-of-the-art facility. Jim Stover, chairman and CEO of Eaton Corporation, agreed to chair our fundraising campaign. Al Higley's company served as the construction manager at no cost, which was a great contribution to the Red Cross. We made arrangements to borrow from the national office if necessary. It was not.

Thankfully, we completed the $12.5 million operation with no debt. Mayor Mike White and many other dignitaries attended our grand opening ribbon-cutting ceremony. I was extremely honored to oversee construction of what became known as "the building that Bullock built."

"You've made your mark now," someone from the foundation told me.

The three-story, brick and glass building at 3747 Euclid Avenue housed laboratories on the first floor, along with client services, disaster relief, and service to military families. Education programs were on the second level. Programs, administrative offices, and conference rooms were on the third floor. The building also had free, outdoor parking for staff and visitors.

My office was on the third floor, on the corner, facing Euclid Avenue. The office of the blood services director on the back side of the building had a nice view of Lake Erie.

As CEO of the American Red Cross of Greater Cleveland, it was a tremendous honor to lead the design and construction of our chapter's new headquarters. The endeavor exemplified teamwork because every employee had the opportunity to contribute ideas for how the building would look and function. *Photo Credit: Brian Bullock.*

"It didn't dawn on me how important he was until we came to Cleveland," Kelly says. "He had a corner office with lots of windows. When I visited, I'd sit in the big chair behind his shiny desk. People would come in and ask, 'Where's your dad?' and I would say, 'I don't know, I'm just playing around in his chair.' But I was really proud of my dad."

A Racial Slight

African American professionals deal with slights daily. Rather than react angrily with verbal outbursts, I chose to channel any emotional response into my continued determination to make change on an institutional level. Angry outbursts tend only to add fuel to the fire as opposed to educating people who may, through no fault of their own, be speaking from stereotypical perceptions fostered by the media and exacerbated by lack of exposure to people of color who demonstrate otherwise.

I experienced an example of this shortly after the unveiling of our new Red Cross building in Cleveland. I had just attended a big meeting with two top-ranking leaders of the top-ranking leaders at the national Red Cross. While they were visiting our chapter, I chose to drive them back to the hotel myself, rather than hire a limousine or a taxi. When the three of us headed to the car, one person entered the back seat, and I expected the second person to join me in the front passenger seat. But he got in the back seat. That created a feeling that I was their chauffeur.

As I navigated through traffic, they marveled at the beauty and functionality of the new building. Apparently, the gentleman whom I had expected to join me in the front seat had forgotten that I was the chapter's CEO who had overseen every detail of planning, building, and operating our new building.

"This is a new building," he exclaimed. "They built it, and they had no debts! Can you imagine that?"

I really believe that he had forgotten who I was. Still, I explained, "We initially arranged to borrow money with the national Red Cross, which had a special program where local chapters could borrow money for facilities or buy equipment, which included a very large lab facility."

The next day, the other Red Cross leader apologized that the other individual had spoken about something I had done as if I were not there.

I am never one to play the victim. Instead, I am pointing out an instance of something that is often experienced by women, minorities, and other groups that face prejudice: being overlooked.

Boosting Our Fund-Raising with Great Success

Fundraising had not historically been a strength of the American Red Cross in Cleveland and other communities. Our chapters received most our funding from the United Way and other donations. For the Greater Cleveland chapter specifically, we needed to raise $10 million every year. I wanted to make our chapter as financially and independent strong as possible.

So, I spearheaded the complete redesign and reinvention of the fundraising program, which now raises more than $9 to $10 million annually in donations from foundations, corporations, and the general public. In addition, I created a $1 million grant department and a planned giving department. At the same time, these endeavors reduced reliance on United Way funding.

In 1996, American Red Cross President Elizabeth Dole recognized my efforts, and asked me to apply this successful model to the national organization. She appointed me as Director of the 1996 National American Red Cross Campaign. This happened when she took a leave of absence to work in her husband Bob Dole's presidential campaign. She asked me to run the campaign while she was away. As my friend Bob Bender had done, I eagerly stepped up to the plate to shoulder this tremendous responsibility. At times, it was extremely fast-paced. For example, I recall a day when I flew out of Cleveland in the morning for a 10:00 a.m. meeting with an advertising agency in New York. Then I flew to Washington, D.C. for an afternoon meeting. After that, I boarded a plane for Los Angeles, where I was the speaker at the annual meeting for Los Angeles area chapters. Again, this was all in one day!

For a full year, I spent two days each week in Washington. As a result, the campaign was very successful. My hard work was recognized when I received the 1997 President's Tiffany Award for Employee Excellence in Management.

Upgrading Profesional Staffing

When I arrived at the Greater Cleveland Chapter in 1982, I discovered some archaic practices, a lack of credentialing requirements for professional staff, and issues with workplace culture and morale. So, I embarked on a campaign to improve all of that.

Archaic Practices

The PR director was using a manual typewriter, and we could not convince him to use an electric one or a computer. This, and his research skills, became a problem shortly after I arrived and was required to make a presentation to the Board of Directors. The PR director helped me write my speech, and he inserted numbers that included that we had 50,000 volunteers. I began giving the speech, then it hit me: I didn't believe we had that many volunteers. So, I talked with him afterward.

"We recruited 900 this year and 3,000 last year," he said, "so now we have 4,000."

I was uncomfortable with his accounting method, so we consulted our volunteer list. Many of the people named had since died, but the list was never updated, thus accounting for the inaccuracy. As a result, we upgraded our record keeping to ensure that the volunteer rolls were updated regularly, and that our facts and figures – especially those provided to me for presentations and press conferences – were accurate.

Credentialing Requirements for Professional Staff

The directors of major departments – Disaster, Social Work, and Health & Safety – all lacked college degrees. Because no professional credentialing requirements had been established for our professional staff, we implemented a scale as we slowly began to expand our staff in the new building.

For example, anyone hired as a social worker was required to have a college degree. If he or she wanted to ascend into leadership ranks, a master's degree in social work would be required.

Likewise, counselors needed training and licenses that would be renewed when required.

It was imperative for us to elevate the professional qualifications of the leadership staff. We also changed the structure of some departments to improve effectiveness and efficiency. This overhaul sparked tremendous improvements. For example, we hired additional fundraising professionals, including Evelyn Faulkner. Her outstanding work enabled our chapter to make exponential increases in our fundraising efforts and improvements. Our staff overhaul boosted morale and inspired a better work ethic, higher quality work, and better productivity among the staff.

Workplace Culture and Morale
When I was CEO of the Cleveland chapter, my reserved parking space served as a launch point for important conversations that helped improve our workplace culture. When my car was in the space, the employees believed I was in the building. That may or may not have been true, as I could have departed with a colleague in another vehicle to attend an off-site meeting. When my car was not in my parking spot, this signaled to the men and women who worked in our building that the boss was off the premises.

Some employees became preoccupied with whether I was in the building. Unfortunately, their presumption was that if I were not there, then I was not working. That could not have been farther from the truth. My position required me to attend many meetings in the state capitol of Columbus, and to take trips to the national office in Washington.

In addition, serving as the leader of the Red Cross in Cleveland required my extensive interaction with the community. It was my responsibility to act as an ambassador and quite frankly a promoter for the services that we provided. We needed the community to know that we were there, and we wanted their participation as volunteers, financial contributors, and participants in our safety courses, events, and programs. To accomplish this, I attended many meetings, and was often invited to events to represent the Red Cross.

On top of that, I was a member of the board of directors for the United Way and University Hospitals, as well as boards for several neighborhood organizations. These required my attendance at meetings, which were extremely beneficial because they provided opportunities to maintain a close working relationship with these organizations. Maintaining an active presence in the community also enabled me to stay aware of trends and needs of the people we served.

It was also imperative for me to build relationships with the mayor, business leaders, and health care executives such as the CEO of the Metropolitan Hospital. This could not be achieved by sitting in my office. Meeting and greeting people face-to-face facilitated the building of important relationships that created win-win opportunities for the community to benefit from the mission of the Greater Cleveland Red Cross.

All of this left my parking space vacant, which triggered chatter that the boss was not working. Not only was this counterproductive as employees spent time talking about my whereabouts, but it also fueled negative morale rooted in assumptions about poor work ethic.

This had to stop.

So, I used a staff meeting as an opportunity to transform some employees' negative mindset on this matter. First, I explained that many of our employees performed important aspects of our jobs outside the building. My deputy, for example, supervised five branch offices simultaneously; that meant she might be working in another county on any given day.

"The Red Cross is here in Cleveland to serve the community," I explained, "and to do that well, many of us need to be outside of this building, interacting with leaders and everyday people to let them know about all the services we provide. It's important to assume that when someone is not here, he or she is working elsewhere, doing something helpful for our organization and for the people that we're here to help."

In addition, one solution for alleviating the preoccupation with other employees' whereabouts was to eliminate reserved parking spaces, even for myself, when we moved into the new building.

As I became further acclimated to the culture of the Cleveland office, I was deeply disturbed to discover a lack of cohesion and interaction between departments. These revelations occurred as I explored the building. For example, one day I ventured to the tenth floor, which housed Safety Services such as water safety, first aid, and CPR training. When I chatted with the staff, they wanted to know what I wanted. A man asked me:

"Why does management need to know anything about what we do in Safety?"

This is a sick place, I thought. *This guy doesn't even know he's part of the Red Cross organization.* I also encountered employees who referred to the Red Cross as "they" rather than "we." This indicated a disconnection from the organization where they spent eight hours working every day. I was so astounded by the lack of unity, I hired a consultant to cultivate team-building for our staff.

While her "close your eyes and visualize" style did not appeal to me, she told us about David Cooperrider, a psychologist who was looking for a non-profit organization where he could test his theories. We volunteered, and he presented to us a concept called "Appreciative Inquiry" that was being designed to cultivate team-building in organizations.

Since this occurred concurrently with our brainstorming sessions to construct the new building, I turned that endeavor into an exercise for testing his theory. Basically "Appreciative Inquiry" means inquiring within the organization to ask employees and volunteers for ideas, solutions, and strategies to help improve the workplace for themselves and the people we served. At the core of this exercise was the question: What do you believe are the most important qualities that must be retained in the organization?

This process enabled us to identify our core values at the Red Cross, and ranking at the top was volunteer spirit. Once people began to share their concerns and ideas, and feel that their viewpoints were valued, their morale spiked. They contributed ideas for how to design the new building, based on their experiences with working in different departments and what improvements could be made over the old building. The lab staff was especially insightful. And some of the suggestions – such as installing a swimming pool on the roof – were downright hilarious.

What made this process successful was that management truly listened to what the staff and volunteers were saying, and implemented some of the best ideas during the design and construction process for our building.

Amazingly, this process of giving everyone a voice in the process worked wonders. It cultivated honesty, effective communication, transparent leadership practices, and volunteer spirit. One woman in particular became a superstar leader. When we moved into the new building, productivity spiked. People bought new outfits, worked harder, and had a much more upbeat mood in the office. We rewarded them by recognizing their hard work and by putting in place a more competitive pay structure.

Our team-building work continued as we held regular meetings, events, and communications that cultivated a spirit of inclusion and importance for every employee.

This included management meetings twice each month, and we held all-staff meetings every two or three months during which I communicated what was happening in the organization and the progress we were making, as well as new activities and goals. We also created newsletters and special bulletins to keep the staff informed of the latest news, for example, about our chapter's disaster response services for multiple families impacted by a big fire. We let everybody know what went on, how we responded, and how we were supportive for the people affected.

The importance and value of synergy in organizational effectiveness is a critical area for leadership attention and focus over time. The goal is for the organization to be able to achieve a level of success that "is greater than the sum of the whole." So, the sum of five departments, committees or units will be greater when there is synergy between the departments than when those departments operate independently of each other. The organization is more effective and that is what leaders want to achieve.

Also, related to synergy, a long time ago, I encouraged our employee participation by sharing another core belief: that life is far more about additions than it is about subtractions. I encouraged everyone to feel they were adding value to our Red Cross chapter and the people we served, while our staff concurrently felt that their work was adding value to their lives through fulfillment, compensation, and teamwork that was improving the greater good of our community. These dynamics underscored the importance of inclusion; our success was rooted in making every person at every level of the organization feel that he or she was included in the decision-making process, from start to finish.

All these philosophies have proven true in both my personal life and professional work, and it is immeasurably fulfilling to know that I passed along these practices to the hundreds of people with whom I have worked across the country. I say this not to boast in any way; I say this to echo the Biblical verse that to whom much is given, much is required.

My intention for my work with the Red Cross was to exemplify and teach the values that were instilled in me by the three other pillars in my life, specifically, my mother, my college professors, and the church. As one of W.E.B. DuBois' "Talented Tenth," I was leading a major Red Cross chapter. And I was demonstrating The Parable of the Talents by sharing what I knew about leadership to multiply that as each individual went out into the world teaching the same knowledge to others.

This ripple effect over time and distance compounded the positive actions that truly enabled me to achieve my life purpose of improving the human condition.

Success Rooted in Mother's Work Ethic Focuses on Preparation and Productivity

Back when I was growing up on the farm in North Carolina, my mother used to say that we had a lot to accomplish between the time we started in the morning and the end of the day.

"We need to work harder," she'd say. "We need not be afraid of work. Our work never killed anyone. You need to be about the business that you're about, not just trifling." She used the word "trifling" a lot. For example: "There's no reason to be trifling about anything. Do what you're going to do. Do it well. Get on with it."

That edict motivated me to approach every day with purpose and a sense of urgency to get things done. To master this, I began my preparation the night before. When I arrived home from work, I went to the closet and removed the suit, dress shirt, tie, and shoes that I planned to wear the next day. I organized my clothing in the place where I dressed, so it was ready the next morning. Two or three times each month, my board chairman liked to meet at 6:00 a.m. or 6:30 a.m.; he was president of the gas company and needed to arrive at his office for 7:30 a.m. staff meetings. I was fine with this schedule. It made me extremely productive; I accomplished a tremendous amount of work before noon.

I was very organized, and my executive assistant helped me. I tried to organize my work according to what needed to be completed tomorrow, or the day after tomorrow, et cetera.

My typical day would start with picking up where I had left off yesterday, and delegating tasks. Two or three times each week, I led an executive session with the Chief Operating Officer, the HR director, the finance director, and the PR/development/fundraising team. Sometimes program people from disaster services, blood services, health and safety, would join us for strategy sessions.

My job was to create the vision and the strategies for accomplishing the goals that we established. Every day involved planning, strategizing, implementing, and evaluating while developing resources for funding and recruiting volunteers. This included working a lot with other organizations and people in the community, corporations, and so forth. This interaction enabled us to meet potential new board members and encourage donations.

I was also appointed Coordinating Manager for the State of Ohio, representing statewide interests to national ARC leadership and participating in nationwide public relations and community awareness programs. This required me to spend time with other large chapters within the state, while my two field reps visited smaller chapters. I also visited small chapters as often as possible. I often drove two hours to the state capital of Columbus, a central location where I met with other chapter executives to plan work and do goal checking. We had to ensure that chapters were prepared and responding to local disasters in their communities such as tornadoes and annual flooding in southern Ohio after the snow melted and ran down the Ohio River.

House fires were a major problem in Cleveland and other large cities because the neighborhoods have an abundance of wood-frame houses that frequently caught fire, and the Red Cross was always on hand to provide food, blankets, emergency shelter, and counseling.

We started the "Save a Life" program that distributed free smoke detectors to residents of Greater Cleveland. I actually walked the streets with Mayor White to give out smoke detectors and encourage people to install them in their homes. We partnered with the city in this endeavor, enabling Fire Department staff to install the smoke detectors in residents' homes. The Save a Life program is a major nationwide program today; smoke detectors are proven to save lives by alerting people with an alarm so they can escape from burning houses and buildings.

We distributed American Red Cross fact sheets about fire prevention and safety in the home, and it says, "Having a working smoke alarm reduces one's chances of dying in a fire by nearly half."

Building Relationships for the Greater Good

When I arrived in Ohio, I heeded St. Paul Mayor George Latimer's advice to call Cleveland Mayor George Voinovich. Well, I met his delightful mother first, because she insisted on having lunch. I quickly accepted and learned that Mrs. Josephine Voinovich was a United Way volunteer.

"I'm going to talk with George and tell him to do whatever he can do to help you be successful at the Red Cross," she told me.

I thanked her. Then I met with Mayor Voinovich; he became a personal friend who continued his advocacy for the Red Cross. Having endured the tragedy of losing his daughter in an accident years before had inspired him to get involved in humanitarian endeavors.

Mayor Voinovich, his mother, and his wife, Janet, were well-known and well-liked in Cleveland. Their endorsement of me opened many doors and facilitated many collaborations for our organization and its programs. Later, George became Governor of Ohio, then a U.S. Senator. He died in 2016, as did John Glenn, who with his wife, Annie, were big supporters of the Red Cross after Elizabeth Dole became president.

My relationship with George Voinovich continued to prove beneficial throughout my public service in Cleveland.

And that was extensive. Throughout the course of my tenure as CEO of the Greater Cleveland Red Cross, I served on the Board of Education of the Cleveland-Heights-University Heights City School District, becoming president in 1991. I also served seven years on the University Heights city council. (I am a registered Democrat and I am identified by Democrats as a liberal or progressive Democrat. My commitment is to what Dr. Orr challenged me to do – and that is to be right more often than I am wrong).

Mayor Mike White appointed me as co-chairman of the Operation Desert Storm Homecoming Committee. I served on the Board of Trustees for the Cleveland Campaign, and chaired the Marketing Cleveland-to-Clevelanders Committee. For a time, I was chairman of the Mandel Center for Nonprofit Organizations Case Western Reserve University Executive

Advisory Network. And I worked as President of the Council of United Way Services Agency Executives.

I served on the Board of Directors for National City Bank; the Board of Trustees for University Hospitals Health System; the Board of Trustees for University Hospitals of Cleveland; the Board of Trustees for Leadership Cleveland; the Board of Trustees for the Ohio Motorists Association; and the Board of Trustees for the Greater Cleveland Roundtable for which I chaired the Education Committee.

In addition, I served as Mayor White's Black on Black Crime Commission, the African American Cultural Gardens Advisory Board, the Mt. Sinai Urban Health Council, and The City Club's Program Committee and president of the Board.

I was a member of the Rotary Club of Cleveland, The Club, The Play House Club, The City Club, and the University Club. I had memberships in the Association of MBA Executives, the American Management Association, the American Society for Training and Development, the NAACP, the Urban League, and Alpha Phi Alpha Fraternity, Incoporated.

"Steve was never one to flaunt his power and influence," says attorney Donet G. Graves, who performed legal work for the Cleveland Red Cross Chapter and became a lifelong friend. "He was very effective in his many roles without striking discord in the community. He was very genteel, but stood his ground on the issues. I don't think Steve ever lost his grounding in his commitment to not only the greater community, but in endeavors that were unique and significant to him."

Donet, who is a member of the Boulé, served on the Board of the Red Cross after I left the organization, adds that it was very unusual for a person of color to hold a leadership role in corporate Cleveland during the 1980s and 1990s.

"The message I have for Steve regarding the impact that he had on the community is, 'Thank you for your tenacity,' because he was regularly called upon to provide that kind of perspective to ensure his board composition was representative of everyone."

Leading By Example to Impart Leadership Skills to Others

A major motivation for writing this book is to share the behaviors and practices that have enabled me to serve as an effective leader. Throughout my career, I have demonstrated these tenets. The passage above provided an overview.

Below, a long-term colleague and friend elaborates on what she observed, and how she applied my example to her own successful career.

"I learned how to be a manager from him," says Jennifer Baker, who began working in marketing at the Cleveland chapter in 1987 after she graduated from college. She rose to become Director of Development and Public Relations for the American Red Cross. Because she so impressed me and I found confidence and comfort in her, I asked her to work with me as a consultant with The Bullock Group, after I retired from the American Red Cross.

"I can attribute every good thing that I know about managing people," says Jenni, who is now Development Officer at University Hospitals in Cleveland. "I learned from him. The overall way that he managed teams was the greatest gift he gave me."

The passages below are italicized to indicate that they are told by Jennifer.

Let Everyone Know Their Role Is Important to the Organization

Steve would walk around the building, and he knew everybody's name, from the guys who drove the disaster relief vans, all the way up. It didn't matter what anyone's job was. He made them feel their jobs were absolutely essential to the success of the organization. I've never seen a CEO like him, walking around and saying, "Nice to see you," or "Glad you're here," or "Hi, Darryl, how's your wife? How are the kids?" It was genuine, and people responded to that. He was a very well-respected leader.

Cultivate Teamwork

Steve's method for leading meetings focused on what we were looking at as a group, and what each person's role was in achieving that. So instead of going around the room and having each person regurgitate their "to-do list" to the team, we talked about the organization's goal and each person's role in addressing it as a whole, so that everybody felt that their piece in it was valued. Steve's subtle, nice way of looking at it from the organizational point of view has served me and everything I do.

Give Everyone a Voice, and Really Listen to What They Say

Steve always allowed time for everybody to be heard in the right way. He taught me the importance of letting everybody be heard, and considering their input when decisions are made.

Think Before You Speak or Act

Steve taught me that there's nothing wrong with taking your time to make a decision before taking action. Acting too quickly can cause mistakes. Instead, Steve demonstrated the importance of consulting with people for their opinions and expertise, as well as thinking through options and solutions. He taught me not to have knee-jerk reactions, even during a crisis.

Maintain Grace Under Pressure

Steve has the unique ability to remain calm, even when people are angry, or getting worked up, dealing with something controversial. He never wavered from who he is: a kind, humble person who's calm.

People really respond to that, even in tense situations. I

learned from that. I've never been as good at it as him. You learn how important it is to just listen. People just want to be heard. He was good at listening and responding, even if his point was the opposite of what someone wanted. The essence of who he is came through, and that made a deep impression on me.

We've all seen situations where people let situations overtake who they are. It's hard to not get worked up when things are not going your way. He can be true to who he is.

The Bullock Style: Demonstration, Not Confrontation

When I was CEO of the Greater Cleveland chapter, Bob Bender was CEO of the American Red Cross in Greater New York. Unfortunately, a few people in the organization accused him of being racist.

I knew better. But rather than loudly contest their accusations, I demonstrated my personal endorsement of Bob as a valued colleague, as a good friend, and very importantly, as an individual who embraced and celebrated diversity and inclusion.

I did this by inviting Bob to attend a large meeting in Cleveland. As CEO of the host chapter, and organizer of the event, I orchestrated Bob's involvement in the business meetings as well as the social events.

"It was not traditional for me as head of the New York chapter to attend some of the social events," Bob recalls.

The handful of individuals who had been antagonistic witnessed how I showcased Bob in this capacity; this silenced their criticism. In addition, this display nullified his critics' ability to taint others' opinions about Bob, because their observance of his interaction with me had already convinced them that Bob is a good guy.

"Steve is like melted butter," Bob says. "He can spread out and smooth things over and influence other people and somebody like me in a lot of different ways."

This was evident when I visited the New York chapter and was impressed by Bob's ability to recruit and maintain a very diverse staff that included African Americans, Hispanics, and Muslims for whom worship rooms were provided.

"Steve taught me a lot about being inclusive, and making sure there was representation," Bob says. "More than 50 percent of our staff, including top managers, represented non-white groups. I watched Steve bring people of different backgrounds and cultures together when I ran Boston after Minneapolis, and then when I went to New York. Steve really influenced my style. When we used headhunters to recruit for top management jobs, we specifically told them that we wanted to see a variety of different candidates with different backgrounds and so forth. It all worked and that was great."

Leading the Five Commitments Seminars as CEO of the Cleveland Chapter

My commitment to becoming better every day inspired a deepening passion for learning about leadership and applying it to my work with the American Red Cross.

At the time, Dick Schubert was President of the American Red Cross, having begun on January 1, 1983. Dick was a strong leader who endorsed the progressive trajectory that George Elsey had established to relinquish the ARC's position as a follower and instead strengthen its leadership and create strategies that enabled the organization to transform from simply responding to emergencies and disasters, to serving as a catalyst to prevent them or lessen the potential for damage and death.

To do this, the national Red Cross hired a consulting company that helped us implement a concept known as "In Search of Excellence." The purpose was to achieve excellent personal and organizational performance, by building stronger teams composed of individuals who were committed to being their best. This required that each person understood the definition of commitment.

The Merriam-Webster dictionary defines it as: "the state or an instance of being obligated or emotionally impelled." In addition, commitment results from a unique blending of one's strong beliefs and one's actions. If you believe strongly in something and you are committed, you will be motivated to do something about it. On that premise, our consultant presented "The Five Key Commitments." They are:

- Commitment to the Organization – Embracing the organization's work and purpose.

- Commitment to your Task – Having passion for what you do in your individual position and for what you do as part of a team that works to achieve the organization's mission.

- Commitment to the People in the Organization – Valuing your colleagues, their roles, and the work they do to advance the organization's work.

- Commitment to the Customer – Wanting to do your best in your position to provide the best services for the people who rely on your organization for help.

- Commitment to Yourself – Being confident, willing to take risks, actively involved, self-aware, and improving yourself by learning and expanding your skills.

This information fascinated me. It was exciting and fulfilling to learn and teach philosophies and strategies for the Red Cross that mirrored my personal beliefs. As such, I was the senior executive and captain on one of two teams of four leaders who traveled the country teaching the Five Key Commitments. I did this during Dick Schubert's entire tenure, until he left the Red Cross on May 31, 1989. In 1988, on the recommendation of my peers, he appointed me as Chairman of the President's Advisory Committee, leading a group of senior Red Cross field executives advising national ARC management on key strategic and organizational issues.

It was especially exciting to lead corporate retreats 10 times each year. We brought people from chapters across America to conference centers and resort areas in places such as New York, Atlanta, Phoenix, and St. Paul. Over three days of workshops, we included a lot of exercises that fostered working together and problem solving. I often quoted that great philosopher, Butch Cassidy, by saying, "We're not going to fight until we have discussed the rules."

Each time, I emphasized the importance of knowing the rules and following them, but changing the rules when situations required doing so.

During the course of our leadership meetings, I met Linda Mathes, who had served in several leadership positions at the national headquarters of the American Red Cross in Washington, D.C. between 1978 and 1986. She then became Executive Director of the Pittsburgh-Allegheny County Red Cross Chapter in Pennsylvania until 1991, and was appointed CEO of the American Red Cross of the National Capital Area in 1991.

As such, Linda Mathes became the first-ever female CEO of a Big 12 Red Cross chapter.

"I began meeting with Steve and other colleagues of major chapters," she says. "It was a daunting experience. Steve always encouraged me to be myself and to feel that I deserved to take a seat at the all-male leadership table. He was sensitive to my feelings in an environment that did not have many women leaders at the time. Steve was very thoughtful in helping me feel included and respected. He encouraged me to speak up and add my perspective. He took the time to listen. It sounds so simple, but it was very significant. Some people had confrontational communication styles. But Steve was very principled and thoughtful about different perspectives on the local and national levels. He always said his mother told him to 'make some dust' by making a difference, and Steve was definitely trying to kick up some dust."

Linda watched me do that many times.

"Wherever he was," she recalls, "Steve would look very thoughtfully at an issue for solutions and ways to effect positive relationships. He'd make a mark. You knew he was there. He would make some dust and make a difference. He was always listening for a way to make things better. We had many difficult days dealing with controversial issues. But Steve had a way of dealing with them in a way that maintained everyone's dignity and integrity."

Linda says I provided a model of how to be a successful Red Cross executive, which included being balanced with my family.

"He inspired me to model my career after his example," she says. "Very importantly, Steve helped increase my own sensitivity to inclusion of everyone. When I looked around the professional ranks, we did not for years have many people of color. Steve helped me and many others understand and become more sensitive to inclusion of people of all kinds. He showed us how to 'make some dust' to create a more diverse professional base."

Linda and I had many conversations about leadership. She asked me, "What are some experiences you had, so I can learn and do everything I can to recruit people who reflect diversity, to make an environment where people feel celebrated?"

She recognized that it was sometimes difficult to encourage diversity among those who resisted it. "Steve never let that get in the way of his commitment and his positive attitude and his professionalism," she says. "He was ahead of his time in many ways, being a very accomplished African American in our organization. He was not bitter. He continued his commitment and modeled integrity and professionalism in a way that stands out. He did a lot to foster the field leaders and chapters across the country, by giving them a voice and enabling them to work with national to develop plans and have dialogue. We're stronger when that happens."

The Annual Red Cross Ball: "A Stunning Success"
As we explored new fundraising opportunities for the Greater Cleveland Red Cross, I tasked our Fund Development Committee with brainstorming ideas. This happened at a time when 40,000 disasters had zapped the Red Cross relief program, prompting our national board to set a quota for our chapter to raise $156,000 for disaster relief funds.

In 1983, two members – the wife of board chairman David Ludwick and her friend – suggested several options, including that we host a black-tie gala called the Red Cross Ball.

I expressed serious concerns that a high society and exclusive event costing $250 or $500 per couple would exclude many people. Very few black people were involved at that level in the Red Cross. I didn't want to do anything that would brand us as an elitist organization that was not concerned about the rest of the community.

When presented with a clear choice of inclusion or exclusion, if it is not criminal or evil, I will almost always choose inclusion. Generally, it makes me, the team, the organization, and the outcome better. I was determined to achieve that in this instance.

"I need to do my own research," I told the committee.

I met with Cheryl Wills, whose family owned a large funeral home with several locations in northeast Ohio. She was on the national board of directors for the United Way.

"Here's my dilemma," I told her. "I don't want to send the wrong message to the broader community."

"Okay, Steve," she said, "you have to figure out how to do both. If you want to raise money, you have to go the people who have money. The ball might be for the people who have money, and maybe you can provide opportunities for other folks to participate."

After meeting with Cheryl Wills, I gave the Fund Development Committee the green light for our chapter to host the first Red Cross Ball. We also found ways to include people who were unable to purchase tickets. For example, the director of a community center asked, "Can you provide two seats for me and a senior citizen so we can be at your ball?" We agreed. This director, Rubie McCullough, had come to Cleveland as a teenager from Enfield, North Carolina.

More than 700 people attended the Inaugural Red Cross Ball for the Greater Cleveland Chapter on Saturday, November 12, 1983, at Stouffer's Inn on the Square in Cleveland. The program booklet included an introductory letter from President Ronald Reagan, who was the Honorary Chairman of the American Red Cross.

When I was CEO of the Greater Cleveland Chapter of the American Red Cross, we established the Red Cross Ball. It became a hugely successful fundraiser and highly anticipated social event that Doris and I greatly enjoyed attending. One photo shows us with Dr. Floyd Loop, then-CEO of the Cleveland Clinic, and his wife, Dr. Bernadine Healy, who served in several government positions, including National Institutes of Health. Dr. Loop and Dr. Healy received the American Red Cross Award at the first Red Cross Ball. She followed me as ARC president. One year, the legendary singer, actress, and civil rights activist Lena Horne performed at the Ball, and it was a delight to meet her. *Photo Credit: American Red Cross*

The event was lauded as the social fundraiser of the year, attracting the who's who of Cleveland's leaders in business, education, government, non-profit organizations, and philanthropy. It helped our organization meet the emergency disaster relief campaign quota of $156,000 that the national board had set months before.

"A stunning success," read an article in the Red Cross newsletter. "The Ball rivaled the annual Red Cross balls held at Monte Carlo, Monaco, and Palm Beach, Florida. Maddy Joseph and Marion Ludwick, co-chairpersons of the Ball, and their Ball committee, gave thousands of hours preparing this dazzling event."

I wore a tuxedo, and Doris wore a long, red satin skirt with a white blouse; most of the women wore the theme colors of red and white to match the Red Cross flags draped over the ballroom balcony. Everything about it was grand; we descended the stairs into the ballroom under the raised sabers held by uniformed members of the U.S. Air Force Sabre Drill Team.

"This was the most elegant affair I've ever attended," Doris told one local newspaper.

Our photograph was printed in many local publications that were part of the extensive radio, TV, newspaper, and magazine reports about the Ball. Our own family photo album includes many pictures, including those showing Kelly wearing a long, white dress, while Eric and Brian sported tuxedoes.

After that, the Red Cross Ball was held every two years; in 1985, 650 people attended. Doris, wearing a sparkling red jacket and long skirt, and I were photographed in the *Call and Post* newspaper; the picture showed us introducing Cleveland Browns defensive back Frank Minnifield to our friends, Robert P. Madison and his wife, Leatrice.

Doris and I met Bob and Leatrice shortly after we moved to Cleveland. Bob is a World War II Purple Heart Veteran, a trailblazer in the architecture profession, and a member of my fraternity, Alpha Phi Alpha. Now 95 years old, he attributes his active lifestyle and longevity to strong faith and living the principles of the Bible. He vividly recalls our first meeting.

"My wife and I were attending the annual Christmas pageant that's put on every year by the Junior League in Cleveland," Bob says from his home in Cleveland. "They had an exhibit where they brought organizations in to decorate trees that were displayed on the public square. While we were looking at trees, we saw three black people, including this African American couple at the end of the line of trees. That was unusual; we did not see other African Americans at this program. So, we stopped, waited for them, and introduced ourselves. We learned that Steve was President of the Cleveland Red Cross, which was remarkable. We chatted with him and Doris. They decided they liked us, and we've been friends ever since. I was involved with one of Steve's Red Cross boards because he asked me."

Bob and Leatrice, who died five years ago, became true friends and supporters, and we were honored for them to join us at the Red Cross Ball every year it was held. In fact, the local newspapers published several photographs of us together at the Ball, along with a picture of Doris and me with ball chairwoman Carol Markey in the *Cleveland Plain Dealer*. On November 14, 1985, the *Call and Post* published an extremely flattering feature story about Doris with the headline: *Introducing the Red Cross "First Lady"* with two photographs of her.

"Doris Bullock stands just a little over five feet and, one would guess, tips the scales just a bit over or under 100," said the article written by Madeline L. Cargill. "She's our 'First Lady' at the Greater Cleveland Chapter of the American Red Cross. She is Mrs. Steve Bullock, the lovely and demure wife of our executive director. To talk to Doris Bullock is quite a pleasure… it is completely relaxing to spend a few unhurried minutes reviewing 24 years of a happy marriage and productive life with this diminutive lady of Southern heritage who is the strength behind the local Red Cross throne."

The article went on to provide an overview of our life together, including details about our children's schooling and activities.

"Dear Mrs. Bullock," wrote Rubie J. McCullough, Executive Director of the Harvard Community Services Center in Cleveland, in a letter to Doris. "Congratulations on your well-deserved recognition. Behind every 'Big Man' is a 'Bigger Woman.' Keep up the good work."

When we attended the Balls, Doris and I really enjoyed celebrating together for a great cause.

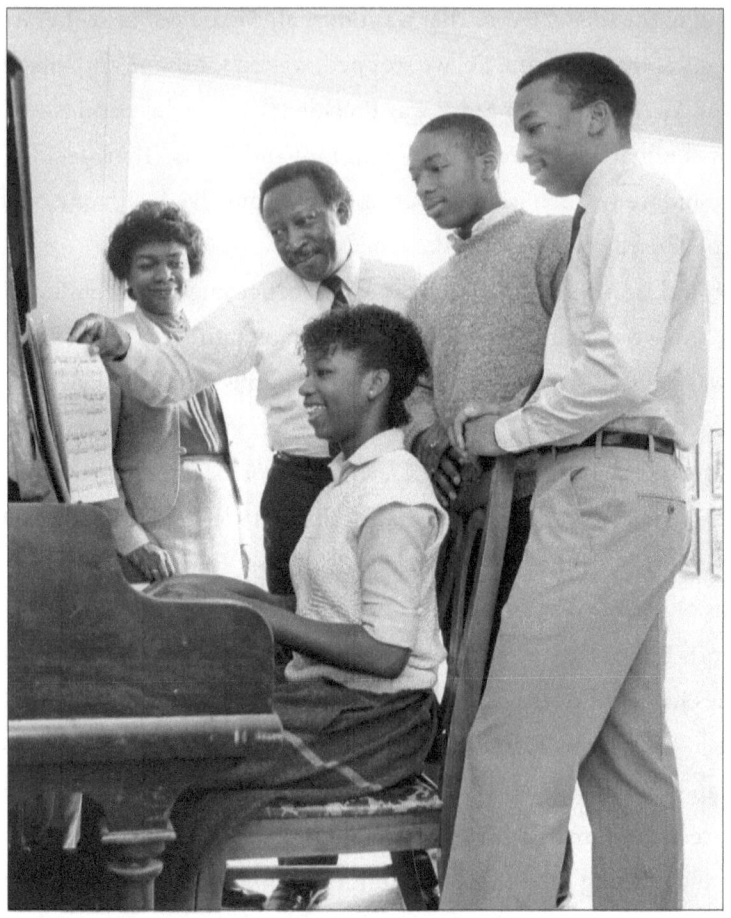

Enjoying time as a family is one of the Four Pillars of my life: God, family, Virginia Union University, and the American Red Cross.

"I loved the people," she recalls. "I always wore a different hairstyle and a different dress. In 1987, for our third ball, I had a lady help me find a dress. The color scheme that year was royal blue. I came down the steps into the ballroom, and when I got about halfway there, I looked around. Every other dress was just like mine. The fashion writer at the *Cleveland Plain Dealer* didn't have to write about it; she was wearing the same dress, too. She walked up to me and said, 'I love your taste in clothes.' I was not amused. I made it through the night, but I was just mortified that so many of us had on the same dress. After that, I gave the dress to someone and said this will never happen again. The first lady will never be copied. Then I got a dresser and she found my gown every year, and that didn't happen again."

Kelly, like many children of administrators, served as a hostess at the Red Cross Ball during high school. That year, among 750 guests, she wore a royal blue satin gown, as she and her friend Leslie Cole handed out programs. They were photographed in the *Call and Post* newspaper with Doris' brother, Colonel Needham Kelly of Washington, D.C. Her brother Mark also came to town to attend the Ball.

"I was impressed when I saw my father speaking to hundreds of people in the ballroom at the Red Cross Ball," Kelly recalls. "I saw him on TV, and in a magazine, and when he won the Black Professional of the Year, and the mayor was there. I thought, 'Wow, he knows everyone.' People would ask me, 'Are you Steve Bullock's daughter? You look just like him.' That's when I knew, 'Okay, everyone knows him.' That made me feel that I had to be on my best behavior during my high school years."

Hosting the National Boulé Conference

In 1983, I joined Sigma Pi Phi fraternity, which is also known as the Boulé and means "a council of noblemen." Its 5,000 members in 126 local member boulés in the United States, the Caribbean, and Europe are educated black men who have achieved significant professional accomplishments.

In 1988, the Cleveland local boulé hosted the Boulé's national conference, with Bob Madison serving as the lead organizer as the Sire. While the Red Cross did not sponsor the event, I did head the finance committee which funded this extremely successful gathering of 1,300 men committed to leadership and service.

"Steve was tremendous in getting organizations to join, securing venues, and setting up programs, particularly with respect to young people," Bob recalls. "He was critically involved in trying to realize what we need to do to help these young African American boys and girls become better citizens. Steve spearheaded that effort."

The event included opening ceremonies, businesses sessions from Monday through Wednesday, and many discussions about how Boulé members could make a positive impact on society.

"The Boulé is the Talented Tenth among black folks, as W.E.B. DuBois said," Bob recalls. "It's our responsibility to use our education and professional skills to uplift everyone, and Steve definitely does his part to do that."

"Steve Put Me on a Trajectory to Where I Am Now"

A few years ago, I was sitting on the dais at the UNCF dinner in Cleveland, when a man named Timothy D. Goler approached me.

"I just wanted to say thank you," he said. "I want to share with you on how you have impacted my life. You put me on a trajectory to where I am today. I appreciate that, and feel extremely blessed that you helped me."

Timothy is a member of my fraternity, and he is Founder and CEO of HBCU Preparatory Schools Network, a $2.5 million company with 40 employees that is preparing more than 300 black students to attend HBCUs. He proceeded to tell me his story, italicized here, in his own words:

> *I grew up in a rough section of Cleveland during the early eighties. I had to leave town or I was going to kill somebody. Although I had track and football scholarships, I wasn't prepared for school, and no one was encouraging me to attend college. So, I joined the Marine Corps for eight years, then went to Norfolk State University in Virginia.*
>
> *I returned to Cleveland, working toward a master's degree. I was in my early 30s, and I wanted to embark on a career that would help black people, and I earned an internship at The George Gund Foundation, a nonprofit institution founded*

with a mission of "contributing to human well-being and the progress of society."

They sent letters of introduction on my behalf to top companies in the city. I met with leaders in our community – head of the Urban League, the NAACP, and the Transit Authority.

But none of the black business leaders would meet with me. I would arrive for my meeting, only to be greeted with, "Unfortunately, I can't meet with you. I'm going to have my assistant meet with you."

This pattern of putting me off on somebody else raised questions: You don't have enough time to spend 15-30 minutes with me? Am I not worthy of you, of your time? The purpose of the meeting was for me to meet YOU, not your assistant or second-in-charge.

I was so put off by that. It left a mark. No matter where you are in your life, everybody has worth!

When I met Steve, he affirmed that self-worth in me. He proved that everybody was not like those who had passed me off to someone else in their office. As busy as he was as head of the Red Cross in Cleveland, he took the time in his plush office to talk with me. I didn't want anything from him: not a job, not money. I just wanted advice, mentorship. I wanted somebody to give me some direction as a grown man.

He took the time. It was really a big deal to me. I didn't know who he was. It was the fact that he was a black man in a leadership position running this organization. He embodied this wisdom with the way he spoke and how he allowed me to sit there and talk to him about my life and my future. I said, "Here's my dream," and he never busted my bubble. He was encouraging and made me feel like I could do it.

All these years later, I still remember how we sat in his office:

he was distinguished. He was a strong man, but he also had a strong humility about him. He engaged with me and I was very appreciative for that. I said, "I will never ever treat anybody like these other people treated me; instead, I will always treat people the way Steve treated me."

I carried his encouragement with me as I established two schools modeled after HBCUs, with 300 students, and have since earned my PhD from Case Western Reserve University.

And like Steve, I always take the time to talk with young men and young ladies just to hear them. I never got a chance to tell him what a powerful impact his time and attention had on me and the future I have created for myself and hundreds of young people.

He taught me the profound lesson that you never know what you say to somebody or how you say it will affect their life – not just the day – but their LIFE!

Receiving the Black Professional of the Year Award

One of the most tremendous honors of my career occurred on Saturday, February 15, 1997, when I received the Black Professional of the Year Award.

The Cleveland Black Professionals Association provided this honor before 1,100 people at the formal 17th Annual Scholarship and Awards Gala in the Renaissance Cleveland Hotel. The event included showing the audience a videotape of my life and an interview with local TV news anchor Romona Robinson.

Doris, Eric, Brian, and Kelly were with us. Making the evening even more special was that my older brother, Reverend Floyd Bullock, who was then pastor of Living Word Baptist Church in Riverside, California, introduced me. In doing so, he recounted our upbringing in North Carolina.

"Think of it," he said. "It is by the grace of God that my brother is here tonight."

A previous award winner, Carole Hoover, CEO and president of the Greater Cleveland Growth Association, handed me the inscribed vase that was the award. She is also a friend.

"This award," she said, "is an earned honor, not a given honor. He has high standards of excellence."

Eric, Brian, and Kelly all said that witnessing this event was one of the proudest moments of their lives.

"That was when I really realized how much of an impact our father was having on our community," Kelly says. "And that he was doing such important work to help people. That made me want to emulate him in my future career."

It was an absolute honor to receive the Black Professional of the Year Award from the Cleveland Black Professionals Association at a black-tie gala attended by 1,100 people. The celebration was extra special because I was surrounded by my family, including my brother, Reverend Floyd Bullock, who introduced me. Pictured above are, from left to right: Eric and his wife, Cathy; Kelly; me; Doris; Patricia, holding four-month-old Marcus; Brian; and Brandon.

Encouraging Achievement and Work Ethic in Our Children

When we moved to Cleveland, Eric was a freshman at St. Cloud State University in Minnesota. Brian was in tenth grade, and Kelly was in fifth grade. I decided that I was not going to work seven days a week, and that I would stay home with my children as often as possible on weekends rather than taking them to the office with me. They presented many opportunities for Doris and me to teach them about character, values, and work ethic. My success thus far was rooted in the lessons my mother had taught me, so it was my mission to instill that wisdom in our children. For example, my mother urged us to move quickly and, "Act like you have someplace to go."

Sometimes Brian failed to heed that advice, and paid the consequences.

"My brother and I shared a room in Minnesota," he recalls, "but we all had our own rooms when we moved to Cleveland. I had the smallest bedroom in the house, but the trade-off was that I got a phone in my room. That was a mistake; being a teenager, I'd be up until one or two in the morning on the phone talking to girls. I was tired in the morning! Days when Dad gave me a ride to school, if I wasn't ready to go when he was ready – this is one of those lessons – he would leave me. He'd say, 'I told you to get up; now I'm leaving.' And he would leave, so I'd be late! I remember asking him, 'Dad, are you tired in the morning? Don't you get tired?' And he said, 'No. I sleep, and when I get up, I'm ready to go. I'm refreshed. I'm ready to work.' I learned that getting enough rest gave him the stamina to succeed."

Brian finally paid attention and understood the importance of getting enough sleep to prepare to work hard the next day.

"Dad loved his job and his career," he says. "Work ethic is the biggest lesson he's taught me. Like him, I love my work right now as a producer on a Discovery Channel show called *Copycat Killers*. I'm up ready to go with the same stamina he had. I delivered 13 episodes in one month. I didn't want to sit down as I put in those long days. I do that now because of what I learned from Dad."

Brian sums it up: "He has leadership skills, work ethic, compassion, and humility all rolled into one person. Both our parents encouraged passion for our careers. I liked a few different things and changed along the way to my present career, and my parents absolutely encouraged and were fully supportive of us. They told us, 'If you pursue what you love, you'll make the money. You have to be happy.'"

Meanwhile, Kelly was learning about the importance of reputation and proper behavior.

"I understood that people knew Dad wherever we went," she recalls. "I also understood the importance of his reputation, how he carried himself, and how people viewed him. I knew the way we carried ourselves was important. He also talked to us about our choice in friends and what we did with them."

We had many discussions about my pet peeve: kids hanging out on the front porch and in the front yard. We had a spacious back yard, which I thought was the better place for Kelly to socialize with her friends because it was private and safer. She argued that because we lacked a back patio, it was more fun for her and her friends to sit on the front stoop when the weather was nice.

When I got home from work, I asked, "Why are you sitting on the front porch?"

"Everything is happening here," Kelly said. "There's nothing in the back."

Kelly now understands the feelings behind my pet peeve. "Sometimes we got loud and rowdy with our friends, and this affected the way people viewed us and that represented who he was," she says. "Sometimes what we talked about with our friends wasn't for other people to hear. Dad enjoys having fun in a confined space. He instilled high expectations, and always offered words of wisdom."

Eric remembers that I was strict, but so was Doris.

"Mom has been the rock of the family," he says. "She has kept me on the straight and narrow whenever I needed to be! When I was a 17-year-old, she told me which of my friends she didn't approve of. She tells it like it is. I learned to pay more attention to who I talk to."

Kelly learned the same lesson. "When I was focused on boys, playing sports, and being popular," she says, "Dad was always concerned about the way I dressed because I'm a girl. Back then, in the eighties in the time of *Flashdance* and off-the-shoulder shirts, wearing a miniskirt without stockings was in. Stockings were big for Dad! He would get on my case and tell me, 'Get some stockings on! Cover your legs!' He couldn't understand this new style, and I couldn't understand why he hated it. He believed that by being conservative in your dress, you are sending a positive message to people. Everything you do communicates something to other people, down to my red nail polish! Mom allowed us to come into who we were as individuals."

In fact, Doris says, "I let them pick their own personalities."

Of miniskirts, Kelly adds, "Mom had an opinion, but she let me wear them. She made certain that I looked my part and that I was not sending a derogatory message. When I appeared in my prom dress – a fitted white dress with spaghetti straps and a high slit up the leg, my dad about had a heart attack. He said, 'Where is she going dressed like that?'"

"Steve, stop it!" Doris exclaimed. "She's a senior in high school."

Kelly's high school sweetheart, when she was a senior and he was a junior, became her husband. She dated Leroy Daugherty III for a decade, and they've been married for 18 years. After studying animal science at Virginia State University, he has become an elephant trainer at the Cleveland Metroparks Zoo. Kelly recently earned her PhD and is an educator in the Cleveland area. Their children are: Blair Ali Daugherty, 16; Steven Kyle Daugherty, 14; and Kylee Alicia Daugherty, 10.

When Eric, Brian, and Kelly were small and through their teen years, Doris and I were always teaching them the importance of honesty and proper behavior. In turn, they provided many "teachable moments." For example, when Kelly was a teenager, she wanted to hang out at the shopping centers on Saturdays with a group of boys and girls.

"Are you going shopping?" I asked. "Do you have money?"

"No, we're going to have fun," she said.

"You can't do that," I said. "You could go to a museum together."

I knew of other kids getting into trouble, storming through the mall with no money and no intention of shopping. The merchants didn't like it, nor did the customers. Now as an adult and as a parent, Kelly tells us she's glad we did not allow her, Brian, or Eric to spend their time that way.

Another situation occurred when Kelly graduated from high school. It was Seniors Night, and the kids convened downtown to go to teenaged dance clubs. She was with her boyfriend, Leroy, and two other couples. All were college-bound, and one boy had a football scholarship to a small school in Pennsylvania.

"You cannot go to The Flats," I said. That was an area downtown along the river with nightclubs and restaurants. It was notorious for problems caused by teenagers who were hanging out, getting in fights, even carrying guns.

"Dad," Kelly said, "we're going to behave."

"I'm not concerned about how you'll behave," I said. "I'm concerned about others. I don't want you in an environment where you'll get in trouble."

She finally convinced me to allow her to go there for a while. At 2:00 a.m., Kelly called to say, "We're going to breakfast, then I will come home."

At 4:30 a.m., Doris and I woke up. Kelly was not home.

"Are they still at breakfast?" we wondered. At that point, Kelly came into the house, walked in our room, and got in bed between the two of us.

"What's wrong, Kelly?" we asked.

"Dad, when I called you, I lied. We weren't going to breakfast. We were going to the hospital. We went to The Flats, and when we were leaving, we were walking past a group of other kids. A fight started. Somebody fired a gun and a bullet ricocheted and hit the boy with the scholarship in the leg. We weren't at breakfast. We were at the hospital."

"I'm glad nobody got killed," I said, "and that you survived what happened and will not go down there again."

Kelly was scared and wanted to confess. She had lied to us because she didn't want us to be worried. This was a very good learning experience for her to always be honest and to heed warnings about dangerous situations. Meanwhile, the boy lost his scholarship and did not attend the college in Pennsylvania.

"This Is Elizabeth Dole"

On occasion, Eric visited from college, and though he had witnessed my steady career ascension, one phone call had a big impact on him.

"It wasn't until we got to Cleveland that I understood how important my dad was, as the first African American leader of a Red Cross chapter," Eric recalls. "I realized this when I was house-sitting my parents' house while they were on a trip. The phone rang and I answered; a woman with a Southern accent was on the line and said: 'This is Elizabeth Dole.' I knew she was the President of the American Red Cross, and it was really impressive that she was calling for my father. I took a message, wrote her name down, and called my dad and said, 'Elizabeth Dole just called.' I was awestruck!"

The Four Pillars: Church

Doris and I joined Antioch Baptist Church, which was established in 1893 and became Cleveland's second African American Baptist church. Today, we are among 1,500 members, and I sing in the gospel choir and serve as a member of the board of deacons. When we first joined, I greatly respected the spiritual leadership of Reverend Dr. Marvin A. McMickle; we bonded over the fact that former VUU President Samuel Proctor was one of his mentors.

"Often Steve was out of town," recalls Reverend McMickle, who remains a good friend today. "Because he wasn't sending a team to a disaster. He was taking a team to a disaster. He had the same hands-on approach to helping people in Cleveland, by taking the tenets of our religious foundation out of the church and applying them to the people who needed help most."

Reverend McMickle remembers watching the local news media showing live video of an aerial view of the accident scene. "Suddenly," he says, "there's Steve Bullock on TV, pulling over on the opposite side of the highway, parking his car, running in the middle of traffic, across the median, getting to the scene of this accident to see what he could do to be helpful. I saw this on television! Steve was in Red Cross mode, coming to the aid of those in distress. I can't think of a story that's any better to tell about his character. He was always on duty."

Reverend McMickle, who is now President of Colgate Rochester Divinity School in Rochester, New York, also remembers when I joined him on several occasions for a two-hour bus ride to a prison in Ohio, where we provided a worship service and gospel singing for inmates and guards.

"When we arrived, we had to remove our coats to go through the metal detectors before entering the prison," Reverend McMickle recalls. "I noticed Steve was wearing a custom-made suit with STEVE BULLOCK stitched inside the jacket lapel. Here's a guy who can afford to wear a custom-made suit with his name stitched on the inside, and he's taking it off to go sing to prisoners and inmates in a state prison. It speaks to his capacity as a person and his humility to go participate with his church in a worship service behind bars. Not all deacons would take that trip to a prison. He had a very deep commitment not just to going to church, but doing the work of the church, even if it meant going to the prison."

My involvement with the church facilitated frequent blood drives there, with the Red Cross truck setting up in the church parking lot so that the church members and others could donate blood.

Another spiritual leader who became a true friend and trusted counselor is Reverend Dr. Otis Moss Jr. Doris and I befriend him and his wife, Edwina, during our early years in Cleveland, after I participated in a conference on the black family that was sponsored by Olivet Institutional Baptist Church.

"Steve became one of the key participants," recalls Dr. Moss, now Pastor Emeritus of Olivet Institutional Baptist Church. "The event was exceptionally successful. We had people from across the country, including scholars and writers. Steve shared himself and encouraged the support of the staff of the Red Cross. He was a tremendous resource in both church and community."

During the 10 years that he and his wife worked with Dr. King during the Civil Rights Movement, Dr. Moss was jailed as an activist, and learned first-hand the power of change that one person can make.

"I have to salute a person like Steve Bullock," Dr. Moss says. "He is part of that tradition that created a Dr. Martin Luther King Jr., a Muhammad Ali, a Mary McCloud Bethune, a Dorothy Height, and a Barack Obama. Steve is an individual of great integrity, great commitment and esteem. I cannot think of anyone over my six decades of public service for whom I have greater respect and admiration than Steve Bullock."

Over the years, Dr. Moss has followed my career with the Red Cross.

"Steve has been able to move courageously against racial barriers to effect change within the Red Cross. Through his long and fruitful career to fight with courage, ability and preparation, he built a staff within the organization by implementing the concepts of diversity and inclusion. Most of the time, he did it without announcement or fanfare. Some people don't even realize that he did it. Change came about as he moved with a steady hand and he opened doors in a quiet way."

Doris and I remain good friends with Dr. Moss and Mrs. Edwina Moss, who became a member of the board of the Greater Cleveland Red Cross.

"Steve had a stellar reputation in Cleveland," she recalls, "and he communicated extremely well with all of the board members, who represented major corporations in the area. Many of the people on the board were CEOs of major corporations, and they had great respect for him. Steve was forceful but gentle. He communicated with a sense of firmness and was always very fair with the staff, as well as with the board. All the staff liked him a lot. Steve was an excellent leader."

Serving on the Board of Education

Doris and I established rules for our children to speak proper English, use good manners, and excel in school to the best of their ability. We set high expectations for them, and we insisted that they follow suit by doing the same for themselves. We also expected their teachers to hold them to high standards in the classroom.

Unfortunately, when we first moved to Cleveland, a black teacher looked at Brian and said he would be a good candidate for the lower-achieving education track that led to vocational and technical school rather than college.

I was furious! How could she look at a child and make that assumption? Why couldn't she have just as easily designated him for the honors program? I was extremely disturbed that a culture of low expectations was handicapping the educational environment of the Cleveland Heights-University Heights school district. It was unacceptable that teachers, parents, and students failed to aim high and instead settled for mediocrity. Nothing of the sort was tolerated in the Bullock home, and Doris and I would not allow for it in the classrooms where our children were supposed to be educated and prepared for college and life. I was not shy about expressing this, and in fact, I got in trouble by voicing my opinions at meetings.

"I don't know why you think everybody has to be an Einstein," the black teacher countered.

"I accept your criticism of me," I said, "but there ought to be some real credible criteria for determining who does, or doesn't, get steered into these programs."

Another experience with Kelly's teacher underscored the desperate need for change in the district. She and Brian attended a high school that was so huge, it was like a college campus. It began with grades 10 through 12, then ninth grade was added when Kelly began high school.

"Why do you have a C in English?" Doris and I asked Kelly when she brought home her report card.

"I did my best," she said.

"Average is not your best," I told her. "Why would you think you're average? If you think of yourself as average, you'll perform average."

"At the time," Kelly says now, "I'm like, 'Oh, man, you're so hard on me! I don't understand; I'm doing the best I can!' It didn't start to click until I was a freshman in college. I had graduated high school with less than a 3.0, and went to Virginia State University (down the street from VUU), still thinking I was average, that this was the best I could do."

Kelly earned straight A's during her first semester of college.

"I thought I was average because that's how I performed, that was my effort level," she adds. "Later, while getting my master's degree, if I brought an A home, they'd say, 'Why isn't it an A plus?' That's heavy pressure to put on a young person. Now at age 44, I absolutely understand it's a mindset that my parents tried to instill in us at a very early age, and I'm instilling in my own children. I say to them when they bring home C's, that 'a C is not acceptable because you are not average.' It took me a long time to believe that I'm not average and perform above average. That's what I mean by Dad's belief in high expectations: if you think it, it will be. That is what he instilled in us."

Kelly sums it up by saying, "Watching him in Minnesota as an executive director, then coming to Cleveland as a CEO then going to DC as the national president – all those moves were showing me what it looked like to get to the next level. The next level is not given to you. You had to work hard for it."

While Kelly ultimately learned that, Doris and I talked with her teacher to find solutions. He invited me to sit in the classroom. I did, and talked with him afterward.

"What's going on with Kelly," I asked, "that she can't get better grades?"

"Not everybody is an A student," the teacher responded. "I don't know why you're worried about it."

"Okay," I said, you answered my question. "I think part of the problem is you." From there I went to the superintendent's office and told him.

"Well, you know we have some problems with some of our teachers," he said. "I need people like you to come in here and help me fix it."

I agreed. And that's how I ended up on the Cleveland Heights-University Heights school board. I was elected in 1989, after running as a group of three men; two of us were elected. I called VUU alumnus and former Virginia Governor Douglas Wilder for guidance.

"We talked about how he offered to run for political office and was successful," Governor Wilder says. "He told me why he was inspired to do that. We exchanged pointers. Steve is involved in trying to educate people to effective government and how they should and could be. I discussed with him that you never get too old to make a difference."

On the board, we immediately began pushing for having high expectations for our teachers and the students. The school board had never done a strategic plan, so we walked the board and administration through creation of a strategic plan which focused on what everybody was concerned about but was failing to take action to correct. I served for two years as president of the school board, juggling this huge responsibility while also running our Red Cross chapter.

On the school board, we enjoyed some success and definitely made a difference. For example, after three failed attempts, we convinced voters to approve an 8.9 mill operational levy as well as a $15 million plan to upgrade and renovate 13 buildings in the district, thanks to another millage increase. In addition, we saved the district $150,000 in annual maintenance costs by selling the Northwood School to a Jewish day school called Bet Sefer Mizrachi. Very importantly, we ended years of contentious relationships between the teacher's union and the district; we abolished threats of walkouts by fostering harmony in negotiations and overall relationships. We also established organizations for parents and alumni, to get people involved and enthusiastic about raising expectations for the students' performance and the quality of education that teachers would provide. One way I measured our progress was that I never had another experience like the one with Kelly's ninth grade English teacher. We felt good that our work had elevated everyone's expectations.

"Dad set a great example for us," Eric says, "that when you see something you don't like, do something about it. At the same time, he always said, 'Say what you mean and mean what you say.' He put his money where his mouth is, and he told us to do the same."

The highlight of my service as President of the Board of Education was that I had the pleasure of presenting Kelly with her high school diploma.

As President of the Board of Education in Cleveland Heights, I had the unique honor of presenting our daughter Kelly with her high school diploma.

Brian Goes to College

In 1985, Brian attended Syracuse University on a football scholarship. But when his coach asked him to change his major so he would not have to take a biology lab on Sunday so he could attend practice instead, Brian realized that his education was not the school's priority; his athletic prowess was.

So, he transferred to Virginia Union University. He was very much aware of my experience there, and had heard me tell stories about the racism I had experienced during the Summer from Hell while working in Virginia Beach.

"Dad," Brian said, calling home shortly after he arrived on campus. "I want to go with my friends to Virginia Beach for HBCU weekend. Can you please put some money in my account?"

"You know what?" I responded. "I'm going to put some money in that account because when I was at VUU, I wasn't allowed on that beach."

Brian attended and "had a blast" with his friends. That inspired me to reflect on just how much times had changed for black people in Virginia. I was grateful that my son was free to enjoy himself in an environment that was void of the racial oppression that I had experienced.

On campus, Brian enjoyed some fun moments, like learning that his Spanish teacher had taught me and Doris back when we were students. He also met some of my other professors.

"Dad's experience there shaped my drive and stamina to do things," Brian says. So much so, that years later in a questionnaire for alumni, he said VUU saved his life, because it enabled him to become an independent, free thinker in a nurturing environment.

"I got one F," Brian says, "and it stopped me from graduating on time. I had to call and tell my dad. It was two weeks before graduation when the professor, Dr. Watson, said, 'Your father is not going to be so happy about this. I'm not happy.'"

Brian then earned a master's degree in film at American University, specializing in historical and social issue documentaries.

Exposing Our Children to Diverse People

When we moved to Cleveland, we got involved with Youth for Understanding, an organization that enabled us to host an exchange student for nine months. He was from Mexico. The goal was for our family to enjoy an intercultural experience while exposing the student to life in America.

This experience was not a positive one for Doris because, unfortunately, the only black people this young man had ever seen were those who worked for his family. He and Doris did not get along.

Our children remember our many guests from distant places who enhanced their understanding of people and the world.

"Dad traveled a lot but always came home with stuff," Eric recalls. "He had interesting stories. He met these people who came to the house; they were from Germany, Africa, and different places. He opened our world to different people and things that he would bring home."

During the 1980s, Doris and I worked with two graduate students from Malawi. They were in the United States working on degrees and special training in education for the deaf. They lived with us and we provided them with housing and other logistics in support of their education and training in Cleveland, Washington, D.C., and Rochester, New York.

During the late 1990s, both Eric and Brian got married. Kelly was 17, and we wanted her to focus on school rather than marriage.

"I told Kelly, 'Cool your heels and go to college,'" Doris recalls.

CHAPTER 7

Interim President of the American Red Cross Taking the Helm in Washington, D.C.

ON JANUARY 4, 1999, I was named Interim President of the American Red Cross at the recommendation of the departing President Elizabeth Dole and Chairman Norman Augustine.

This occurred after Mrs. Dole announced her run for the U.S. Presidency. Mrs. Dole, who would ultimately leave the race and become a U.S. Senator, told me that my unprecedented record of service and contribution to the organization had inspired her and Board Chairman Norman Augustine to personally select me to serve in this position.

The announcement was made at a press conference that was covered by the national media. I was overwhelmed with gratitude and excitement that my service in this capacity would enable me to execute my life's Purpose across America and around the world.

I did not know whether I would hold the position of Interim President for a month, a year, or longer, while the Red Cross determined who would become president on a permanent basis. What I did know was that I would give this my absolute best effort, using all my experience, expertise, and energy to lead the American Red Cross to realize its greatest potential. I also took comfort in the fact that I had left the Cleveland chapter in the able hands of Mary Alice Frank, Chief Operating Officer.

I sat with Elizabeth Dole, the departing President of the American Red Cross, during an event during which I was named Interim President of the American Red Cross. Mrs. Dole had announced her candidacy for President of the United States, and ultimately became the first female U.S. Senator in North Carolina. *Photo Credit: American Red Cross*

As I moved to an apartment in Washington during the week, with the goal of making frequent trips to Cleveland with Doris, I relished the idea of applying the leadership skills that I had learned during my 37 years thus far with the organization, as well as the insights that I had gained about how the Red Cross operated and how it might be improved. I often chuckled about the number of times over the years I would jokingly say, "Those people at national headquarters need to move over and let me run this organization."

When I took the helm of the world's greatest humanitarian organization, we had 1,302 chapters. We provided more than half of America's blood supply, and every year, we taught lifesaving skills to 8.5 million people. We helped victims of more than 68,000 disasters across the nation. We aided international disaster and conflict victims in more than 40 countries, and we transmitted more than 14 million emergency messages to members of the Armed Forces and their families. We provided direct health services to 2.8 million people.

It was a weighty and exhilarating moment as I assumed leadership for 31,000 employees, 1.3 million volunteers, and a $2.1 billion budget.

In this position, I was challenged to maintain organizational stability, provide strong leadership, and initiate several innovative grassroots and community outreach programs. It was also my intention to maintain the strong forward momentum as the ARC had reinvented and revitalized itself under Mrs. Dole's leadership. I did this by designing and launching a 100-day plan with five key initiatives to further strengthen organizational performance:

- Enhancing programs for America's youth, diversity, and partnerships;

- Boosting chapter development & support;

- Expanding the organization's use of information technology to enhance its internal efficiency and outreach;

- Strengthening and applying organizational values; and

- Pioneering efforts to define core values and their worth to the organization.

My duties also included responding to emergencies and natural disasters across America and around the world. On Thursday, February 25, 1999, I sent a memo to our field colleagues. It follows here in its entirety:

I am announcing a major service and visibility agenda to benefit the entire Red Cross family called the 100-Day Plan. During this period, select internal and external events have been scheduled to raise public awareness, educate and inspire Red Cross paid and volunteer staff, and, most importantly, support the critical work of Red Crossers in communities everywhere. The 100-Day Plan will maintain the momentum of recent months by keeping Red Cross in the public eye, continue our pace-setting path and reinforce the vital services, programs and fund-raising activities taking place in chapters, stations and Biomedical Services units.

As your Acting President, my time with you will be defined by action and tangible results. We have not put the organization on hold as we search for a permanent leader. Through this 100-Day Plan, we will showcase progress toward corporate goals and strengthen our promise of, "We'll be there."

In the context of our breakthrough performance gains, I have chosen, in concert with field and national sector leadership, four priorities where I feel I can have the greatest impact. They are technology, chapter development, cultural diversity and youth involvement. To highlight these priorities, we have planned promotional campaigns and events. All will include internal elements and the advance distribution of communication and marketing materials that include our key message and support similar activities locally.

The Many Faces of the Red Cross

Using Black History Month as a springboard, activities celebrating The Many Faces of the Red Cross will highlight our continued commitment to diversity through the year. We will be focusing on our past, highlighting our present and issuing a call to action for the future – that we want African Americans, women, Asian Americans, Hispanics, and Native Americans to be part of our organization.

Our strategy includes expanding our partnerships with the NAACP, the National Association for Equal Opportunity for Historically Black Colleges and Universities, the Hispanic Association of Colleges and Universities and the United States Pan Asian American Chamber of Commerce. Media interviews will also be conducted to reinforce the message of the Red Cross' continued commitment to fully reflecting and serving diverse communities everywhere. I will help focus media attention on the best practices of our service delivery units.

In Communities Nationwide

In Communities Nationwide is a March effort that combines Community Campaign activities and the launch of a new and exciting lifesaving innovation in our Health and Safety Services workplace program: the Automatic External Defibrillator (AED). In addition to the many chapter Community Campaign activities taking place around the country, we will stimulate additional interest in Red Cross with media events in cooperation with chapters involved with the AED pilot program. These chapters are among the 17 units participating in the testing and refining of the program for organization-wide release. I will be speaking at several of these media events where the Red Cross will be staking our claim as the industry leader in workplace AED training.

Simultaneously, NHQ has created a number of March visibility efforts nationwide including sponsored advertising on major television networks, donated ad space and partnership activities with major companies. National visibility efforts are strong with hundreds of chapters planning concurrent public relations activities.

Saving Lives in New Ways into the 21st Century

To highlight technology, we have targeted the advances of our Biomedical Services as a way of demonstrating how the Red Cross never stops inventing new ways to care. Entitled Saving Lives in New Ways into the 21st Century, our event will feature an open-house day in early April at the Jerome H. Holland Laboratory for the Biomedical Sciences, the world's premier blood research facility where lab and other innovations will be showcased.

According to extensive internal research, many Red Cross paid and volunteer staff are not aware of the mission-related biomedical research being done at the Lab and throughout the organization. Our celebration open house at the Holland Lab will feature demonstrations and tours for Red Cross staff and the BoG, as well as media, government and community officials.

Similar events can be planned locally. A field unit communication packet featuring a 12-minute video on the Holland Lab and biomedical research, ideas for local activities, information materials, pins, and other promotional elements will be sent to each of you in March. We also plan to air the event on ARC-TV the day of the open house.

The Promise of Humanity

Our final initiative elevates attention to Red Cross humanitarian principles and our commitment as part of the International Red Cross movement, showcasing the work of International Services, a MUST service for chapters. Through a Capitol Hill event early in May, entitled The Promise of Humanity, we will be drawing attention to the 50th Anniversary of the Geneva Conventions and the work of chapters. At this presentation, we will initiate a joint resolution, in concert with key congressional leaders, to highlight the importance of these Conventions, the role of the Red Cross and the need for greater compliance in conflict areas.

This is an outstanding opportunity not only to educate field unit staff on our work in the Red Cross movement but also to build public awareness. We are encouraging local events that piggyback on this national exposure and will be distributing numerous turnkey promotional and communication materials to assist with those efforts.

National Convention

At the National Convention, we will be able to join together and celebrate what we have accomplished in four key priority areas: technology, chapter development, cultural diversity and youth involvement. We will have tangible results of our actions in each area. We will have a better-educated and informed Red Cross family and public. We will have expanded our diversity agenda, increased our visibility, strengthened the position of the Red Cross as an innovator of life-saving research and technology and reinforced our continued progress toward *humanitarian goals. And we will have set the course for our great organization for the 21st century.*

This is an ambitious plan, but one I believe is vital in keeping us on our pace-setting path. It combines not only opportunities for increased awareness and support, but ways to educate staff and build pride in what we do. I will keep you posted on these efforts through special communiqués detailing plan developments and with materials to support your local activities. With your support, this 100-Day Plan will resonate with our promise of being there for people in communities everywhere.

Fast forward eight months. On Wednesday, August 25, 1999, ARC Chief of Staff Jan Cook wrote in an internal communication: "When Steve Bullock became acting president last January, he promised his tenure would be characterized by 'action and results.' During his first 100 days in office, he launched a whirlwind of activity centered around initiatives that promoted automated external defibrillators, youth, diversity, information technology, chapter development, and organizational values. He maintained a demanding travel schedule that took him 37,000 miles – across the United States, and to Honduras and Macedonia."

"It was a Golden Year for the American Red Cross"

Before I showcase the details of this pinnacle of my life and career, please allow me to describe it through the words of one of my most respected peers: Harold Brooks, whom you may recall I met when I was CEO of the St. Paul Chapter, and with whom I had since developed a deep friendship.

"Steve led a rebirth of the Red Cross that was extraordinary," says Harold, who became senior vice president, International Operations. "We have had, unfortunately, many interim presidents at the American Red Cross. Steve served as Interim President like no other. He started by setting goals for his first 100 days, and during that time he visited many chapters around the country.

His tireless effort invigorated the organization at a time when the RC needed it. He understood the organization on every level because he had worked in so many capacities. And his familiarity with national headquarters enabled him to inspire leaders to do their best. As a result, the organization was having one of its best periods with him in that role. It was a golden year for the Red Cross. It convinced me without question that the organization should have removed the title interim and installed him as the president. Truly."

Getting to Work as President

During my first day on the job, an eagle appeared outside my window as I was sitting in my office in the Red Cross headquarters at 17th and E Streets N.W. I didn't know if that was a normal sight for downtown Washington, but I took it as a welcome sign. Inside my office, I hung three huge portraits: Red Cross Founder Clara Barton; Charles Drew, the African American physician who perfected the procedure for blood transfusions; and Dr. Charles Orr.

I was grateful to receive a phone call from former American Red Cross President George Elsey, who wanted to wish me well and encourage me in the new position. My future success as Interim President depended upon building a team of talented individuals, so I brought Dave Therkelsen to national headquarters as my co-chief of staff with Jan Cook.

They made a tremendous partnership. When I was asked to come to Washington and serve as president, the first thing that hit me was, *Okay, I'm going to need my own team. But I don't want to make it look like I'm getting rid of everybody.* I had seen that happen way too often. Instead, I had to figure out how to make it my own team. Jan had worked for Elizabeth Dole, and she wanted to stay and work for me. Knowing who she was inspired me to agree. But I still wanted somebody who knew me, so I hired David Therkelsen.

Jan's experience with former President Dole provided institutional memory for our planning and response. Likewise, Dave knew my workstyle and my history. Together they made an excellent, highly effective team as we embarked on our 100-day plan.

"He was not going to be a lame duck," Dave says. "He was going to push the organization forward with the five initiatives that were important to the president of the organization."

To do so, I gave explicit instructions to my senior staff. First, I wanted our chapters to view a presidential visit as a positive experience that would inspire great conversations to push the organization forward.

"Elizabeth Dole had an imperial presidency," Dave recalls. "When she visited a chapter or blood region – she demanded that briefings be prepared on everybody she met, whether they were contributors, longtime board members, et cetera. As a result, someone on the local staff spent a lot of their time a week or two before her visit just preparing for it. Steve said, 'When I travel to chapters, I don't want that. I just want to go in, meet people, and have good conversations. I don't want a presidential visit to be a burden. I want it to be a plus.' That was one instruction to me and senior members of his own staff, that a president's visit is something to be welcomed, not feared."

Dave was one of two people on my senior staff who controlled my calendar. At the time, I was 63, with great mental energy, and my ideas were flowing. But I realized that my physical energy was limited.

"I'll go anywhere to represent the Red Cross, but please try hard to get me back to Cleveland or Washington every night," I told my staff, which tried hard to accommodate my request. "Every day, I'll have a breakfast meeting and a dinner meeting, but please try not to give me both."

Helping After Hurricane Mitch in Honduras

In November of 1998, Hurricane Mitch tore through Central America, Mexico, Florida, and Jamaica, killing nearly 20,000 people. In March of 1999, I traveled there with an American Red Cross delegation to deliver humanitarian aid for some of the 1.5 million people left homeless. I also toured the damage with local Red Cross leaders; stone buildings had been reduced to piles of rubble, homes were demolished, and the country's infrastructure was nonfunctional.

The American Red Cross published a 12-page booklet called "Hurricane Mitch: Bringing Healing and Hope to Central America." It detailed our efforts for: food and essential relief supplies; agricultural assistance; water and sanitation; transitional support housing; health services; capacity building of the national societies; disaster preparedness; help to remote areas; cooperative efforts; and long-term recovery plans. It also listed the names of people, companies, and organizations that donated $48 million for emergency and long-term community needs in Central America. The booklet, which included many photographs of children eating food provided by the Red Cross, as well as myself and other Red Cross employees distributing goods, quoted me in large text on page three:

"In my 37 years with the American Red Cross, I have witnessed a lot of suffering, from wars abroad to countless natural disasters back home. But, Hurricane Mitch is an event without parallel, a story that must be told and retold. The generosity of countless Americans is today creating a better future for thousands in Honduras, Nicaragua, El Salvador, and Guatemala. Regardless of how far from home it is, when the generosity of some meets the courage and hope of others, the future is ours."

Throughout the hurricane-demolished areas of El Salvador, Guatemala, Honduras, and Nicaragua, the American Red Cross distributed rice, beans, corn, sugar, salt and cooking oil to nearly a half million people. In Honduras, I assisted in the distribution of 110-pound sacks of food while riding in a Red Cross truck. In Tegucigalpa, a group of elderly women came in search of food.

"How are you going to carry these heavy sacks?" I asked.

"Put them on our heads," they answered.

"Do you want me to help?" I asked.

"Yes," they said.

So, I carried four, 110-pound sacks for the women. My muscles ached something terrible after that, and reminded me that I was no longer a teenager. But the experience of doing the work of the Red Cross by helping people in need was immeasurably fulfilling.

"When I saw pictures of Steve in Honduras carrying sacks of food on his shoulder," Jim Krueger says, "I was amazed that he was doing that during the time of his first 100 days of goals. I thought, 'Oh my gosh, he's acting president and doing all these things, and these photos exemplify his work great work ethic. Steve was hands-on and showed that no job is too small, no matter what your level is in the organization."

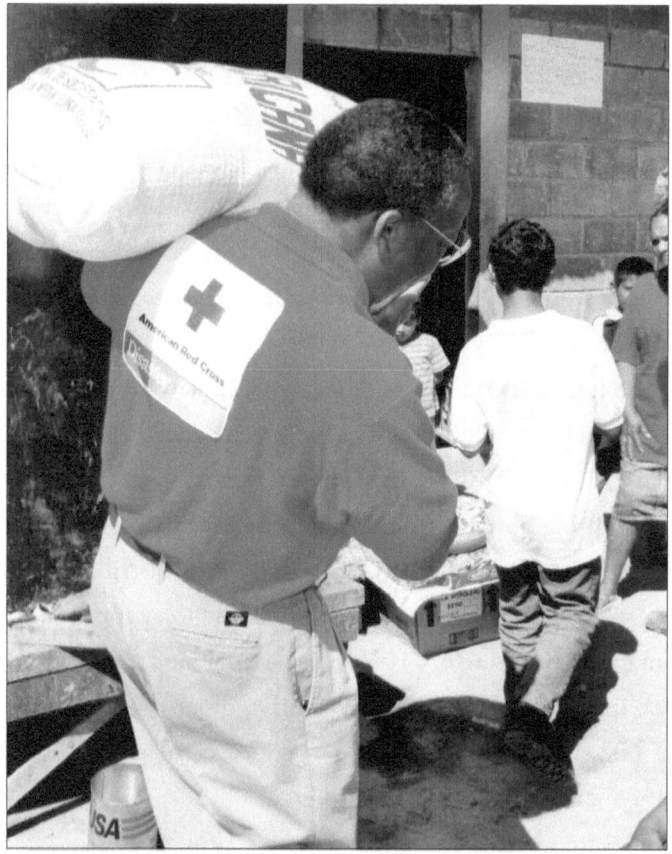

After Hurricane Mitch struck Central America, I traveled with an American Red Cross delegation to Honduras, where we delivered humanitarian aid. We carried 110-pound sacks of food that helped feed many of the 1.5 million people left homeless by the storm that demolished homes and buildings. *Photo by Daniel Cima. ©The American National Red Cross.*

Helping Bosnian Refugees

A visit to refugee camps in the Eastern European country of Macedonia was one of my most memorable and impactful experiences as President of the American Red Cross. My mission was to deliver relief supplies and visit refugee camps on April 29, 1999. At that point, the American Red Cross had raised $9.7 million for relief efforts in that region and was spearheading an intensive effort to assist refugees in locating family members who were separated. Two dozen people traveled with me to Macedonia, where I visited a warehouse facility, inspected the Tetvo Refugee Camp's family tracing center, and distributed supplies in the Brazda Refugee Camp.

I spoke to media from around the world about how the American Red Cross was providing relief supplies and visiting camps in Macedonia, where thousands of people were seeking shelter and safety after fleeing their war-torn homeland of Bosnia. *Photo by Daniel Cima. ©The American National Red Cross.*

I also spoke with community and government leadership to commit our support in the form of both finances and staff who could help the hundreds of thousands of people who had fled war-torn Bosnia. I and my delegation delivered a $750,000 check to provide humanitarian aid to assist the men, women, and children who had been forced from their homes across Bosnia and the surrounding region. What impressed me was that while some of them wanted to get out of this refugee camp and go somewhere else, the greater percentage wanted to return to their homes, which was not going to happen.

"What would be the first thing you want to do if you could?" I asked many of the people who were living in endless rows of white tents.

"I'd like to go home," they responded.

Unfortunately, that was not going to happen. The Red Cross was not allowed in the negotiations about the refugees being able to return home. Instead, as I stated at meetings and at press conferences, we were there to send two messages to the world: "Don't abandon these people," and "The American Red Cross is here to provide help for the long haul."

We took hundreds of photographs, including many of me with children who are holding my hand, as well as shots of me speaking with the elderly and women who had given birth in a hospital tent. The CEO of the Philadelphia chapter, A. Frank Donaghue, described our experience in detail in a letter that was sent to Red Cross colleagues and supporters. Frank had accompanied me on many trips, and I had invited him to participate in this one. Here is the letter, typed and dated April 29, 1999 on American Red Cross letterhead:

> *Dear Friend:*
>
> *I'm writing this letter aboard a chartered cargo flight returning from a long 36 hours in Macedonia – an amazing experience. I'm honored to be among the 24 passengers who are accompanying National Red Cross President, Steve Bullock, on this humanitarian flight.*
>
> *Today, we delivered 60,000 pounds of desperately needed blankets, tents, and comfort kits to Macedonia. We met with the head of the local Macedonian Red Cross, International Committee of the Red Cross (ICRC) and the Federation*

leadership. We then went to a local branch of the Red Cross in Tetovo, where hundreds of refugees lined the narrow stairs waiting to register with the Red Cross in order to get medical and relief supplies. We went to a warehouse where the supplies we brought would be quickly inventoried and distributed to refugees. Finally, we spent a few hours simply roaming around the largest refugee camp, a temporary home to 26,000 people, in Brazda, Macedonia. There were rows upon rows of tents, one after the other, in this beautiful countryside within miles of the Kosovo/Macedonia border. Snow-capped mountains a few miles away marked the path of the exodus followed by these refugees, and about 150,000 others fleeing Kosovo. Having left the area only hours ago, the memory remains vivid and heartbreaking for me. These 26,000 people are locked in a camp of canvas and cyclone fencing, some standing eagerly around a makeshift bulletin board that periodically lists the names of refugees located in other camps. Others circle a huge satellite dish and microphone where, one by one, they read their names to be aired on radio stations in the hope of locating a husband, son, daughter or parent.*

I was moved to tears upon entering one tent. The outside appeared to be just like all the others, but that was in fact a Red Cross hospital. In a sweltering hot room inside this tent, five women had just given birth, not knowing whether their husbands were alive or dead. In the shadow of a drape, another new life was being born. I was alone in my awe and surprised when a young refugee girl, who volunteers in the hospital, said hello (only two weeks earlier, she was a graduate student in Prestina, Kosovo). She spoke great English and offered to introduce me to the new mothers. One young woman, who looked about 28, proudly showed me her newborn son whom she had named Victor. She told me she named him purposely so that he would be victorious over this horrible time. I have enclosed a picture of Victor and his mom. It was so incredible on this day, April 29, 1999, six new lives were beginning in this tragic place. They were the lucky ones and I, like this young mother, can only hope that they will all be victorious over this place and time.

After that, I began to explore and take in the essence of this camp on my own. I came upon two young high school-aged boys. We were able to talk a little. They had just met here three weeks earlier. Both of them were alone in this place – neither knew what had happened to their parents, brothers and sisters – they clung to each other for support and friendship. I noticed there were few boys and young men in the camp – most never made it out of Kosovo. Every once in a while, a new family came by – moving in – carrying all they owned in a bag. Children everywhere seemed to love strangers' visits and were particularly willing to be photographed by us. I asked one of the workers walking by to snap a photo of my new friends and me. (Enclosed is a picture). Everywhere you turned there were tents for refugees: young, old, disabled – alone, or in groups, here for only God knows how long.

The Red Cross workers, some American, others from all over the world, are unsung heroes – each and every one of them.

When we visited the small town of Tetovo to see the local chapter and the refugee registration center, I was overwhelmed by the hundreds of people who came out to welcome us. High school students in Red Cross uniforms lined the streets and sidewalks. The police escorted our bus and closed the streets. I had one of those moments James Joyce describes as an epiphany moment – "a quick and sudden discovery of whatness." The Red

Cross, a symbol of incredible hope, respected, if not honored, everywhere. In this country of 2.1 million people, the impact of 200,000 refugees would be comparable to 21 million refugees arriving in the United States within two weeks. Here and everywhere in this conflict, Red Cross does what it does best by helping people respond to life's emergencies, whatever they might be. No other movement has touched so many areas of this conflict and gained the love and respect of so many people.

We are caring for the refugees in the surrounding countries and the Yugoslav Red Cross is helping their neighbors. We are in every country in the Balkans. With the U.S. military, we are providing emergency communications with their families here at home. The International Committee of the Red Cross (ICRC) is involved in visiting those who have been detained and works to ensure the Geneva Conventions are honored. We helped bring little Victor into the world. We developed websites to help trace refugees, and provided equipment to train the local Red Cross to learn how to use that information.

These 26,000 people I had the honor to see today only make up a small part of the world-wide population of 22 million refugees and displaced people. Red Cross is with all of them in one way or another.

We haven't slept in 40 hours and yet I feel somewhat exhilarated, because, despite all of the suffering, there is only hope. Hope brought to life by a girl, a refugee herself, who volunteered to work in the maternity hospital – just to help; a mother so in love with her son she only wants victory for him; two boys lost, alone, and separated from everyone in their lives who found each other for support. Exhilarated by hundreds of Red Cross workers, and workers from many other organizations, who are truly tireless in giving of themselves to those who have nothing.

Excited in knowing that the goods we have brought, the technology developed and shared, will reunite those separated by war and help them begin again.

This trip, like my previous trip to Bosnia and Armenia, made me aware of a lesson that a Red Cross friend, Ann Stingle, once told me of her trip to Somalia. Telling these stories about Victor and two high school students may never change their suffering, but together Victor, the young men and I can perhaps save others by telling the story of their incredible suffering.

Best Regards, A. Frank Donaghue

P.S. Shortly after arriving home, the devastating tornadoes hit Oklahoma City. As you know, the Red Cross is very active – approximately 400 volunteers and staff are at the scene. Meanwhile, we are also at Ft. Dix, welcoming refugees in America. A busy and very important time for Red Cross. Our promise is more real than ever – We'll be there when help can't wait… thanks to you.

Responding to Disasters

When I was president, I had a team at most of the disasters, including a hurricane that struck Harrisburg, Pennsylvania, and did a lot of flooding and wind damage.

Oklahoma seemed to get frequently hit by tornadoes. When I traveled there with our response teams, I saw that the force of the winds had driven a piece of wheat through a brick. It was amazing, and I wondered what that could do if it struck someone's head.

Responding to these deadly disasters, and seeing the devastation firsthand, made me think extensively about how the Red Cross could educate people on preparation and prevention. What do you do when you know a tornado is coming? You find cover, because it's not something you can survive.

After a tornado destroyed her home and the surrounding houses, this woman led me on a tour of the damage. I'm holding a beanie baby, which she gave me from her collection. *Photo by Daniel Cima.* ©*The American National Red Cross.*

Visiting the White House

My role as Interim President of the American Red Cross provided several opportunities to visit the White House, as well as participate in national ceremonies.

On Memorial Day of 1999, Doris and I attended a morning reception at The White House, where we spoke with President Bill Clinton. Then we joined him and other dignitaries, including Secretary of Defense William Cohen, at a ceremony at Arlington National Cemetery. There I had the honor of making remarks about our fallen service members, before placing a wreath on the Tomb of the Unknown Soldier. President Clinton also spoke and presented a wreath. This extremely poignant experience inspired deep reflection about my own service in the U.S. Army, as well as the important role that our military plays in the world, and the human toll that it takes.

Doris shakes hands with President Bill Clinton during one of our many visits to the White House in 1999 when I was Interim President of the American Red Cross. *Photo Credit: American Red Cross*

It was an extraordinary honor to represent the American Red Cross at White House events. On this occasion on Memorial Day in 1999, Doris and I joined President Bill Clinton at a reception that preceded a ceremony at Arlington National Cemetery where I spoke and laid a wreath on the Tomb of the Unknown Soldier. *Photo Credit: American Red Cross*

Mistaken for the Driver – Again, Years Later

While traveling the world to help people, I had a déjà-vu moment, unfortunately, showing that some perceptions of black men had not changed over three decades. It happened shortly after I returned to Washington, D.C. As president, I had a driver and a car. Well, one particular weekend, I told my driver that I would drive myself over the weekend. Doris was not with me, and I needed to go shopping for towels and other items for our apartment. My car was black, with a light in the back, the kind that are recognized in Washington as chauffeured vehicles for executives who ride in the back seat. In fact, that was what typically happened when my driver was with me. Now alone, I parked the car near the department store where I would shop. It was located next to a big restaurant. The valet attendant came out and asked me, "Who are you here to pick up?"

"I'm not picking anyone up," I said. "I'm driving myself."

That Monday morning, I returned the car to the facilities person at the Red Cross.

"Please get me a regular car," I said. They got me a Buick sedan, and I had the same car in Cleveland. No more was I mistaken as a chauffeur.

The Steve Bullock Humanitarian Award at the Red Cross Ball

When I was in Washington, the staff of the Cleveland chapter presented a proposal to the Board to rename the American Red Cross Humanitarian Award as The Steve D. Bullock Humanitarian Award. The board approved it, and it was first presented at the Red Cross Ball in 2001.

Doris and I attended the Ball that was chaired by the wife of Al Lerner, who owned the Cleveland Browns at the time. He was a billionaire who made his money through credit cards.

The award was usually given to a CEO or private philanthropist who worked to improve the condition of humanity. That year the ball raised $1 million, more money than ever, compared to the usual half million other years.

Over time, the award was given, but they forgot to put Steve D. Bullock on it. In 2017, Mike Parks, the new CEO of the Greater Cleveland Chapter, called me and we met.

"I stand in this position on the shoulders of Steve D. Bullock," he said, "and we need to make sure that you are recognized."

In March of 2017, the chapter awarded The Steve D. Bullock Humanitarian Award to Beth Mooney, CEO of Key Bank, the largest bank in Cleveland, at the Red Cross Ball. Mike invited Doris and me to the event, and he honored me with praiseful words.

"I want you to know how honored I am to see your name on the award I'm going to receive," Mrs. Mooney told me.

The event was wonderful, and drew significant publicity in the local press. As a result, I received an outpouring of phone calls and emails, including from members of the Boulé chapter who were pleased to see that I was being honored and recognized. Doris and I wrote a letter to Mike Parks:

> *Michael,*
>
> *On behalf of my wife Doris and the Bullock family, I want to thank you, the Red Cross Board and your delightful team for a most enjoyable and inspiring evening at The Red Cross Ball last Saturday. We thoroughly enjoyed being with you and wish we could have stayed a little longer after the program, but at this age, we know our limitations. We came home and went to bed and got some rest for the next day.*
>
> *Congratulations to you and the Board for selecting Beth Mooney to receive the Steve D. Bullock Humanitarian Award for 2017. Beth Mooney is a humble giant in this community and beyond and we love her. We also love Key Bank… The most important characteristic about Beth for us, is that she values humanity and shares her blessings with others. Great Choice.*

Finally, Michael, I want to express our most sincere best wishes to you, the Board and your team as you lead your unit of the Red Cross into the future. You are leading a great organization, you are doing good work, you are doing it well and we thank you.

Steve and Doris Bullock

Leading the National Convention in Richmond, Virginia

When I was president, I led the National Red Cross Convention that was hosted by the Richmond, Virginia chapter in May of 1999. The event included meetings, panel discussions, dinners, and a formal gala featuring performances by the Richmond Ballet, the Virginia Symphony, and the Richmond Boys Choir.

"It was one of the best Red Cross conventions ever," Harold Brooks recalls. "The sheer excitement of having thousands of people coming to this mid-sized town was a big deal. The newspapers talked about the pride of having this President of the Red Cross as being one of their own because he attended Virginia Union University. Richmond's hotels, restaurants, and other businesses enjoyed the financial benefits of hosting the convention. When the different groups came to participate, they could not express enough just how proud they were that Steve was one of their own. Steve brought in stellar people to present and be part of the convention."

Bullock 1999 National Red Cross Convention

One of my most memorable experiences as Interim President of the American Red Cross was leading the National Red Cross Convention hosted by the Richmond, Virginia chapter in May of 1999.

As part of an event honoring past American Red Cross leaders, I interviewed George Elsey about his work with the organization as well as his opinion about our organization's impact on the communities we served. *Photo Credit: American Red Cross*

I also coordinated a special event to honor past Presidents George Elsey, Dick Schubert, and Elizabeth Dole. As part of this, I interviewed George Elsey about his experience, vision, and evaluation of the Red Cross, as we sat on a stage before an audience. During a second such interview session, I spoke with Walter Cronkite about his life's work as a legendary broadcast journalist, as well as his assessment of the Red Cross, and his perceptions about how our organization was responding to people.

... Taking the Helm in Washington, D.C.

In a unique role reversal, I interviewed legendary broadcast journalist Walter Cronkite about his accomplishments, as well as his thoughts about how the Red Cross was serving people across America. *Photo Credit: American Red Cross*

The convention provided many opportunities to connect with colleagues from across the country, as well as the organization's leaders. Here I am photographed with American Red Cross Chairman Norman Augustine and esteemed colleague James Thomas. *Photo Credit: American Red Cross*

"It was quite wonderful at the convention when Steve honored our elders," Harold Brooks recalls. "George Elsey was president during the seventies and early eighties. Steve consulted with him and brought a lot of the brainpower and the kind of spiritual connection to the Red Cross mission that George Elsey held. Steve looked to George Elsey for a good amount of mentorship and inspiration."

In closing remarks before the thousands of people attending the convention, I aimed to inspire them with one of my mother's sayings: "We're going to go off from this convention and we're going to make some dust!"

I concluded the convention with a rousing speech that encouraged everyone in attendance to return to their communities across the country and the world to aggressively execute the mission of the American Red Cross. *Photo Credit: American Red Cross*

Harold Brooks appreciated that. "That's a cool way to get us pumped up and go out there. Steve was a wonderful, wonderful leader. He provided excellent inspiration and mentoring to many of us. He'll always have a place in the heart of the Red Cross because the organization is only great because of great people and Steve was definitely one of the greater ones to come and share his talents with the organization."

Celebrating the 50th Anniversary of the Geneva Conventions

On August 12, 1999, I joined the International Red Cross community in Geneva, Switzerland for a moving public ceremony that marked the 50th anniversary of the Geneva Conventions.

In 1999, I developed a relationship with General Colin Powell, as he frequently visited Cleveland to engage young people in motivational events for America's Promise, an organization he founded with his wife, Alma. The American Red Cross was one of 380 organizations that participated in America's Promise, which mentored boys and girls nationwide on the importance of education, healthy lifestyles, goal-setting, and all the tenets of success. General Powell and I shared many impactful discussions about leadership and personal achievement. *Photo Credit: American Red Cross*

I represented the American Red Cross, and sat among 12 world-renowned humanitarian leaders who delivered powerful remarks. They included: U.N. Secretary-General Kofi Annan; Prince El Hassan Bin Talal of Jordan; Ruth Dreifuss, President of Switzerland; Prince Sadruddin Aga Khan of Saudi Arabia; Shabana Azmi, Indian actress and member of Parliament; noted Nazi-hunter Serge Klarsfeld; and Marian Wright Edelman, president of the Children's Defense Fund.

"I am pleased and honored to join you in honor of the commemoration of the 50th anniversary of the Geneva Conventions," Annan said. "However, in this final year of the final decade of a century of war, genocide and immense suffering, we do not meet in celebration of the respect for these conventions. We cannot say that civilian populations have been spared in the conflicts of the last decade. Indeed, the ethnic wars of the 1990s have been characterized by the abominable practice of making civilians the very targets of war."

Edelman spoke about how war crimes cause children to suffer. She said two million children had died due to armed conflict between 1986 and 1996, 4.5 million were disabled, and 12 million became homeless. "Through our individual and collective actions, we can dismantle the arsenals of death and replace them with tools for life for the hungry, homeless, sick and uneducated people around the globe."

Chris Moon of Great Britain, who had lost a leg and arm while working for a charity to clear land mines, gave an impassioned speech asking world leaders to invest resources to clear land mines from areas where people live and work.

As part of the commemoration, world leaders signed a solemn appeal for the international community to respect the rules and limits of warfare.

The Geneva Conventions, signed on August 12, 1949, are the collection of laws that govern the rules and regulations for providing protection and assistance to victims of armed conflict. They represent a milestone achievement for the Red Cross Movement.

The celebration marked a half-century of the Geneva Conventions being used to defend human dignity in war. It also highlighted the Red Cross' historic role in alleviating human suffering. For example, the largest relief effort that the Red Cross has ever led since World War II occurred in the Balkans as a result of a mandate under the Geneva Conventions. The Red Cross has also worked around the world to unite families separated by crisis and war. At the Geneva celebration, a Cambodian family was reunited after 24 years apart, with the help of Boston's Mass Bay Chapter of the American Red Cross.

During the event, I was quoted as saying, "The Geneva Conventions are central to the backbone of our mission to provide neutral, impartial and independent assistance to people in need and serve as a powerful ideal that guides our work every day. Because of our unique role under the Geneva Conventions, the Red Cross makes a simple promise to anyone, anywhere who is touched by war. And that promise is: We'll be there caring for the wounded and sick, providing relief shipments, visiting prisoners and tracing family members. We at the American Red Cross are committed to making our bedrock principle of humanity a living ideal."

During my visit, I met with Federation President Astrid Heiberg and International Red Cross President Cornelio Sommaruga. Earlier that year, on May 6, I spoke at a commemoration of the 50th anniversary of the Geneva Conventions at the American Red Cross' national headquarters in Washington, D.C. Joining me were President Sommaruga, Senator John McCain, Congressman Sam Johnson, Secretary of the Army Louis Caldera, and Under Secretary for Global Affairs Frank E. Loy, along with paid staff and volunteer staff of the Red Cross. It was an honor to participate in a global endeavor to do what I love most: helping people.

Recognition By My Alma Mater and Fraternity

The Virginia Union University's magazine, *Unionite*, featured a two-page article in its Summer 1999 issue about me being named Acting President of the American Red Cross. I'm photographed at my desk at the Red Cross while talking with Jason Johnson, a VUU student and editor of the campus magazine, and a member of the graduating class of 2000. I facilitated Jason's hiring as a summer intern at the American Red Cross headquarters in Washington, D.C.

A second photograph showed me with former Virginia Governor Douglas Wilder, after he interviewed me on the Doug Wilder Talk Show of WRVA Radio. As a graduate of the Virginia Union University and America's first black governor, he and I shared many parallel experiences.

"Steve is a very good man," says former Governor Wilder. "I'm very proud of his accomplishment. We have both embarked on a common mission during our lifetimes. Steve and I have parallel situations in being the first African Americans to serve in high profile, public service positions. We've both aimed to help restore people's confidence in America's leaders."

The Sphinx magazine published by Alpha Phi Alpha Fraternity, Inc. also wrote a one-page story for its Summer 1999 issue. The headline read: "Alpha Phi Alpha Brother at Top of American Red Cross Looks to Diversity Organization and Gets More Youth Involved." The article recounted my international travel and commitment to diversify the ranks of the ARC.

Both articles inspired countless telephone calls, letters and emails from fellow alumni and fraternity brothers across America who congratulated me on the service I was providing to help people.

Staying Humble in the Spotlight

As Interim President of the American Red Cross, I worked in Washington during the week and when possible returned to Cleveland for weekends with my family. I also traveled frequently for the organization. I was treated like a dignitary, often attracting media attention and meeting with high-ranking leaders across the country. I even had the privilege of meeting Queen Raina of Jordan on May 17, 1999.

Likewise, if I arrived in Austin, Texas, or Seattle, Washington, in response to a natural disaster, a small army of reporters would be waiting for me to comment on camera as soon as I stepped off the airplane. For other trips, a sign saying WELCOME STEVE BULLOCK AMERICAN RED CROSS would greet me at the airport, along with a driver who would take me to my hotel. There, I didn't have to check in; I was given a key and went straight to my room.

In Washington, when I had a car and a driver, he took me to the airport on Fridays. After spending the weekend with my family in Cleveland, I flew back to Washington, where my driver picked me up. The Red Cross also provided a car for me in Cleveland; a driver would either pick me up or leave it at the airport for me to drive myself home.

Once, however, when I was flying home, the car was not available. I called Doris, who told me that neither she nor our children were available to pick me up.

"Do you know who I am?" I demanded.

"Yeah," Doris quipped, "you're Steve Bullock, and you can take the train from the airport."

So, I did. I took the train to the Red Cross office, where I retrieved my car.

Similarly, I experienced the phenomenon of people with questionable motivations attempting to get close to me because I was in a leadership position.

Concurrent with this, frequent moves and my own ego sometimes pulled me away from one of my four pillars: church. At times, we did not belong to a church. In Maryland, I occasionally attended services at a big church down the street that was mostly white. But I never joined. Doris and I found ourselves spending more time focusing on my job and social relationships than staying on the church path; that's not good. My heavy workload became an easy excuse, and perhaps I was getting a little too big for my britches, as my mother would say.

"Do I need to go to church?" I once asked myself when we lived in Atlanta. "I know God. I can talk to Him directly."

I arrogantly declared this to myself after a conversation with a colleague who never attended church. It happened one day after work, when we met to enjoy a cocktail and listen to music. Our discussion reminded me how far I'd come from working barefoot on the peanut farm, to a comfortable life in which I could stop for a martini anytime.

Thankfully, I realized that God had carried me up and out of poverty and the oppression of a sharecropper's life in the rural South, and I came to my senses. Actually, I kicked myself! I remembered that the church is one of the Four Pillars of my life, and without it, I could crumble. So, I resumed regular church attendance and participation.

Doris kept me grounded.

"Don't lose your perspective," she warned. "All this attention is because of the position, not you personally." She reminded me that the illusion of celebrity is just that. An illusion. I am immensely grateful to Doris for that.

This keeps me cognizant of Pride, one of the seven sins when misused. When used correctly, pride keeps you grounded. You should be proud of who you are, including your name. Your name is part of your brand. But you should not exalt yourself. The Bible says in James 23:12: "Whoever exalts himself shall be humbled; and whoever humbles himself shall be exalted."

The healthiest and most humble way to live is with a good balance of pride and humility.

"The Red Cross Missed a Phenomenal Opportunity"

In August of 1999, the Red Cross selected Dr. Bernadine P. Healy as president. She took office on September 1, and I returned to Cleveland.

"The national Red Cross missed a phenomenal opportunity when Steve did not become the permanent director," says Dr. Moss.

Reverend McMickle agreed. "All of us in Cleveland were hoping that he would become the acting director of the national office of the Red Cross on a permanent basis. We thought it was a terrible mistake that a man who had proven himself to be absolutely devoted to the work of the Red Cross in word and in deed was not chosen because they wanted a national name. It was their loss."

Linda Mathes added, "I so wish he had been selected to be president of the organization. Many others wanted that as well. It was a real blow when he was not."

On Wednesday, August 25, 1999, the Red Cross hosted three farewell receptions for me.

"As he moves to new opportunities," said the email to all staff, "Steve would like to say goodbye to the old and new friends at national headquarters who have provided support and encouragement during his tenure as acting president."

I retired from the American Red Cross, reflecting on how far I had come from my childhood on my father's sharecropper's farm in North Carolina during the oppressive 1930s and 1940s. Back then, I had longed to help people and be a leader. I dreamed of traveling the world and fulfilling my life's Purpose. Thankfully, God had placed people, places, and opportunities in my life to enable all of these dreams to become reality.

And so it was with a deep sense of fulfillment and gratitude that I concluded my tenure as Interim President of the American Red Cross, because it had enabled me to truly improve the human condition on a global scale.

... Taking the Helm in Washington, D.C.

> THE WHITE HOUSE
> WASHINGTON
>
> May 26, 2000
>
> Mr. Steve D. Bullock
> Chief Executive Officer, Greater Cleveland Chapter
> American Red Cross
> Cleveland, Ohio
>
> Dear Steve:
>
> Congratulations on your retirement from the American Red Cross.
>
> America's tradition of hard work has made our country strong, and you can be proud of your contribution to that legacy. Your dedication to the public is an inspiration to others. On behalf of all those who have benefited from your service, I thank you for a job well done.
>
> Hillary and I wish you good health and every future success.
>
> Sincerely,
>
> Bill Clinton

I cherish this letter from President Bill Clinton and keep it framed and on display in our home.

CHAPTER 8

Making Change with The Bullock Group

A TRADEMARK OF MY life and career has been my commitment to cultivating strong relationships with people I've met and continue to meet along the way. When God is involved, we are blessed by these relationships that blossom into professional collaborations and lifelong friendships.

Bob Bender and Jim Krueger exemplify this, as we worked together for many years and continue to enjoy meaningful social gatherings. In fact, Doris and I recently traveled to Maine to celebrate my 80th birthday with Bob, Jim, and their wives at Bob's home.

Likewise, many of the relationships that I have cultivated throughout my career came back into play after I retired from the American Red Cross. As I strategized the next phase of my career, I thought about whom I might call upon to assist me in the founding and operation of a Cleveland-based consulting company that would enable me to continue helping people by contributing the knowledge that I had gleaned over 38 years of service in the non-profit sector.

"He could have just hung a shingle the next day and capitalized on the prestige of the position that he just left," says Jennifer Baker, who became a Senior Associate with The Bullock Group. "It would have been easy for Steve to say, 'Yesterday I was the CEO of a large organization, and today I'm a consultant because I have all this experience and wisdom to share with non-profits.' He could have had a group of clients immediately. Instead, he chose to take the time to do it the right way before he entered the next phase. In fact, he took at least six months to strategize how to proceed. We worked with a firm in Chicago on structuring not just what the organization should look like, but how he would be as a consultant. I was impressed by how much soul-searching he did."

Jennifer has embraced the tenets of my leadership style and implemented them in her own career as a manager. She credits that with her success, which led to becoming Director of Public Relations and Marketing for the Greater Cleveland Red Cross Chapter.

My lifetime of professional experience served as the template for The Bullock Group to provide high quality leadership and management consulting services to nonprofit and public institutions. To do that, we assembled a team of nonprofit management experts representing a variety of disciplines and specialties. Our work focuses on strategic planning, fund development, collaborative and merger relationships, feasibility studies, dissolutions, crisis management, and executive coaching.

Here again, relationships became the magic sauce for the company, because some of my former colleagues sought guidance from us on how to improve their services.

One of our first clients was Linda Mathes, who by then had become Chief Executive Officer of the American Red Cross in the National Capital Region, which includes: the District of Columbia; the Virginia counties of Arlington, Fairfax, Loudoun, and Prince William; the Maryland counties of Montgomery and Prince George's; and the Virginia cities of Alexandria, Fairfax, Falls Church, Manassas, and Manassas Park.

In that capacity, Linda was charged with the responsibility of carrying out the American Red Cross' mission throughout this region while supporting other communities across America and around the globe. Unfortunately, she discovered that the organizations were operating as separate entities; she wanted to create a cohesive team of chapters that could collaborate for the greater good of the region.

I was delighted to meet with Dr. Condoleezza Rice, who gave an inspiring speech as the keynote speaker at The City Club Forum sponsored by The City Club of Greater Cleveland, an organization of which I am a member. At the time, Dr. Rice was National Security Advisor for President George W. Bush. She later became Secretary of State.

So, she called The Bullock Group, and became one of our first clients.

"I reached out to Steve to consult and help with some strategic planning in my community, because we used to have 10 different units," Linda recalls. "I reached out to him to help facilitate strategic planning in the area. And I did so because of his wisdom and experience in the Red Cross, his knowledge in the community, and my ability to trust and respect his experience. It was very controversial planning. But Steve was uniquely trusted because he's a person of real integrity. As a result, we consolidated." And that aimed to create a more effective, efficient operation that can better serve people in need.

The Benjamin Rose Institute on Aging, whose motto is, "Helping people age successfully since 1908" featured me on a poster under the title, "I'm not used up." The poster showed my photo as well as a quote about how I had worked around the world for the American Red Cross, and learned just as much from my parents, who lived into their 90s. I was 65 years old at the time, and was proud to serve as a voice of encouragement to other men and women who had reached retirement age and know that they still had many valuable contributions to make to the world.

Likewise, I remained active in our community and participated in many events that enabled me to carry on my life's Purpose to help people improve their lives. At one such event, The City Club Forum sponsored by Key Bank on October 15, 2004, I had the honor of meeting Dr. Condoleezza Rice. She was the first woman to become National Security Advisor, and later became the first female African American Secretary of State.

Tribute to the Life and Legacy of George Mckee Elsey, President Emeritus, American Red Cross

After former American Red Cross President George Elsey died on December 30, 2015 in Tustin, California, I had the privilege of speaking at a memorial service for him at Red Cross headquarters in Washington, D.C. Many of my Red Cross friends and colleagues, including Jim Krueger, Harold Brooks, Linda Mathes, and Dave Therkelsen, were there. Here follow my remarks in their entirety:

> *Good afternoon all. I would like to extend special greetings to the Elsey family, to the American Red Cross family, and friends.*
>
> *It is with honor, privilege, and humility that I speak today of the life and legacy of George M. Elsey, President Emeritus of the American Red Cross. I will share some of my experience*

with and my appreciation for this man of vision, courage, and commitment, commitment to the mission of the Red Cross and people we serve.

Let me set the stage. After graduating from college in May 1959, I served in the U.S. Army until February 1962 and joined the American Red Cross in March 1962.

I was happy and honored to be able to join a large organization that was well known, highly respected and greatly valued throughout America and in many places around the world. In my role as a member of service at military installations in the United States, Europe, and Vietnam, I found a sense of satisfaction in knowing we were doing good work. However, after some time, I began to wonder if good work was enough. Perhaps we could be more effective, and achieve more lasting results, in my opinion, based on my experience and observations.

We suffered from a degree of malaises that was not taking us beyond where we were. Some of the leaders of the organization seemed to be followers at best. Followers in our approach in the use of the state of the art leadership and management practices, related to societal norms, civil and human rights, and most of all, effective service delivery.

After serving overseas, I came back to the United States in 1969 and Mr. Elsey was appointed president in 1970. Again, in my opinion, this was one of the wisest decisions made by the organization during my almost 40 years of service. This man of vision, courage, and commitment immediately set out to revitalize and energize the organization in every aspect of our work, domestically and abroad. He reconnected us with the rest of the Red Cross world. It was as if he could see around corners and over mountains. He said we must prepare for "a new century." We must be able to avoid some crises and cope with those that do occur.

The level of activity created through Mr. Elsey's efforts caused me to remember a charge that my mother gave me over and over again during my early years. She would say "try to leave every situation better than you found it." We were clearly beginning to do this in the Red Cross.

I will briefly share two of my personal experiences with Mr. Elsey during this new century effort. A new initiative was launched known as Serving And Involving The Entire Community (SAITEC). The goal was to both serve and to involve people from all segments of all communities where we served. This focus was on African Americans and other minorities. I was one of five individuals asked to lead that effort. There was pushback, both internally and externally, but the effort went forward.

Secondly, in 1976, in an effort to improve my leadership and management skills, I enrolled in the MBA program at the University of St. Thomas in St. Paul. I asked for support through the American Red Cross education incentive plan. I was told the degree I was seeking had no value for work in the Red Cross. I continued my efforts, and as I approached the final year of the program, I received a call from the national director of training, stating the organization was going to assist me through the balance of the program. I simply said thank you and quietly celebrated the changes taking place under the leadership of George Elsey. We were indeed preparing for a new century.

Finally, let's fast forward to January 1999. I was appointed Interim President of the American Red Cross. George Elsey called me during the first few days and wished me well and *offered his support. We stayed in touch and he spoke at the 1999 Red Cross convention in Richmond, Virginia.*

I thank him for his vision, courage and commitment. I thank God for putting him in our lives, and I thank him for his service to the American public through the American Red Cross.

George, you left us better than you found us. We thank you.

Harold Brooks, who also spoke, said he and many others were moved by my message. "Steve was very powerful and eloquent," he says. "His remarks were pretty fabulous."

Celebrating Lifelong Friendships

My friends from the Red Cross celebrated many family events with me and Doris. Bob Bender and Jim Krueger attended our children's weddings, and we attended the nuptials of their sons and daughters.

"I flew to Cleveland to celebrate the 50th anniversary party for Steve and Doris," says Linda Mathes. "I loved celebrating his relationship with his family. Doris was always by his side. Steve always held her and his family in high priority and never lost sight that his work with the Red Cross was a high priority."

Jim Krueger remembers how, "All the kids shared all these wonderful testimonials about their parents. Steve and Doris attended all the weddings of all three of our children. We had the same concept in terms of family values in terms of how our kids were raised. They got along when together. In a work setting, I can't think of another person that we've had that family exchange."

For years, Doris and I have gathered with Bob Bender and Jim Krueger and their wives, once or twice every year.

"On Steve's 70th birthday," says Jim Krueger, "we had a party at our house in Vienna, Virginia. Fifty people were on our meandering deck, and we invited back his whole leadership team when he was acting president. All the kids were here. The highlight of the evening was a parody (Sheryl Kravitz performed; she was on my team in Washington) that was done honoring him to the Aretha Franklin song *Respect*. It was so much fun, not too long after he'd been acting president. We all saluted him because we respected him. They were all delighted to be at the party to celebrate his 70th birthday."

A decade later, Bob Bender and his wife, Katherine Theodore, hosted us at their house in Seco, Maine, along with Jim and Noreen Krueger, for three days to celebrate my 80th birthday.

"It's been a bond over the years," Jim says. "I'm proud to know both of them. We've been through a lot together. We had a lot of discussions in times of troubles, both personal and professional. You are blessed to find friends like that in your lifetime."

The Four Pillars: Church

When I returned to Cleveland, Doris and I continued attending Antioch Baptist Church. In 2012, Reverend McMickle left for New York, and was succeeded by Reverend Dr. Todd C. Davidson. He was only 34 years old at the time, and we found common ground very early on because he attended graduate school at Virginia Union University.

"We often talk about how VUU can make an impact in this region," Reverend Davidson says. "I have seen Steve help numerous students get into college and secure financial resources. We're trying to start an alumni association in the greater Cleveland area."

When Reverend Davidson's father was hospitalized, Doris and I provided moral support for him, his wife, and their three daughters.

"My father has always been my hero, and he passed two years ago," Reverend Davidson says. "Steve reminds me of my own dad. That's really the highest compliment I can give to anyone."

He goes on to say that when church members and their relatives are hospitalized, "Steve is always right there. He is very compassionate and cares about their family's well-being. I hold him in the highest regard because he's a man of the highest integrity. He has a tremendous work ethic and commitment to other people, and he's a model father and husband."

From the beginning, I have supported him in his leadership role.

"Steve is somebody I can depend on as a pastor," he says. "You need deacons like Steve, who hold up your arms, who share your vision, who believe in, buy in, support, and nurture your talents."

As such, I have used my contacts to uplift Reverend Davidson.

"Steve really is a champion for change, for young people becoming leaders and being given opportunities to lead internal and external organizations with committee work," he adds. "I spoke at the City Club because he recommended me. I was invited to deliver a baccalaureate keynote address at our alma mater because he recommended me. He believes in me and has afforded me opportunities to participate in the larger Cleveland community because he believes in whatever strengths he thinks I have, and supports them wholeheartedly."

Serving on the Board of Virginia Union University

When I was Interim President of the American Red Cross, I visited Virginia Union University several times. Having graduated from there 40 years earlier, in 1959, it was a tremendous honor to return and show what my educational foundation from the university had enabled me to achieve. Even more so, I was happy to serve as an example for the current students to show what could be accomplished with the strong education, values, and life skills obtained at VUU.

The following year, after I retired from the Red Cross, I was invited to serve on the VUU Board of Trustees. I am currently serving as Vice Chair of the Board, which requires me to oversee and monitor all of the Board's committees, while cultivating synergy between them. Meanwhile, I play a very hands-on role with the Presidential Search Committee. After eight years of service, having led us beyond many of our aspirational goals, VUU President Dr. Claude G. Perkins stepped down. As we searched for an outstanding individual to replace him, I traveled frequently by car from our home in Cleveland to the VUU campus for Search Committee meetings.

After an extensive search, we selected Hakim J. Lucas, who took the helm as president in August of 2017.

My participation with VUU has also provided some wonderful experiences, such as hearing Johnny Cochran, the attorney whose defense of O.J. Simpson led to an acquittal of murder charges, deliver a rousing message as commencement speaker at Virginia Union University. Doris and I had the pleasure of speaking with him after the ceremony, during a reception at the university president's home.

One of my most significant roles as a member of the VUU Board of Trustees has been as Chairman of the Financial Affairs and Endowment Committee, which has provided more than $30 million for scholarships over the past seven years. A portion of that money comes from the endowment that is controlled by the Finance Committee. The remainder of that money comes from the university's four fundraising initiatives that involve cultivating relationships with donors and other revenue sources.

Serving on the Academic Affairs Committee, I have tried to help facilitate the enhancement of the breadth and quality of classroom instruction that VUU can offer to our students. My service has also included participation in: the Enrollment Management Committee, the Audit Committee, and the Facilities and Plant Management Committee.

I believe HBCUs are as necessary today as ever. They provide a unique experience that nourishes the mind, body, and spirit of each student, while preparing students for life in a comprehensive manner. Many of our students are the first generation to attend college. They arrive on campus, as I did, with no information or insight from their parents or relatives about what to expect or how to survive and excel in higher education. Likewise, having no college-educated role models, they lack a frame of reference about the benefits of how a college degree can provide better jobs, benefits, financial security, and personal fulfillment.

HBCUs teach all of this as faculty and staff establish personal relations with each student. It is a transformative experience. For me, being surrounded by people who believed in me and saw something in me that I didn't see in myself, was life-changing for me and my family. Now, my gratitude and spirit of giving back inspires me to work hard as vice chairman of the board of trustees to provide the same life-changing experience for thousands more students who follow in my footsteps.

"Steve Bullock wants to make the world a better place," says former VUU President Dr. Claude G. Perkins. "That's a wild and huge concept. He thinks in that way. He's a very driven and comprehensive type thinker. But his values tend to help him focus toward things that are good for humanity. His engagement and his leadership are designed to go forward with one hand behind him, because he is always thinking about pulling someone up."

Dr. Perkins adds that being very focused enables me to "make sure the organization is functioning with clear goals and pathways that one would establish to achieve those goals. Steve draws upon his experiences in family, education, church, and his Red Cross career to become an invaluable leader at Virginia Union University."

Revamping the school's strategic plan seven years ago exemplified this. As did promoting the power of HBCUs such as VUU. As the oldest HBCU in the South, the school boasts graduates who include 23 college presidents. Most of the mayors of Richmond, Virginia over the past 15 years were VUU graduates. Wyatt T. Walker, who was Dr. King's chief of staff, was a VUU science major. Former President Barack Obama's pastor in Chicago, Reverend Jeremiah Wright, attended VUU, as did his parents.

The mother of artist Romare Bearden attended Horshone College, which merged with VUU and created a co-ed institution. We are very proud of our non-discriminatory history. Starting as a school for former slaves, VUU welcomed Jewish academicians who fled Nazi Germany and were shunned at some institutions in the United States. Our school never discriminated on the basis of race, religion, or nationality.

"Mr. Bullock sees the value of an HBCU as being as great today as it ever has been in our 152-year history," says Dr. Lucille M. Brown, a VUU Board Member and Chair of the Academic Affairs Committee.

"Steve has talked with the president and the board to help us understand the role that HBCUs play in today's world in preparing young students for the future who need an extra measure of attention or confidence in their performance," she says. "We let students know from day one that we're there for them. We commit to enable them to be successful."

As a 1950 magna cum laude graduate of VUU who then graduated with honors with a master's degree from Howard University, Dr. Brown has pursued graduate studies at Virginia State University, Virginia Commonwealth University, and the University of Virginia. She ultimately became Superintendent of Schools in Richmond, Virginia.

"Steve's leadership," she says, "has enabled us to cultivate an understanding of academic needs, to prepare youngsters for a meaningful lifestyle to enable them to improve their own lifestyle, and a level of commitment to serving the community that is unmatched."

Chapter 9

The Bullock Family Legacy

IN CLOSING, I WANT to express my immense gratitude to God for blessing me and our family with a bountiful life that has enabled all of us to serve as agents of positive change for our family, our communities, and the world.

"Yes, we have lived a charmed life," Doris says with a laugh. "I definitely got off the farm in Lawrenceville, Virginia. I was not going to be a farmer's wife! I never got that Corvette that I used to imagine was the potbelly stove when I was a girl, but I did get my luxury car and lived in nice homes with our family. And we traveled the world."

That included celebrating our 50th anniversary in 2011 in the Greek Isles.

"Steve has been really good to my sister," says Charles Kelly, 76. "There was nothing that she wanted that he would not give her. He was solidly as much as she was behind him as he was beside her and cared for her just as much."

Harold Brooks makes a similar observation: "Doris and Steve are a perpetual love affair that's kind of cool to witness. Years ago, he had a health issue. The way she was protective and so loving of him let us all know that this was a special man and you need to pray to help her to get him healed. Then recently she had a health problem. There he was, very similarly just making sure that she knew the most important thing on the planet was her and that for him it was important for her to get well."

Kelly, who lives with Leroy and their three children in Highland Heights, about 20 minutes from me and Doris, now appreciates all that we instilled in her.

"My dad is my hero," she says. "It brings tears to my eyes. It took me a long time to figure it out. Now I respect everything he ever said because I wouldn't be who I am and where I am had I not grown to understand everything that he's done. When I started my undergraduate degree, I never would have believed I would have a doctorate in education. My daughter was four months old when I began taking classes from Walden University online. It took six years, three face-to-face visits with professors, and an intense thesis defense via Skype. My dad taught me the power of hard work and perseverance. I used to think he was mean, but he had values and he stood by them. He taught us that everything is earned. He earned his; I'm going to earn mine."

Kelly, who is the only black educator in her school, says when she encounters challenges, "I could easily walk away and say, 'I'm not doing this. I quit.' But I would feel like I'm letting him down. He said nothing good comes to anyone easily."

Kelly says she holds her children up to high expectations, and devotes significant time and energy to nurturing their values and character.

"God is first in our household," she adds. "He's the mold that holds us together. We have family gatherings. We make sure the kids have time with grandparents, aunts and uncles. And we take trips together. At Christmas, we make sure the kids hear Dad tell his story about feeling blessed when he received only a paper bag with fruit, nuts, and a pair of gloves. I tell them, 'If it were not for God, for Christ, we wouldn't have this roof or your clothes.' I also tell them how I teach in a low-income school district where kids come to school with no coat and holes in their shoes. That makes my own children stop complaining that the TV in their bedroom doesn't work."

Brian cherishes my encouragement that our children become leaders. "Even now, he always stresses leadership and being leaders," he says, "Kelly is a leader in many things. She and I are always the ones who are planning family reunions, and I'm the president of the Maryland VUU alumni chapter."

Brian says he also loves when I call him and ask his opinion about something. He comes home several times each year.

Eric, who has been coping with health challenges, is instilling our family values in his daughter, Elizabeth.

"My dad sets the bar on how to be a good citizen," Eric says. "He's a good man. And that's what he's trying to teach us, to be good men and women. My mom has done the same thing. As leader of the Red Cross, as a city councilman, and as school board president, he set the example that you help your neighbors and your friends. When I worked in a school as a security guard, I tried to get these kids to understand the good values even though they're old fashioned. They're still valuable. Say 'please' and 'thank you' and 'excuse me.' Those things don't go out of style. Dad also taught us to never shy away from your work. You have to get it done. He was always very physical. He'd get out there and get dirty, and he taught us, coming from the farm in Enfield, you've got to get a little dirty sometimes to get the work done."

During recent years, I have received many awards. One especially memorable one occurred in December of 2016, when I was one of 100 Hall of Achievement Inductees at the Case Western Reserve University Mandel Center for Nonprofit Organizations during its 100th anniversary.

I have also been reflecting on some very special experiences that I never dreamed of having when I was growing up in rural North Carolina. One was when Doris and I visited the Cape Coast Dungeons in Ghana a few years ago. I first visited this horrific and haunting slave shipping fort in 1972. President Obama, First Lady Obama, and their daughters made a highly-publicized visit there in 2009.

In addition, in an experience of coming full circle from my childhood, Doris and I visited the Biltmore Estate in Asheville, North Carolina. Though America's largest home was only 318 miles from Enfield where I grew up in poverty and racial segregation, George Vanderbilt's family home was worlds away from me. However, seeing it in the *Life* magazine that my mother brought home from her white employers' home, the Vanderbilt mansion inspired my faith that God had a much better place for me. It became my purpose and divine assignment to find that place. I found it, by the grace of

God, and experiencing the grandeur of Biltmore Estate was nothing short of soul-tingling.

"Steve has turned out to be model of what is possible," says Colonel Mark Kelly. "He was quite the trailblazer."

Let me say more regarding my legacy. I believe that God gives us gifts to achieve more than most of us do. The Bible speaks of a "bountiful life" because He expects us to make the best and greatest use of what He has given us and to share with others. He wants us to grow in our physical, mental, and spiritual capacity to provide for our daily human needs. As we grow, God blesses us with even more. This may include shiny and bright objects, fancy cars, and nice homes. However, first and foremost, He still wants us to love and to bless others.

To do this, we must cultivate faith and hope while never succumbing to defeat. While we may – and will – be victimized, we should never allow ourselves to become a victim. Perseverance is the order for all of us, until we achieve our purpose. My approach was to find a way to get over or around the next hurdle, or to allow God to use me and those around me to deliver us all to what He has planned for us.

As we come to a close, here are some additional points that I want to reinforce:

Apply Purpose, Preparation, Performance, and Results to Everything You Do. Approach every goal with a clear understanding and application of your Purpose. Invest time and energy in Preparation by taking the necessary steps to ready yourself to achieve your Purpose. Execute your best possible Performance by conducting yourself at a level of excellence that will allow you to achieve your purpose. Then evaluate your Results with a critical, objective viewpoint so that you can improve with more efficient and effective techniques for achieving your goals.

Take Risks! Be reasonable and responsible, but take risks. Do not be afraid to fail. If you fail, evaluate the failure and try again. Don't do the same thing over and over and expect a different outcome. Learn from the failure.

Refuse to feel jealousy or envy. A true mark of success is the ability to celebrate another person's good news, blessings, promotions, accomplishments, et cetera. Jealousy and envy are, in a Biblical and practical sense, extremely toxic emotions. The only way to go when one is consumed by these feelings is downward into a negative mindset, which can breed hostile behavior. When you feel tempted to indulge feelings of jealousy and envy, take a moment to realize that God is showing you an examples of blessings that could shower upon you as well, when you maintain a positive and faithful mindset, and engage in behavior that improves yourself and others.

Bless Others! When possible and appropriate, share your success with others who might benefit. Success is a God-given blessing; He works through us to bless others.

Make It Better! Work hard to make every situation better than you found it. My mother drilled this into me when I was young; Dr. Samuel Dewitt Proctor reinforced it in college by what he said, what he did, and how he lived his life. Be that example for young people.

Express Yourself! Express the importance of knowing who you are and being who you want to be. Also understand the importance of what lies within you, versus what exists around you. As stated before, establish a set of core values and guiding principles which will help to keep you focused and grounded. Again, it is what lies within you that matters.

Know Your Worth! Know and use your value. Be aware of the unique assets that you bring to the table. Use everything that God has given you to make a positive difference. Don't be shy about letting others see and feel your value.

Compensate for Your Blind Spots! Regardless of our level of formal and technical education and training, no matter how many years of experience or how tested we are, we all still have some areas and levels of ignorance. Be aware of those in your personal and professional lives. Admit what you don't know, and ask for help. This takes courage, but the results are worth it. Leaders know their blind spots and surround themselves with others who can help them see solutions within their blind spots.

Learn from Your Mistakes! Getting it right is a great experience, but getting it wrong will happen! Make mistakes a great learning experience.

Hunger for Better! Possessing some level of divine dissatisfaction is positive and good. Always want to be better, the best you can be. Successful people will tell you that they are always working to improve their craft or their gift and many leaders will do the same.

"Steve showed what a dream, hard work, determination, and the pursuit of excellence could do for one's life," says my brother-in-law, Charles Kelly. "In everything that he elected to do, and in some things he was pushed to do, he pursued that same excellence with the same dogged determination to succeed."

Charles continues, "As Steve progressed in the Red Cross, he moved progressively forward in his career using techniques that he developed along life's highways. As I view his life and the successes that he has achieved, you have to know that it was not by accident. His plan for a successful life was shaped and carved out of his need and drive to succeed at whatever he set his mind to do. I do not believe that Steve ever met a challenge that hampered his dreams. His legacy to those who will follow him is one that our high school principal wrote in Doris' yearbook: 'You can do anything you think you can, and more.'"

Anything, indeed.

I hope that by experiencing my story, and absorbing my tenets of success, you can apply these values and ideals to your own life. We all have the power to achieve the infinite possibilities of our heart's desire. May you be blessed with the courage and vision to become your absolute best and share the fruits of your labor to inspire and uplift your family, your community, and the world.

Epilogue

As Doris and I celebrate 56 years of marriage, we are awed with gratitude that God elevated us from the difficult circumstances of our youth to enjoy such an abundantly blessed life. We are very thankful for the many people that God put into our lives from all walks of life. Rich and poor, black and white, young and old, we valued them all as additions, not subtractions. In fact, we believe life is more about additions than subtractions.

Because of our shared goals and determination, we are thankful for how far we have been able to come since that day in September of 1957 when we met on the Virginia Union University campus in Richmond, Virginia. What a great day that was! I knew I had met my partner for life, and I hoped she would agree.

Marrying Doris Elizabeth Kelly was one of the greatest blessings of my life. We often reflect on the solid foundation upon which we built our life. Both born into good families, we were blessed with good health, sound purpose, and strong core values. What a great inheritance. We receive and accept it, embrace it, grow it, and pass it on to those who follow us. We were blessed with full employment and many other benefits for 39 years, along with three robust, bright children, and six healthy, intelligent grandchildren. We have taught them to know who they are and to be proud of it. We have taught them to know and stay focused on their Purpose, and to thank God for every moment of success. I have reiterated my mother's wisdom in saying that no one can take these core characteristics from us.

The Bullock Grandchildren: back row, left to right: Elizabeth (Liz), 19; Marcus, 21; Steven, 13. Front row, left to right: Blair, 15; Kylee, 11; Brianna, 16. Inset, Brandon, 32.

Doris and I cherish spending time with our seven grandchildren. We teach them our values that are centered on the four pillars of God, family, education, and careers that make a positive impact on themselves and others.

God's greatest blessings in my life also include two factors to which I credit my success: graduating from college, and serving 27 months in the U.S. Army. These accomplishments, and the successes that Doris and I have cultivated together, have allowed us to help others along the way, thus fulfilling our Purpose through the Four Pillars: God, Family, Education, and the American Red Cross.

While I had many negative experiences during my nearly 40 years with the American Red Cross, Doris and I are better people for it. Romans Chapter 5 tells us that we should glory in tribulation and suffering, knowing that tribulation and suffering produce perseverance. And perseverance produces character, which produces hope. Hope does not fail or disappoint, because the love of God has been poured out for us. In plain English, each negative experience made us stronger and more determined.

The American Red Cross and the International Red Cross are great organizations that are doing meaningful work. Great because the Red Cross mission and purpose are sound and necessary. Great because the organization does excellent work, and most of the time, does it well. The services have been very important during my career, and I do not expect that to change anytime in the future. It is for that reason that I urge the American public to continue its support for the organization in every way possible. I also urge the organization to do its very best to continue earning and deserving that support.

Steve D. Bullock

Appendix

Chapter 13 (The Love Chapter) 1st Corinthians
1 Corinthians 1 King James Version (KJV)

1. Paul called to be an apostle of Jesus Christ through the will of God, and Sosthenes our brother,

2. Unto the church of God which is at Corinth, to them that are sanctified in Christ Jesus, called to be saints, with all that in every place call upon the name of Jesus Christ our Lord, both theirs and ours:

3. Grace be unto you, and peace, from God our Father, and from the Lord Jesus Christ.

4. I thank my God always on your behalf, for the grace of God which is given you by Jesus Christ;

5. That in every thing ye are enriched by him, in all utterance, and in all knowledge;

6. Even as the testimony of Christ was confirmed in you:

7. So that ye come behind in no gift; waiting for the coming of our Lord Jesus Christ:

8. Who shall also confirm you unto the end, that ye may be blameless in the day of our Lord Jesus Christ.

9 God is faithful, by whom ye were called unto the fellowship of his Son Jesus Christ our Lord.

10 Now I beseech you, brethren, by the name of our Lord Jesus Christ, that ye all speak the same thing, and that there be no divisions among you; but that ye be perfectly joined together in the same mind and in the same judgment.

11 For it hath been declared unto me of you, my brethren, by them which are of the house of Chloe, that there are contentions among you.

12 Now this I say, that every one of you saith, I am of Paul; and I of Apollos; and I of Cephas; and I of Christ.

13 Is Christ divided? was Paul crucified for you? or were ye baptized in the name of Paul?

14 I thank God that I baptized none of you, but Crispus and Gaius;

15 Lest any should say that I had baptized in mine own name.

16 And I baptized also the household of Stephanas: besides, I know not whether I baptized any other.

17 For Christ sent me not to baptize, but to preach the gospel: not with wisdom of words, lest the cross of Christ should be made of none effect.

18 For the preaching of the cross is to them that perish foolishness; but unto us which are saved it is the power of God.

19 For it is written, I will destroy the wisdom of the wise, and will bring to nothing the understanding of the prudent.

20 Where is the wise? where is the scribe? where is the disputer of this world? hath not God made foolish the wisdom of this world?

21. For after that in the wisdom of God the world by wisdom knew not God, it pleased God by the foolishness of preaching to save them that believe.

22. For the Jews require a sign, and the Greeks seek after wisdom:

23. But we preach Christ crucified, unto the Jews a stumbling block, and unto the Greeks foolishness;

24. But unto them which are called, both Jews and Greeks, Christ the power of God, and the wisdom of God.

25. Because the foolishness of God is wiser than men; and the weakness of God is stronger than men.

26. For ye see your calling, brethren, how that not many wise men after the flesh, not many mighty, not many noble, are called:

27. But God hath chosen the foolish things of the world to confound the wise; and God hath chosen the weak things of the world to confound the things which are mighty;

28. And base things of the world, and things which are despised, hath God chosen, yea, and things which are not, to bring to nought things that are:

29. That no flesh should glory in his presence.

30. But of him are ye in Christ Jesus, who of God is made unto us wisdom, and righteousness, and sanctification, and redemption:

31. That, according as it is written, He that glorieth, let him glory in the Lord.

Psalm 23
A psalm of David.

[1] The Lord is my shepherd, I lack nothing.

[2] He makes me lie down in green pastures,
he leads me beside quiet waters,

[3] he refreshes my soul.
He guides me along the right paths
for his name's sake.

[4] Even though I walk
through the darkest valley,[a]
I will fear no evil,
for you are with me;
your rod and your staff,
they comfort me.

[5] You prepare a table before me
in the presence of my enemies.
You anoint my head with oil;
my cup overflows.

[6] Surely your goodness and love will follow me
all the days of my life,
and I will dwell in the house of the Lord
forever.

Bullock, Eric Delano v, xiii,
Bullock, Estee 6
Bullock, Floyd Douglas 6, 193, 194,
Bullock, Frank Leon 6
Bullock, Hattie 6
Bullock, Ida Mayo xiii, 7, 8, 9
Bullock, James 6, 9, 28, 35, 36, 62
Bullock, Leslie 6, 7
Bullock, Marcus Delano xiii, 123, 262
Bullock, Morris Vernon 6, 7
Bullock, Patricia Hopewell 123, 154
Bullock, Paul Roman 6
Bullock, Percy Sherrod 6
Bullock, Raymond L. 6,7
Bullock, Savannah Alfonso 6, 7
Bullock, William Harvey xiii, 6, 9
Bullock, William Henry xiii, 1, 7, 9, 10
Bullock, Yvonne 6
Bullock Group, The 177, 243, 244, 245

C
Caldera, Louis 237
Cargill, Madeline L. 188
Case Western Reserve University 193
Case Western Reserve University Mandel Center for Nonprofit Organizations 175, 257
City Club, The 176, 245, 246, 251, 281
Cleveland, Ohio v, 150, 151, 153, 161, 165, 166, 168, 169, 170, 174, 175, 176, 177, 179, 185, 187, 191, 194, 195, 197, 199, 200, 201, 203, 205, 206, 207, 210, 218, 229, 230, 238, 239, 230, 243, 249, 250, 251
Cleveland Black Professionals Association, The 183
Cleveland Campaign 175
Cleveland-to-Clevelanders Committee 175
Cleveland Metroparks Zoo 197
Club, The 176
Cochran, Johnny 252
Cofield, Mr. 30, 31, 37
Cook, Jan 216, 217
Cronkite, Walter 233

D
Daniel's Chapel 17
Daugherty, Blair Ali xiii, 197, 262
Daugherty, Kelly A. Bullock iii, xiii, 122, 123, 124, 126, 152, 153, 154, 155, 156, 159, 165, 187, 190, 193, 194, 195, 196, 197, 198, 202, 203, 204, 205, 207, 256, 258
Daugherty, Kylee Alicia xiii, 197, 262
Daugherty, Leroy 197, 198, 255
Daugherty, Steven Kyle xiii, 197, 262
Davidson, Todd C. xvi, 250, 251
DeCosta, Lillie Bullock 6
DeCosta, Richmond 35
Dole, Elizabeth 166, 175, 199, 209, 210, 211, 217, 218, 233
Donaghue, A. Frank 222, 226
Dreifuss, Ruth 236

E
Eaton Corporation 162, 163
Edelman, Marian Wright 236
Eden Rosenwald School 12, 31
Ellington, Duke 64
Elsey, George McKee 107, 108, 109, 110, 157, 180, 217, 232, 233, 234, 246, 247, 246, 248
Emancipation Proclamation 1
Emerson, Ralph Waldo ix
Emporia, Virginia 7
Enfield, North Carolina 1, 2, 5, 6, 7, 11, 12, 17, 19, 22, 24, 27, 28, 30, 34, 37, 42, 54, 68, 69, 76, 78, 91, 155, 185, 257
Evans, Jack 118, 120

F
4-H 30
Fairfax County, Virginia 81, 96, 102
Fincher, Charlie 111
Fincher, Janet 111
First Baptist Church 17
Fort Belvoir, Virginia 81, 96
Fort Dix, New Jersey 82, 226
Fort Gordon, Georgia 74

Index

A

African American Cultural Gardens 176
Albert M. Higley Company, The 162
Alexandria, Virginia 80, 101, 127, 129, 244
Alpha Phi Alpha Fraternity, Incorporated
    iv, 62, 64, 66, 75, 176, 187, 238
American Management Association 176
American Red Cross
    Community Service Center xv
    Greater Cleveland Chapter 88, 161-
    Greater New York Chapter i, 179
    Greater Washington Chapter 127
    Jacksonville, Florida Chapter 126
Minnesota-Wisconsin Division 129, 131,
    National Capital Region Chapter ii, 244
    President's Advisory Committee 182
    Red Cross Ball 184, 185, 186, 187,
    188, 190, 230, 231,
St. Paul Area Chapter 129, 131, 132, 134,
    137, 140, 143, 144, 145, 146, 147,
    148, 149, 150, 151, 152, 153, 156,
    157, 158, 216
    San Francisco Chapter ii, 139
    Southeast Area Office xv, 98, 107
American Society for Training and Development 176
Annan, Kofi 236
Antioch Baptist Church ii, xv, xvi, 199, 250
Asbury Park, New Jersey 82
Asheville, North Carolina 28, 257
Association of MBA Executives 176
Atkins, Elizabeth Ann xvi
Augustine, Norman 209, 234
Azmi, Shabana 236

B

Baker, Jennifer 177, 217, 243
Battle, K.P. xv, 17
Bellamy's Mill 21
Bender, Robert i, 137, 138, 139, 157, 166,
    179, 243, 249, 250
Benjamin Rose Institute on Aging 246
Black on Black Crime Commission 176
Black Profesional of the Year Award 190,
    193, 194
Black Professionals Association 193, 194
Blaney, South Carolina 23
Boulé, The vi, 176, 190, 191, 230
Boy Scouts of America, The 30, 154
Brooks, Harold ii, 139, 140, 216, 231, 234,
    235, 246, 249, 255
Brown, Lucille M. 254
Bullock, Bertha 28
Bullock, Brian Dennis vi, xiii, 164
Bullock, Brianna Clyde xiii, 123, 262
Bullock, Cathleen 6, 96, 153, 194
Bullock, Doris iii, 58, 59, 60, 61, 62, 65,
    66, 70, 74, 75, 76, 77, 78, 79, 82, 85,
    89, 90, 91, 92, 93, 94, 95, 96, 97, 102,
    103, 104, 107, 110, 111, 112, 113,
    122, 123, 124, 126, 127, 129, 131,
    139, 143, 151, 152, 154, 155, 156,
    158, 159, 186, 187, 188, 190, 193,
    194, 196, 197, 198, 199, 200, 201,
    202, 203, 206, 207, 210, 228, 229,
    230, 231, 239, 240, 243, 249, 250,
    252, 255, 257, 260, 261, 262, 263
Bullock, Elizabeth Lynn xiii, 262

Index

Fort Monmouth, New Jersey 82, 85, 89, 81
Fort Niagara, New York 74, 78
Four Pillars, The xxv, 86, 87, 88, 133, 151, 159, 161, 189, 199, 239, 240, 250, 262

G
Geneva, Switzerland 93, 122, 236
Geneva Conventions 101, 215, 225, 236, 237
Ghana 122, 257
Goler, Timothy D. v, 191
Graves, Donet G. 176
Greater Cleveland Growth Association 193
Greater Cleveland Roundtable 176
Greenbelt, Maryland 127
Greenspan, Catherine M. xvi

H
HBCUs 38, 44, 88, 191, 193, 205, 252, 253, 254
HBCU Preparatory Schools Network v, 191
Halifax County, North Carolina 2, 37, 72
Hamer, Fannie Lou 114
Hardee Elementary School 11
Harrisburg, Pennsylvania 124, 226
Harvard Community Services Center 188
Harvey, Robert 76
Harvey, Selma Doris Bullock xiii, 6, 62
Hassan, Bin Talal El 236
Healy, Bernadine P. 186, 240
Heiberg, Astrid 237
Henderson, Thomas xv, 55, 56, 63, 68
Henley, William Ernest 67
Hill, Oliver 64
Historically Black College and Universities see HBCUs
Hoover, Carole 193
Horshone College 253
Hurricane Mitch 218, 219, 220

I
International Committee of the Red Cross (ICRC) 93, 222, 225
Invictus 67

J
Jefferson Hotel xxi, 39, 40, 46
Johnson, Jason 238
Johnson, Sam 237
Johnson, Willa Cofield xv, 35, 36, 38, 39, 44
Joseph, Maddy 186

K
Kelly, Charles iv, 61
Kelly, Clyde Elizabeth 59
Kelly, Dorothy 76
Kelly, Mark iv, 61, 190
Kelly, Needham Nicholas, Sr. 59
Kelly, Needham, Jr. 61, 190
Kelly, Valerie 76
Kennedy, John F. 76, 90, 92
Khan, Sadruddin Aga 236
King, Martin Luther, Jr. i, xvii, 54, 64, 124, 201
Klarsfeld, Serge 236
Kravitz, Sheryl 249
Krueger, James iii, 139, 220, 243, 246, 249, 250

L
Latimer, George 150, 151, 175
Lawrenceville, Virginia 59, 60, 61, 75, 76, 77, 78, 97, 255
Leadership Cleveland 176
Lerner, Al 230
Lincoln, Abraham 1
Long Transfer Trucking Company 57
Loy, Frank E. 237
Lucas, Hakim J. 252
Ludwick, David 162, 184
Ludwick, Marion 186

M
Madison, Leatrice 187
Madison, Robert P. vi, 187, 190
Mandel Center for Nonprofit Organizations see *Case Western Reserve University Mandel Center for Nonprofit Organizations*
Markey, Carol 188

Mathes, Linda ii, 183, 241, 244, 246, 249
McCain, John 106, 237
McCullough, Jeff 144, 146
McCullough, Rubie J. 185, 188
McGuire Air Force Base 82
McKee, Isaac xv
McMickle, Marvin A. iii, xv, 199, 200, 240, 250
Miller, Earl F. xv, 142, 156
Minnifield, Frank 167,
Miracle, William 126, 127
Missionary Baptist Church xxv, 9, 87
Money, Mississippi xxi, xxiv, 47, 58
Montgomery, Alabama 54, 111
Montgomery Bus Boycott 54, 65
Montgomery, Horace 91, 92, 94
Montgomery, Jane 111
Moon, Chris 236
Mooney, Beth 230, 231
Moore, Cornell 142
Moore, Paul M. xv
Moss, Edwina xvi, 200, 201
Moss, Otis i, xv, xix, 200, 201
Mt. Sinai Urban Health Council 176
Muldrow, Esther Bullock 6

N
NAACP 39, 47, 64, 102, 176, 192, 213
National City Bank 176
National Urban League 69, 102, 113, 176, 192
Neville Store 25
Newburn, North Carolina 9
Newport News, Virginia 59, 60, 61
Newsome, Billy 117
Northey, Don 118

O
Ohio Motorists Association 176
Olivet Institutional Baptist Church i, xv, xix, 200
Oklahoma City, Oklahoma 226
Operation Desert Storm Homecoming Committee 175
Orr, Charles 114, 117, 118, 175, 217

P
Parable of the Talents, The 14, 17, 52, 172
Parks, Mike 230
Parks, Rosa xvii, 53, 54, 112
Perkins, Claude G. 251, 253
Perot, H. Ross 102, 103, 104, 105, 106, 107
Pickford Hall 45, 48
Pilgrim Baptist Church xv, 142, 156
Play House Club, The 176
Pleasant Hill Baptist Church 17
Pollocksville, North Carolina 13
Poplar Mt. Baptist Church 76, 77
Powell, Colin 181, 232
Proctor, Samuel DeWitt xv, xvii, 48, 49, 50, 55, 56, 63, 64, 65, 68, 69, 199, 259
Public Works Administration (PWA) 5

Q
Quad State Project 120, 122
Queen Raina of Jordan 239

R
Rice, Condoleezza 245, 246
Richmond Ballet, The 231
Richmond Boys Choir 231
Richmond, Virginia 38, 43, 44, 64, 65, 129, 231, 232, 249, 253, 254, 261
Rimsky-Korsakov, Nikolai xxiv, 47
Robinson, John 76
Robinson, Randall 45
Robinson, Ramona 193
Robinson, Spottswood William, III 64
Roosevelt, Franklin Delano xxiii, 5, 11, 107
Rose, Ernie 113
Rosenwald, Julius 12
Rotary Club of Cleveland 176
Rotary Club's 4-Way Test 114

S
St. Paul's Baptist Church 17
Scherek, Barbara 140, 149
Schubert, Richard 180, 182, 233
Serving and Involving the Entire Community (SAITEC) 107, 108, 109, 110,

111, 113, 114, 116, 124, 125, 126, 127, 128, 142, 248
Shakespeare, William xxii
Sommaruga, Cornelio 237
Sphinx, The 238
Spraggins, Tinsley L. 50
Steve D. Bullock Humanitarian Award 230, 231
Stover, Jim 163

T
T.S. Inborden High School 34, 37, 38
Therkelsen, David 134, 135, 157, 217, 246
Till, Emmett 42, 43, 46, 47, 49, 53
Till, Mamie 42
Tolka, North Carolina 7
Townsend, Terry 108

U
Union Missionary Baptist Church 9
Unionite 238
United States Army Vietnam Headquarters (USAV) 100
United Way 148, 149, 166, 159, 175, 176, 185
University Club 176
University Hospitals Health System 176
University Hospitals of Cleveland 169, 176, 177

V
Vaughan, Margaret Bullock 6
Virginia Beach, Virginia xxi, 39, 42, 43, 45, 73, 155, 205,

Virginia State University 197, 202, 254
Virginia Symphony 231
Virginia Union University xv, xviii, xxi, xxiv, xxv, 38, 43, 44, 45, 46, 48, 49, 50, 55, 56, 61, 62, 63, 64, 65, 66, 69, 75, 86, 88, 129, 142, 151, 156, 158, 189, 199, 202, 203, 205, 206, 232, 238, 250, 251, 252, 253, 254, 256, 261,
Voinovich, George 151, 175
Voinovich, Janet 175
Voinovich, Josephine 175

W
Walker, Wyatt T. 253,
Wallace, Ben 45
Watson, Miss xv, 12, 13
White, Mike 163, 174, 175, 176
Wilder, Aaron 35, 52
Wilder, Douglas 45, 203, 238
Wilkins, Roy 47
Williams, Sheldon 102
Williams, Willie 68
Wills, Cheryl 185
Willocks, Buck 126
Wright, Curtis xxi, 39
Wright, Jeremiah 253
Wright, Marshall 162

Y
Young, Whitney M. 69

www.ingramcontent.com/pod-product-compliance
Lightning Source LLC
Chambersburg PA
CBHW021140080526
44588CB00008B/145